The Nassi-Levy

Spanish

D0999001

FIRST

YEAR

WORKBOOK EDITION

Stephen L. Levy
Former Head, Foreign Language Department
Roslyn (New York) Public Schools

Robert J. Nassi
Former Teacher of Spanish
Los Angeles Valley Junior College
Los Angeles, California

AMSCO

AMSCO SCHOOL PUBLICATIONS, INC.
315 Hudson Street / New York, N.Y. 10013

To Sergio,

You are the wind beneath my wings!
Q.E.P.D.

S.L.L.

Cover Design by: A Good Thing, Inc.
Book Design and Composition by: Sierra Graphics, Inc.
Illustrations by: Felipe Galindo

Please visit our Web site at: *www.amscopub.com*

When ordering this book, please specify: *either* **R 510 W**
or NASSI/LEVY SPANISH FIRST YEAR, FOURTH EDITION WORKBOOK

ISBN: 978-1-56765-814-9 / *NYC Item 56765-814-8*

Preface

The NASSI / LEVY SPANISH FIRST YEAR is designed to give students a comprehensive review and thorough understanding of the elements of the Spanish language that are normally covered in the first year of study. Highlights of Spanish and Spanish-American cultures are provided to familiarize students with the background of native speakers of the language. The book aims to incorporate and reflect the National Standards for Foreign Language Learning in the 21st Century, also known as the 5 C's: communication, cultures, connections, comparisons, and communities. Abundant and varied exercises help students master each phase of the work.

The FOURTH EDITION, while retaining the proven organization and successful program of the previous edition, has been strengthened in several ways:

1. Open-ended writing activities enable students to show their proficiency in using grammatical and lexical elements in personalized, contextually organized tasks.
2. The revised cultural section keeps the narratives clear and readable and provides a wealth of information.
3. Chapters present a cleaner, easier-to-read layout.

ORGANIZATION

For ease of study and reference, the book is divided into six Parts. Parts 1 to 3 are organized around related grammatical topics. Part 4 provides a comprehensive review of vocabulary, presented thematically. It also presents chapters on cognates, synonyms and antonyms. Part 5 covers Spanish and Spanish-American Civilizations. It includes the geography, history, lifestyle, science, literature, music, art, and architecture of both Spain and Spanish America. Part 6 provides materials for comprehensive practice and testing of the speaking, listening, reading, and writing skills.

Each grammatical chapter deals fully with one major grammatical topic or several closely related ones. Explanations of structures are brief and clear. All points of grammar are illustrated by many examples, in which the key elements are typographically highlighted.

Care has been taken in this text, which reviews the first stage of a basic sequence, to avoid the use of complex structural elements. To enable students to concentrate on the structural practice, the vocabulary has been carefully controlled and is systematically "recycled" throughout the grammatical chapters.

EXERCISES

For maximum efficiency in learning, the exercises directly follow the points of grammar to which they apply. Carefully graded, the exercises proceed from simple assimilation to more challenging manipulation of elements and communication. To provide meaningful practice of a grammatical topic, the exercises are set in contexts that are both functional and realistic. Many are also personalized to stimulate student response and internalization of the concepts under study.

While the contents of the exercises afford opportunities for extensive oral practice, the book's format also encourages reinforcement through written student responses, including extended written discourse. The grammatical chapters conclude with Mastery Exercises, in which all grammatical aspects in the chapter are again practiced in recombination of previously covered elements. All directions to exercises at this level are in English.

FLEXIBILITY

The topical organization and the integrated completeness of each chapter permit the teacher to follow any sequence suitable to the objectives of the course and the needs of the students. This flexibility is facilitated by the detailed table of contents at the front of the book and the comprehensive grammatical index at the back. Both teachers and students will also find the book a useful reference source.

CULTURE

The cultural chapters in Part 5 are presented in English. Students gain a wealth of knowledge and insight from the information provided as they proceed from Spanish influence in the United States, to Spain, to Spanish America. Each cultural chapter includes exercises designed to facilitate and check learning.

OTHER FEATURES

The Appendix features complete model verb tables and the principal parts of common irregular verbs, along with basic rules of Spanish punctuation, syllabication, and stress. Spanish-English and English-Spanish vocabularies and a comprehensive Index complete the book.

The NASSI / LEVY SPANISH FIRST YEAR is a thoroughly revised and updated edition. Its comprehensive coverage of the elements of Spanish, clear and concise explanations, extensive contextualized practice materials, and functional vocabulary, will help students strengthen their skills in the Spanish language. As they pursue proficiency, they will also gain valuable insights into the cultures of the Spanish-speaking world.

Thanks are due to our consultants, who reviewed substantial parts of the manuscript and made valuable suggestions.

Contents

Part 1
Verbal Structures

Part 2
Noun and Pronoun Structures

Part 3
Adjective/Adverb and Related Structures

Part 4
Word Study

♦ 30 ♦ Topical (Thematic) Vocabulary   **278**

Part 5
Spanish and Spanish-American Civilizations

♦ 31 ♦ Spanish Influence in the United States   **311**

♦ 32 ♦ Geography of Spain   **318**

Part 6
Comprehensive Testing:
Speaking, Listening, Reading, Writing

Verbal Structures

CHAPTER 1

Present Tense of –AR Verbs

♦ 1 ♦ Regular -AR Verbs

a. The present tense of regular -*ar* verbs is formed by dropping the infinitive ending -*ar* and adding the personal endings -*o, -as, -a, -amos, -áis, -an.*

b. The present tense has the following meanings in English:

usted canta	*you sing, you're singing, you do sing*
él canta	*he sings, he's singing, he does sing*

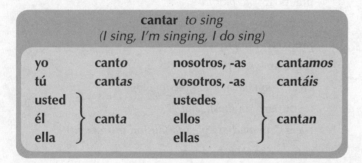

cantar *to sing*
(I sing, I'm singing, I do sing)

yo	cant*o*	nosotros, -as	cant*amos*
tú	cant*as*	vosotros, -as	cant*áis*
usted		ustedes	
él	} cant*a*	ellos	} cant*an*
ella		ellas	

NOTE:

1. The subject pronouns usted *(Ud.)* and ustedes *(Uds.)* are usually expressed in Spanish. The other subject pronouns *(yo, tú, él, ella, nosotros, vosotros, ellos, ellas)* are usually omitted, unless they are required for clarity or emphasis.

Canto bien.	*I sing well.*
Cantan bien.	*They sing well.*

BUT

Ud. canta bien.	*You sing well.*
Ella canta bien pero **él canta** mal.	*She sings well but he sings badly.*
Ella y **yo cantamos** bien.	*She and I sing well.*

2. The feminine forms of *nosotros* and *vosotros* are *nosotras* and *vosotras.*

3. *Tú* and *vosotros* (the familiar forms) are used when addressing close relatives, intimate friends, or small children. In many Spanish–American countries, the *ustedes* form is used instead of the *vosotros* form.

♦ 2 ♦ Common -AR Verbs

admirar *to admire*	ganar *to win*
arreglar *to arrange, fix*	gritar *to shout*
ayudar *to help*	hablar *to speak*
buscar *to look for*	invitar *to invite*
cambiar *to change*	lavar *to wash*
bailar *to dance*	llamar *to call*
bajar *to go down, descend; to lower*	llegar *to arrive*
borrar *to erase*	llevar *to carry, take; wear*
buscar *to look for*	mirar *to look at*
cambiar *to change*	montar *to ride (a horse, bicycle)*
caminar *to walk*	nadar *to swim*
cantar *to sing*	necesitar *to need*
celebrar *to celebrate*	pagar *to pay (for)*
cocinar *to cook*	pasar *to pass; to spend (time)*
comprar *to buy*	patinar *to skate*
contestar *to answer*	practicar *to practice*
cortar *to cut*	preguntar *to ask*
dar *to give*	preparar *to prepare*
decorar *to decorate*	regresar *to return*
descansar *to rest*	sacar *to take out; to take (photo)*
desear *to wish, want*	terminar *to finish, end*
dibujar *to draw*	tocar *to touch; to play (a musical instrument)*
enseñar *to teach*	tomar *to take; to drink*
entrar (en) *to enter (into)*	trabajar *to work*
escuchar *to listen (to)*	usar *to use; to wear*
esperar *to wait; to hope*	viajar *to travel*
estudiar *to study*	visitar *to visit*
explicar *to explain*	

EXERCISE A

Enrique is telling his cousin what they and their friends are going to do after school. Express in complete sentences what he says.

EXAMPLE: Alfredo / montar en bicicleta
         Alfredo **monta** en bicicleta.

1. Sarita / tocar la guitarra

2. Lewis / trabajar en el supermercado

3. Carol y Gloria / bailar el flamenco

4. tú / practicar el piano

5. Uds. / mirar la televisión

6. yo / visitar a mis amigos

7. Roberto y yo / escuchar discos compactos

8. nosotros / pasar un buen rato en la biblioteca

EXERCISE B

Saturday is a day of chores at the Ortegas. Gloria is explaining what each family member does. Tell what she says.

EXAMPLE: Carlos / lavar el carro
Carlos **lava** el carro.

1. mi mamá / comprar la comida

2. yo / usar la aspiradora

3. mi papá / trabajar en el jardín

4. Eduardo y Clara / arreglar la casa

5. mis hermanitos / sacar al perro

6. mi abuela / cocinar la cena

EXERCISE C

You and some friends are planning a party. Mario wants to know who's doing what. Tell him.

EXAMPLE: comprar el pastel (Iggy)
Iggy **compra** el pastel.

1. decorar el salón *(Gunther y Paco)*

2. comprar los refrescos *(tú)*

3. buscar los discos compactos *(yo)*

4. tocar la guitarra *(Marta)*

5. preparar la comida *(Estela y yo)*

6. ayudar con los preparativos *(todos)*

7. cortar las flores *(Silvia e Inés)*

EXERCISE D

You received a note from a friend who's taking a cruise in the Caribbean. Complete the note with the present tense of the verbs in parentheses.

Querida Lucy:

¡Saludos de la República Dominicana! Nosotros _____ ratos agradables aquí: yo
                                        1. (pasar)

_____ en el mar Caribe; mis hermanos y yo _____ en motocicleta
2. (nadar)   *3.* (montar)

todas las tardes; mis padres _____ las tiendas y mi mamá _____

                                            4. (visitar)   *5.* (comprar)

muchos recuerdos. Por la noche, toda la familia _____ un paseo por la playa.

                                                                                 6. (dar)

Mis hermanos no _____ regresar a casa, pero nosotros _____

                                            7. (desear)   *8.* (regresar)

el próximo sábado. Las vacaciones _____ y tú y yo _____ en la

                                                9. (terminar)   *10.* (entrar)

escuela el lunes. Es todo por ahora.

Hasta la vista.

Rick

♦ 3 ♦ -*AR* Verbs in Negative Constructions

A verb is made negative by placing **no** before it.

María **no habla** español.	*María doesn't speak Spanish.*
Yo **no bailo** bien.	*I don't dance well.*

EXERCISE E

Ana and her sister often disagree with each other. Tell what Ana says and how her sister responds.

EXAMPLE: dar un paseo

      ANA: Nosotros **damos** un paseo.
      VIOLETA: **No damos** un paseo.

1. montar en bicicleta

ANA: Rafael _____ .

VIOLETA: _____

2. visitar el museo

ANA: Nosotros _____ .

VIOLETA: _____

3. mirar la televisión

ANA: Mis amigas _____ .

VIOLETA: _____

4. comprar un helado

ANA: Yo _____ .

VIOLETA: _____

5. descansar un poco

ANA: Tú _____ .

VIOLETA: _____

EXERCISE F

Look at the people in the following pictures. Say that they are not doing what they're doing.

EXAMPLE: Pedro *(tocar)*
Pedro **no toca la guitarra.**

1. Las amigas *(mirar)* _____ .

2. Yo *(nadar)* _____ .

3. Carolina *(patinar)* _____ .

4. La familia *(viajar)* _____ .

5. Ellos *(arreglar)* _____ .

♦ 4 ♦ -AR Verbs in Interrogative Constructions

In a statement, the subject usually comes before the verb. In a question (an interrogative sentence), the subject usually comes after the verb.

Ud. contesta correctamente.	*You answer correctly.*
¿**Contesta Ud.** correctamente?	*Do you answer correctly?*
Juan habla inglés.	*Juan speaks English.*
¿**Habla Juan** inglés?	*Does Juan speak English?*

EXERCISE G

Raúl's little brother always questions everything Raúl says. Tell what his little brother says in response to the statements below.

EXAMPLE: Gloria viaja mucho.
        ¿**Viaja Gloria** mucho?

1. David baila bien.

2. Mis amigos patinan en el parque.

3. Tú visitas el museo.

4. Nosotros miramos el cielo.

5. Uds. caminan por la ciudad.

6. Yo canto mal.

7. Wong desea comprar un suéter.

EXERCISE H

Luis never remembers what his friends ask. Write Luis's questions based on the answers given.

EXAMPLE: Yo arreglo bicicletas.
¿**Arreglas tú** bicicletas?

1. Esteban visita la biblioteca todos los días.

2. Los hermanos lavan el carro los sábados.

3. Yo nado en la piscina cada tarde.

4. Nosotros practicamos el béisbol.

5. Luz desea ir al cine.

6. Mi amigo y yo miramos un programa a las ocho.

7. Yo viajo por avión cada verano.

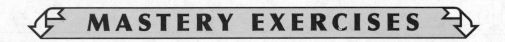

MASTERY EXERCISES

EXERCISE I

While visiting Madrid with a group, you took many pictures. Upon your return, you show them to some friends. Describe what's going on in each picture.

EXAMPLE: Alice (bajar)
Alice **baja del autobús.**

1. Nosotros *(visitar)* _____.

2. Javier, Arthur y Cristina *(entrar)* _____.

3. Javier *(pagar)* _____.

4. Tú *(mirar)* _____.

5. Nosotros *(tomar)* _____.

6. Gregorio *(escuchar)* _____.

7. Kyoko *(comprar)* _____.

8. Este señor *(trabajar)* _____.

9. Nosotros *(llegar)* _____.

10. Yo *(sacar)* _____.

EXERCISE J

A new classmate is asking you about yourself and your friends. Answer the questions as indicated.

EXAMPLE: ¿Deseas tú mirar la televisión? *(sí)*
 Sí, deseo mirar la televisión.

1. ¿Trabajas tú después de las clases? *(no)*

2. ¿Visitas tú a tus parientes a menudo? *(sí)*

3. ¿Sacan Uds. fotografías? *(sí)*

4. ¿Baila bien Alfredo? *(no)*

5. ¿Toman Uds. el autobús al centro? *(sí)*

6. ¿Dan Elena y Joe un paseo por el parque? *(sí)*

7. ¿Escuchas tú discos de rock? *(no)*

EXERCISE K

Working with a classmate, discuss a television reality show that you have both watched recently. Then write a summary of your discussion. You may wish to include the following: the title of the program, the type of program it is, when you watch it, why you watch it, what generally happens in the program, something unusual/interesting that happens, what you admire about the program, and when the program ends.

2

Present Tense of
−*ER* and −*IR* Verbs

◆ 1 ◆ Regular *-ER* Verbs

a. The present tense of regular *-er* verbs is formed by dropping the infinitive ending *-er* and adding the personal endings *-o, -es, -e, -emos, -éis, -en*.

b. The present tense has the following meanings in English:

usted come   *you eat, you're eating, you do eat*
ella come   *she eats, she's eating, she does eat*

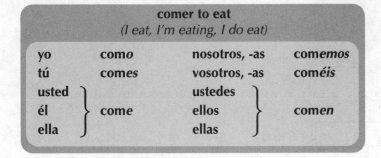

comer to eat			
(I eat, I'm eating, I do eat)			
yo	com*o*	nosotros, -as	com*emos*
tú	com*es*	vosotros, -as	com*éis*
usted		ustedes	
él }	com*e*	ellos }	com*en*
ella		ellas	

◆ 2 ◆ Common *-ER* Verbs

aprender *to learn*   esconder *to hide (something)*
beber *to drink*   leer *to read*
comer *to eat*   prometer *to promise*
correr *to run*   responder *to answer*
creer *to believe*   vender *to sell*

EXERCISE A

Mike and a friend describe their first day at school. What do they say?

EXAMPLE: el señor Bilbao / vender libros
         El señor Bilbao **vende** libros.

1. los alumnos / comer en la cafetería

2. David / beber jugo

3. tú / aprender el español

4. Angel y yo / correr en el patio

5. la maestra / leer una novela

6. yo / responder en la clase

7. ustedes / comprender la lección

8. nosotros / prometer estudiar mucho

EXERCISE B

Tell what each person is doing in the pictures below.

EXAMPLE: Guillermo **esconde la tiza**.

1. Phil _____.

2. Shakeela y Víctor _____.

3. Yo _____.

4. Cristina _____.

5. El hombre _____.

6. Enrique y yo _____.

EXERCISE C

Alfredo is baby-sitting his younger brother, who asks a lot of questions. Answer his questions according to the cues provided.

EXAMPLE:　¿Quién vende helados? *(el señor Rossi)*
　　　　　El señor Rossi **vende** helados.

1. ¿Quién aprende a nadar? *(Rafael)*

2. ¿Quién comprende el japonés? *(los señores Uchida)*

3. ¿Quién bebe una leche batida? *(tú)*

4. ¿Quién debe comprar unos dulces? *(mamá)*

5. ¿Quiénes comen en el restaurante? *(Grace y Rocío)*

6. ¿Quién responde a todas mis preguntas? *(yo)*

◆ 3 ◆ -ER Verbs in Negative and Interrogative Constructions

a. A verb is made negative by placing *no* before it.

Felipe **no bebe** leche.   *Felipe doesn't drink milk.*

Yo **no leo** novelas.   *I don't read novels.*

EXERCISE D

Pedro's sister often disagrees with him. Tell what Pedro says and how his sister responds.

EXAMPLE: aprender a jugar al tenis

PEDRO: Luis **aprende** a jugar al tenis.
GLORIA: Luis **no aprende** a jugar al tenis.

1. leer el periódico todos los días

PEDRO: Tony _____.

GLORIA: _____.

2. vender tortillas

PEDRO: El señor Galán _____.

GLORIA: _____.

3. comer en un restaurante elegante

PEDRO: Nosotros _____.

GLORIA: _____.

4. correr en el parque

PEDRO: Gabriel y Yuri _____.

GLORIA: _____.

5. esconder el dinero

PEDRO: Mi hermano _____.

GLORIA: _____.

6. prometer ayudar en casa

PEDRO: Yo _____.

GLORIA: _____.

b. In a question (an interrogative sentence), the subject usually comes after the verb.

Felipe corre todos los días.   *Felipe runs every day.*

¿Corre Felipe todos los días?   *Does Felipe run every day?*

(**EXERCISE E**)

Jorge's grandfather is hard of hearing and often repeats what Jorge says in the form of a question. Tell what his grandfather asks after Jorge makes each of the statements below.

EXAMPLE: Mis amigos aprenden el japonés.
          ¿Aprenden el japonés **tus amigos**?

1. Mi papá promete llegar a casa temprano.

2. Yo como demasiado.

3. Tú comprendes mis preguntas.

4. Uds. leen todos los días.

5. El señor Robles vende árboles.

6. Graciela no responde a mis cartas.

7. Los niños beben mucha leche.

8. José corre en el parque todos los días.

♦ 4 ♦ Regular *-IR* Verbs

a. The present tense of regular -*ir* verbs is formed by dropping the infinitive ending –*ir* and adding the personal endings *-o, -es, -e, -imos, -ís, -en.*

b. The present tense has the following meanings in English:

usted vive   *you live, you're living, you do live*

ella vive   *she lives, she's living, she does live*

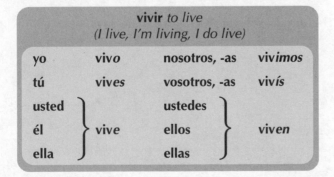

vivir *to live*		
(I live, I'm living, I do live)		
yo	viv**o**	nosotros, -as viv**imos**
tú	viv**es**	vosotros, -as viv**ís**
usted él ella	} viv**e**	ustedes ellos } viv**en** ellas

NOTE:

The endings of *-er* and *-ir* verbs are the same in the present tense except for the *nosotros* and *vosotros* forms.

◊ 5 ◊ Common *-IR* Verbs

asistir (a) *to attend*	insistir (en) *to insist on*
cubrir *to cover*	partir *to leave, depart*
decidir *to decide*	permitir *to permit, allow*
describir *to describe*	recibir *to receive*
descubrir *to discover*	subir *to go up, climb; to raise*
dividir *to divide*	sufrir *to suffer*
escribir *to write*	vivir *to live*

EXERCISE F

Rosita and a friend are visiting some cousins in Mexico. Tell what goes on during their visit.

EXAMPLE: sus primos / vivir en la capital
          Sus primos **viven** en la capital.

1. ellas / decidir visitar Tenochtitlán

2. el autobús / partir a las nueve y media

3. Rosita / insistir en visitar las pirámides

4. Amelia y yo / subir a las pirámides

5. el guardia / permitir cámaras en las pirámides

6. yo / descubrir muchas cosas interesantes

7. tú / escribir muchas tarjetas postales

8. Uds. / describir la experiencia a los primos

EXERCISE G

Yusef tells a sick classmate about the day at school. Write what he says.

1. la maestra / dividir la clase en grupos

2. yo / escribir en la pizarra

3. nosotros / asistir a una asamblea

4. Rogelio / decidir ser cómico en la clase

5. todos los alumnos / subir al laboratorio

6. tú y yo / recibir buenas notas en el examen

7. El equipo de béisbol / partir para México mañana

◆ 6 ◆ -*IR* Verbs in Negative and Interrogative Constructions

a. A verb is made negative by placing *no* before it.

Luz **no escribe** cartas.	*Luz doesn't write letters.*
Nosotros **no cubrimos** la mesa.	*We don't cover the table.*

EXERCISE H

Gabriel meets a friend he hasn't seen since he moved away. He asks about people in his old neighborhood. Answer his questions negatively.

EXAMPLE: ¿Todavía vives en la calle Londres?
No, ya **no vivo** en la calle Londres.

1. ¿Asiste Peter a la escuela contigo?

2. ¿Escriben Pola y Anita muchas poesías?

3. ¿Insistes tú en jugar al béisbol los sábados?

4. ¿Viven tus abuelos en Guadalajara?

5. ¿Permiten tus maestros teléfonos celulares en la escuela?

6. ¿Reciben Uds. tarjetas de Larry?

b. In a statement, the subject usually comes before the verb. In a question (an interrogative sentence), the subject usually comes after the verb.

La madre divide el pastel.	*The mother divides the cake.*
¿Divide la madre el pastel?	*Does the mother divide the cake?*
Tú sufres mucho.	*You suffer a lot.*
¿Sufres tú mucho?	*Do you suffer a lot?*

EXERCISE I

Kim never remembers the questions her friends ask. Write the question asked based on the answer given.

EXAMPLE: Clara y yo asistimos a la misma universidad.
¿Asisten Clara y tú a la misma universidad?

1. Nosotros vivimos en un apartamento.

2. Sanjeetah insiste en alquilar un apartamento.

3. Yo divido los gastos con ella.

4. Nuestras amigas no suben al apartamento por la escalera.

5. Yo parto en autobús el sábado por la mañana.

MASTERY EXERCISES

EXERCISE J

While waiting in line with a friend to buy tickets for a concert, Marisol's conversation jumps from one topic to another. Complete her statements with the appropriate form of the verbs given.

1. *(vivir)* Mi amigo Tomás _____ en el campo. Nosotras _____ en una ciudad

   grande. ¿Dónde _____ tus primos?

2. *(comprender)* Este señor no _____ el español. Tú y yo _____ el español y el

   italiano. ¿Qué lengua _____ ellas?

3. *(responder)* ¿_____ tú bien? Sí, yo siempre _____ bien. Alberto no

   _____ en voz alta.

4. *(asistir)* Carlos no _____ a los conciertos. Tú _____ a los conciertos.

   ¿_____ tus hermanas también?

5. *(leer)* Mi madre _____ el periódico en casa. Yo no _____ el periódico en la

   escuela. ¿_____ tú el periódico los domingos?

6. *(recibir)* ¿_____ tú muchos regalos? Pedro y Alfredo no _____ regalos.

   Yo _____ regalos en mi cumpleaños.

EXERCISE K

A new exchange student at your school is asking you questions about yourself, your friends, and the school. Answer the questions as indicated.

EXAMPLE: ¿Comen Uds. en la cafetería? *(sí)*
      Sí, **nosotros comemos** en la cafetería.

1. ¿Aprendes tú mucho en tus clases? *(sí)*

2. ¿Sufren de alergias Uds.? *(sí)*

3. ¿Recibes tú buenas notas? *(sí)*

4. ¿Venden comida española en la cafetería? *(no)*

5. ¿Beben tus amigos café con leche? *(no)*

6. ¿Permite el maestro dulces en la clase? *(no)*

7. ¿Corren Uds. en el parque después de las clases? *(sí)*

8. ¿Parte el autobús a las cuatro? *(no)*

EXERCISE L

You are preparing an email message to a cousin in which you describe a new friend at your school who is from Ecuador. Include the following: where he/she lives, the school that he/she attends, the language he/she is learning, the language that his/her parents insist on speaking at home, how well his/her parents understand English, the language they use to respond, the sport he/she decides to practice, what you read together, and what you are discovering each day.

Present Tense of Stem-Changing Verbs (*o* to *UE*)

◆1◆ Regular Stem-Changing Verbs (*o* to *UE*)

a. Many verbs that contain *o* in the stem change the *o* to *ue* in the present tense, except in the forms for *nosotros* and *vosotros*.

b. This change occurs in the syllable directly before the verb ending.

c. These verbs have regular endings in the present tense.

	mostrar *to show*	**volver** *to return*	**dormir** *to sleep*
yo	m**ue**stro	v**ue**lvo	d**ue**rmo
tú	m**ue**stras	v**ue**lves	d**ue**rmes
Ud., él, ella	m**ue**stra	v**ue**lve	d**ue**rme
nosotros, -as	mostramos	volvemos	dormimos
vosotros, -as	mostráis	volvéis	dormís
Uds., ellos, ellas	m**ue**stran	v**ue**lven	d**ue**rmen

NOTE:

1. All stem-changing verbs that change *o* to *ue* are identified in the end vocabulary by *(ue)* after the verb.

2. The verb *jugar* (to play) follows the same pattern in that the stem vowel changes in all present-tense forms except those for *nosotros* and *vosotros*: *juego, juegas, juega, jugamos, jugáis, juegan.*

◆2◆ Common Stem-Changing Verbs (*o* to *UE*)

almorzar *to eat lunch*	mostrar *to show*
contar *to count*	poder *to be able; can, may*
costar *to cost*	recordar *to remember*

devolver	*to return, give back*	resolver	*to solve; to resolve*
dormir	*to sleep*	sonar	*to sound; to ring*
encontrar	*to find; to meet*	volar	*to fly*
morir	*to die*	volver	*to return, come (go) back*

EXERCISE A

You're working at the returns desk of a department store. Tell what items various people return. Use the verb *devolver* in each statement.

EXAMPLE: yo / los libros de mis amigos
Yo **devuelvo** los libros de mis amigos.

1. mi madre / el vestido nuevo

2. Dolores / el regalo

3. los niños / los juguetes

4. tú / una cámara

5. Ana y José / los discos compactos de María

6. Uds. / la cinta

EXERCISE B

Tell what each of these people counts.

EXAMPLE: el profesor / los exámenes
El profesor **cuenta** los exámenes.

1. los alumnos / los minutos

2. Sarita / sus blusas

3. el niño / de uno a cinco

4. yo / los días

5. el señor Chomsky / su dinero

6. tú / hasta mil

7. Luigi y yo / los libros

EXERCISE C

Tell what each of these people does.

EXAMPLE: el niño / contar de uno a diez
El niño **cuenta** de uno a diez.

1. los alumnos / almorzar en la cafetería

2. el matemático / resolver el problema

3. yo / encontrar a mis amigos en el parque

4. nosotros / volver a la tienda

5. Elsa / jugar en el parque

6. tú / devolver los libros a la biblioteca

7. mi hermano / dormir doce horas

8. mi mamá / poder hablar dos lenguas

9. el despertador / sonar a las siete de la mañana

10. los turistas / volar en avión a Madrid

EXERCISE D

Some of your friends are excited about going on a youth trip to Spain. Write what each one says.

EXAMPLE: yo / no poder esperar más
Yo **no puedo** esperar más.

1. Gloria y Lourdes / contar los días

2. nosotros / volar el sábado

3. Clara / resolver hablar solamente en español

4. yo / encontrar al guía en el aeropuerto

5. tú / mostrar el boleto a todo el mundo

6. el viaje / costar mil dólares

7. nosotros / dormir en ocho hoteles

8. yo / no recordar cuando nosotros / volver

EXERCISE E

You call the telephone operator to locate a number for your sister. Complete your dialogue with the operator, using the appropriate form of the following verbs.

costar   encontrar   poder   recordar   volver

TELEFONISTA: ¿En qué _____ ayudarle?

TÚ: ¿_____ Ud. darme un número de teléfono, por favor? Mi hermana no _____

el número de teléfono de Aerolíneas Españolas y nosotros no lo _____ en la guía

telefónica. Nuestros padres _____ de Madrid esta noche.

TELEFONISTA: Un momento, por favor. Es el 555-3333.

TÚ: Muchas gracias.

TELEFONISTA: De nada. Este servicio _____ un dólar.

EXERCISE F

Answer the questions a Spanish-speaking student is asking about you and your friends.

1. ¿Dónde juegas tú con tus amigos?

2. ¿Qué deporte juegan Uds.?

3. ¿A qué hora vuelves tú a casa por la tarde?

4. ¿Dónde almuerzan los alumnos?

5. ¿Muestran Uds. películas en tu casa?

6. ¿Puedes tú ver televisión cada noche?

7. ¿Cuántas horas duermes tú por lo general?

MASTERY EXERCISES

EXERCISE G

Using the cues provided, tell how these people react.

EXAMPLE: Gregorio tiene hambre. *(almorzar)*
              Gregorio **almuerza**.

1. Jorge está muy cansado. *(dormir toda la noche)*

2. Yo necesito diez dólares para comprar un regalo. *(contar mi dinero)*

3. A mi mamá no le gusta el regalo. *(devolver el regalo)*

4. A mis amigos les gustan los deportes. *(jugar al béisbol y al voleibol)*

5. Mi papá debe llegar a Chicago rápido. *(volar en avión)*

6. Tú encuentras la tienda de música cerrada. *(volver mañana)*

7. Nosotros buscamos un restaurante bueno. *(encontrar uno cerca del cine)*

EXERCISE H

Your little cousin likes to ask questions about everything and anything. Answer his questions.

1. ¿Puedes tú vivir sin aire?

2. ¿Duermes tú en la cocina?

3. ¿Mueren las plantas en la primavera?

4. ¿Almuerzan Uds. a medianoche?

5. ¿Vuelan tus amigos como los pájaros?

6. ¿Suenan las campanas mientras Uds. duermen?

7. ¿Resuelven tus amigos tus problemas?

8. ¿Recuerdas tú las fechas importantes de tu familia?

9. ¿Juegan Uds. al tenis en la piscina?

10. ¿Cuentas tú el dinero de tus amigos?

EXERCISE I

You are writing a description in your journal of how you spend a typical Saturday with your friends. Include the following:

> ➤ where and when you meet your friends
> ➤ what you are able to do there (play electronic games, shop, see a film, etc.)
> ➤ where you can have lunch
> ➤ how you return home (bus, train, etc.)
> ➤ what you are able to do on the train/bus (sleep, read, etc.)
> ➤ when you return home

Present Tense of
Stem-Changing Verbs (*E* to *IE*)

♦ 1 ♦ Regular Stem-Changing Verbs (*E* to *IE*)

a. Many verbs that contain *e* in the stem change the *e* to *ie* in all present-tense forms except those for *nosotros* and *vosotros*.

b. This change occurs in the syllable directly before the verb ending.

c. The verbs *cerrar, perder,* and *sentir* have regular endings in the present tense.

	cerrar *to close*	**perder** *to loose*	**sentir** *to regret*
yo	c*ie*rro	p*ie*rdo	s*ie*nto
tú	c*ie*rras	p*ie*rdes	s*ie*ntes
Ud., él, ella	c*ie*rra	p*ie*rde	s*ie*nte
nosotros, -as	cerramos	perdemos	sentimos
vosotros, -as	cerráis	perdéis	sentís
Uds., ellos, ellas	c*ie*rran	p*ie*rden	s*ie*nten

NOTE:

All stem–changing verbs that change *e* to *ie* are identified in the end vocabulary by (*ie*) after the verb.

♦ 2 ♦ Common Stem-Changing Verbs (*E* to *IE*)

cerrar *to close*	pensar *to think; to intend*
comenzar *to begin*	perder *to lose; to waste; to miss (train, bus…)*
confesar *to confess*	preferir *to prefer*
defender *to defend*	querer *to want; to wish; to love*
empezar *to begin*	referir *to tell; to narrate*
entender *to understand*	sentir *to regret, be sorry; to feel*

EXERCISE A

Write the favorite pastime of these people.

EXAMPLE: Eduardo / coleccionar monedas
Eduardo **prefiere** coleccionar monedas.

1. Federico / el dominó
2. tú / la natación
3. yo / jugar a las damas
4. Isabel y Luis / el tenis
5. Javier / el béisbol
6. Ricardo y yo / el voleibol
7. mi hermano / la lectura
8. mis hermanas / la escritura

EXERCISE B

Tell what each of these people loses.

EXAMPLE: yo / la cartera
Yo **pierdo** la cartera.

1. Elsa / el dinero
2. tú / los libros
3. Rafael y Carlos / las llaves
4. mi mamá / las recetas
5. yo / el tiempo
6. Jorge y yo / el partido
7. mi abuelo / la memoria
8. mi padre / la paciencia

EXERCISE C

Tell what these people do.

EXAMPLE: la señora / cerrar la puerta
La señora **cierra** la puerta.

1. el niño / confesar la verdad a su madre
2. Carlos y Enrique / no entender el francés
3. yo / defender a mi hermano menor
4. los señores Galván / pensar visitar un museo
5. tú / preferir ver una telenovela
6. Roberto y yo / perder el autobús todos los días
7. la profesora / comenzar la clase a las ocho
8. Ud. / empezar a leer una novela
9. Francisco / querer ir al cine
10. yo / sentir mucho el accidente

EXERCISE D

Mrs. Madrigal talks about the things her family does and doesn't do. Write what she says.

EXAMPLE: Arturito / perder sus juguetes
Arturito **pierde** sus juguetes.

1. Alfonso / no cerrar el refrigerador
2. la abuela / referir cuentos antiguos
3. mi esposo / preferir jugar al golf
4. yo / siempre defender a mis hijos
5. los gemelos / no entender la palabra «no»
6. toda la familia / querer ser buena
7. mi papá / pensar viajar en abril
8. tú / empezar a estudiar más

EXERCISE E

You're living with a Costa Rican family during the summer. Answer their questions about yourself and your life at home.

1. ¿Comienzan las clases en septiembre?
2. ¿Empiezas tú a estudiar después de la cena?
3. ¿Prefieres tú el verano o el invierno?
4. ¿Piensas tú asistir a la universidad?
5. ¿Qué quieres tú estudiar allí?
6. ¿Cuántas lenguas entiendes tú?
7. ¿Qué pierdes tú a menudo?
8. ¿Quieres tú volver a tu casa pronto?

MASTERY EXERCISES

EXERCISE F

Fill in the missing verbs in this entry in Arturo's diary.

El partido _____ al mediodía pero yo no _____ a jugar hasta la una.
      1. (comenzar)   *2.* (empezar)

Carlos no _____ las reglas y el árbitro _____ a explicar las reglas
      3. (entender)   *4.* (empezar)

otra vez. Yo _____ ser deportista profesional. Todos los jugadores
           5. (pensar)

_____ ganar este partido. El entrenador del equipo _____ mucho
6. (querer)   7. (perder)

tiempo porque él nos _____ muchas jugadas antiguas. Yo _____ algo.
                      8. (referir)   9. (confesar)

Nosotros _____ jugar un buen partido a escuchar sus cuentos. ¡Nosotros
         10. (preferir)

_____ ganar este partido!
11. (pensar)

EXERCISE G

Using the cues provided, tell who does the following:

defender la patria   perder el autobús

empezar una carrera nueva   perder las llaves de la casa

entender varias lenguas   preferir jugar

querer visitar otro país   no cerrar la puerta de la casa

referir cuentos de su juventud pensar graduarse en junio

1. Tú   **3.** Los niños   **5.** El ejército   **7.** Yo   **9.** La niña
2. Mi papá   **4.** Mi hermano **6.** Los abuelos   **8.** El profesor   **10.** Mis hermanos

EXERCISE H

Use the following verbs to write a paragraph in which you reflect on your parents and how you (and your siblings) interact with them: *cerrar, comenzar, confesar, defender, entender, pensar, perder, preferir, referir, querer.*

Present Tense of Stem-Changing Verbs (*E* to *I*)

◆ 1 ◆ Regular Stem-Changing Verbs (*E* to *I*)

a. A few *-ir* verbs that contain an *e* in the stem change the *e* to *i* in all present-tense forms except those for *nosotros* and *vosotros*.

b. The change occurs in the syllable directly before the verb ending.

c. The verb *servir* has regular endings in the present tense.

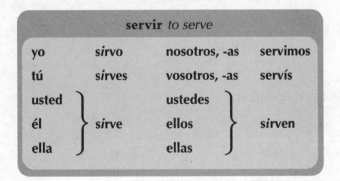

servir *to serve*			
yo	s*i*rvo	nosotros, -as	servimos
tú	s*i*rves	vosotros, -as	servís
usted		ustedes	
él	s*i*rve	ellos	s*i*rven
ella		ellas	

NOTE:

All stem-changing verbs that change *e* to *i* are identified in the end vocabulary by (*i*) after the verb.

◆ 2 ◆ Common Stem-Changing Verbs (*E* to *I*)

medir   *to measure*

pedir   *to ask for, request; to order (food)*

reñir   *to quarrel; to scold*

repetir   *to repeat*

servir   *to serve*

31

EXERCISE A

Tell what each person orders in the restaurant.

EXAMPLE: mi padre / pescado
Mi padre **pide** pescado.

1. yo / chuletas de cerdo

2. mi hermana / arroz con pollo

3. mis abuelos / paella

4. tú / una hamburguesa

5. todo el mundo / una ensalada

6. nosotros / helado de chocolate

EXERCISE B

Your shop class is planning a model house. Tell which part of the house each student is measuring.

EXAMPLE: Gabriel / el jardín
Gabriel **mide** el jardín.

1. Rosa / las ventanas

2. Javier y Enrique / el piso

3. yo / la sala

4. tú / las puertas

5. Petra y yo / las paredes

6. Alfonso / la cocina

7. Silvia y Néstor / el comedor

EXERCISE C

Tell what the students in the Spanish class repeat.

EXAMPLE: Jaime / la pregunta
Jaime **repite** la pregunta.

1. yo / la palabra

2. todo el mundo / la fecha de hoy

3. tú / la regla de gramática

4. Rosa / el trabalenguas

5. Antonio y yo / la respuesta

6. David y Luis / la frase

EXERCISE D

Complete this entry in Raquel's diary by filling in the missing verbs.

Cada miércoles yo voy a un restaurante con mi abuela. Dos meseros siempre _____
                                                                        1. (servir)

nuestra mesa. Mi abuela siempre _____ lo mismo: pollo, papas fritas y una ensalada.
                                  2. (pedir)

Yo _____ una hamburguesa, papas fritas y una ensalada. El primer mesero
    3. (pedir)

_____ las ensaladas. Mi abuela y yo _____ salsa de tomate. En otra

    4. (servir)   **5.** (pedir)

mesa, una madre _____ a su hijo porque habla en voz muy alta.

                           6. (reñir)

A veces mi abuela me dice: «Tú _____ la cuenta hoy».

                                     7. (pedir)

⇜ MASTERY EXERCISES ⇝

EXERCISE E

Using the cues provided, answer the questions posed by a new friend.

1. ¿Quién sirve la comida en tu casa? *(mi madre)*

2. ¿A qué hora sirven Uds. la comida en tu casa? *(6:30)*

3. ¿Qué plato pides tú a menudo? *(papas fritas)*

4. ¿Qué piden Uds. de postre? *(pastel de coco)*

5. ¿Qué bebida pide tu papá? *(café con leche)*

6. ¿Pides tú té con limón a veces? *(no)*

7. ¿Qué sirves tú a tus amigos en tu casa? *(helado)*

EXERCISE F

In an e-mail message to a Spanish-speaking key pal, describe a festive meal in your grandparents' home. You may wish to include the following:

> ➤ where they serve the meal
> ➤ who serves the meal
> ➤ at what time
> ➤ who always asks for soup
> ➤ what you always ask for
> ➤ the desserts everyone requests
> ➤ why your grandmother scolds you

CHAPTER 6

Verbs Irregular in the Present Tense

♦ 1 ♦ Verbs With Irregular *yo* Forms

a. In the present tense, the following verbs are irregular only in the first-person singular (*yo*):

hacer *to make, do*	**hago, haces, hace, hacemos, hacéis, hacen**
poner *to put, place*	**pongo, pones, pone, ponemos, ponéis, ponen**
saber *to know*	**sé, sabes, sabe, sabemos, sabéis, saben**
salir *to go out*	**salgo, sales, sale, salimos, salís, salen**
ver *to see; to watch*	**veo, ves, ve, vemos, véis, ven**

b. The verbs *caer* (to fall) and *traer* (to bring) have an *i* between the stem and the first-person singular ending (*-go*). Their other present-tense forms are regular.

caer *to fall*	**caigo, caes, cae, caemos, caéis, caen**
traer *to bring*	**traigo, traes, trae, traemos, traéis, traen**

<hr>

EXERCISE A

Sarita's younger sister is very proud of herself and what she does. Write what she says.

EXAMPLE: saber montar en bicicleta
        Yo **sé** montar en bicicleta.

1. ver a mis amigos todos los días

2. saber jugar al voleibol

3. hacer la ensalada todos los días

4. salir con mis amigas

5. poner la mesa cada día

EXERCISE B

Omar is being punished. His parents are making him write a statement about his responsibilities. Fill in the missing verb in each sentence.

Yo _____ que debo estudiar más. Yo no _____ programas de
    1. (saber)   **2.** (ver)

televisión durante la semana. Cuando llego de la escuela, yo _____ mis libros
                                                          3. (poner)

en el escritorio y _____ la tarea. Yo no _____ con mis amigos por la tarde.
                      4. (hacer)   **5.** (salir)

EXERCISE C

María is having a terrible day. Everything around her is falling. Describe what's happening.

EXAMPLE: la botella de leche / al suelo
         La botella de leche **cae** al suelo.

1. las monedas / detrás del escritorio

2. el niño / en el jardín

3. yo / en el sillón

4. la cuchara / al suelo

5. Carmen y yo / en el patio

6. tú / en la calle

EXERCISE D

Jorge is organizing a picnic at the beach. What do his friends bring to the picnic?

EXAMPLE: Mario / los refrescos
         Mario **trae** los refrescos.

1. Gilberto / los platos

2. Susan y yo / los sándwiches

3. Virginia / los vasos

4. tú / el pastel

5. Vicente y Gerardo / el estéreo

6. yo / las palomitas

♦ 2 ♦ Irregular Present-Tense Forms

The verbs *oír*, *decir*, *tener*, and *venir* are irregular in the present tense.

oír *to listen*	**oigo, oyes, oye, oímos, oís, oyen**
decir *to say*	**digo, dices, dice, decimos, decís, dicen**
tener *to have*	**tengo, tienes, tiene, tenemos, tenéis, tienen**
venir *to come*	**vengo, vienes, viene, venimos, venís, vienen**

EXERCISE E

Several friends are discussing the types of music they listen to. Tell what they say.

EXAMPLE: Roberto / la música clásica
          Roberto **oye** la música clásica.

1. Yusef y Luis / la música rock

2. yo / la música de jazz

3. mi padre / la música clásica

4. tú / la música de guitarra

5. Alicia y yo / las sinfonías

6. Josefina / la música romántica

EXERCISE F

Tomás is helping his younger sister master the rules of etiquette. Tell what she says in each situation Tomás presents to her.

EXAMPLE: Tú quieres otro pedazo de pastel. *(por favor)*
          Yo **digo** «por favor».

1. Juan recibe muchos regalos. *(gracias)*

   Él _____

2. Nosotros saludamos al maestro. *(buenos días)*

   Nosotros _____

3. Tú conoces a un amigo de tus padres. *(mucho gusto)*

   Yo _____

Verbs Irregular in the Present Tense

4. Elena sale de su casa. *(adiós)*

Ella _____

5. Los niños pasan delante de una persona. *(con permiso)*

Ellos _____

6. Tú entras en la casa. *(hola)*

Yo _____

EXERCISE G

Some young people are talking about what they and their friends have to do on Saturday. Using the expression tener que (to have to), write what they say.

EXAMPLE: Isabel / ir al supermercado
        Isabel **tiene que** ir al supermercado.

1. yo / arreglar mi cuarto

2. Pablo / trabajar

3. Ramona y yo / devolver los libros a la biblioteca

4. tú / ayudar en casa

5. Lorenzo y Esteban / ir a un partido de fútbol

EXERCISE H

Tell at what time these people come home.

EXAMPLE: Rosa / 4:00
        Rosa **viene a casa** a las cuatro.

1. yo / 5:30

2. mis padres / 6:00

3. tú / 12:00

4. Laura y yo / 9:15

5. Antonio / 11:00

EXERCISE I

Answer the following personal questions.

1. ¿Qué oyes tú en la radio por la mañana? *(las noticias)*

2. ¿Qué dices cuando tus amigos vuelven a sus casas? *(hasta luego)*

3. ¿Qué tienes que hacer después de las clases? *(estudiar)*

4. ¿A qué hora vienes a casa todos los días? *(4:30)*

5. ¿Quién tiene que preparar la comida en tu casa? *(mi mamá)*

6. ¿Quién tiene que lavar los platos cada noche? *(mi hermana y yo)*

7. ¿Quién oye el pronóstico del tiempo en tu casa? *(mi papá)*

♦ 3 ♦ Irregular Verbs *DAR* and *IR*

	dar *to give*	**ir** *to go*
yo	doy	voy
tú	das	vas
Ud., él, ella	da	va
nosotros, -as	damos	vamos
vosotros, -as	dais	vais
Uds., ellos, ellas	dan	van

NOTE:

A conjugated form of the verb *ir* followed by the preposition *a* and an infinitive is used to express a future action.

Voy a estudiar.	*I am going to study.*
¿Qué **vas** a hacer?	*What are you going to do?*

♦ 4 ♦ Irregular Verbs *SER* and *ESTAR*

	ser *to be*	**estar** *to be*
yo	soy	estoy
tú	eres	estás
Ud., él, ella	es	está
nosotros, -as	somos	estamos
vosotros, -as	sois	estáis
Uds., ellos, ellas	son	están

EXERCISE J

Tell where each member of your family goes every day.

EXAMPLE: mi padre / a la oficina
          Mi padre **va** a la oficina.

1. mis hermanos / a la universidad

2. mi hermana / a la escuela de enseñanza secundaria

3. mamá / al supermercado

4. yo / a la biblioteca

5. el abuelo y yo / al parque

EXERCISE K

What does each of these people give?

EXAMPLE: Carlos / dinero a los pobres
          Carlos **da** dinero a los pobres.

1. yo / regalos a mis amigos

2. Phil y Juan / problemas a sus padres

3. tú / flores a tu mamá

4. el señor Díaz / dulces a su esposa

5. Carmen y yo / pan a los pájaros

6. el profesor / mucha tarea

EXERCISE L

Gloria and her friends are discussing the nationality of people they know. Write what they say about each person.

EXAMPLE: Lourdes / España
          Lourdes **es** de España.

1 el profesor de español / Colombia

2. mis primas / Venezuela

3. Raquel / Costa Rica

4. Gladys / Honduras

5. Murray y yo / los Estados Unidos

6. tú / Puerto Rico

7. yo / Perú

8. ustedes / Panamá

EXERCISE M

When Mr. Lara calls home, only Tomás is there. Tell where everyone else is.

EXAMPLE: Mamá **está en el supermercado**.

1. Gilberto _____ .

2. Bernardo y Felipe _____ .

3. Yolanda _____ .

4. Tú _____ .

5. Los abuelos _____ .

6. El perro _____ .

EXERCISE N

Complete this note that Ramón left for his parents by filling in the missing verbs. Use an appropriate form of *dar*, *ir*, *ser*, or *estar*.

Queridos padres:

Yo _____ a casa de mi amigo Marcos. Él _____ de México. Nosotros _____
     1.   *2.*   *3.*

a jugar al tenis. Yo _____ a estar en el parque que _____ cerca de la escuela.
                     4.   *5.*

Yo _____ de comer a Fido después. Marcos _____ a cenar con nosotros porque
     6.   *7.*

sus padres _____ en el centro. Hasta luego.
              8.

                                               Ramón

EXERCISE O

Answer the questions that your inquisitive grandmother asks you when some friends come to visit. Use in your responses the cues in parentheses.

1. ¿Quiénes son estos jóvenes? *(mis amigos)*

2. ¿Qué das a tus amigos? *(palomitas)*

3. ¿Dónde está tu hermana? *(en su dormitorio)*

4. ¿Qué van a hacer Uds. ahora? *(jugar a las damas)*

5. ¿De dónde es ese chico? *(Argentina)*

6. ¿Adónde vas tú esta noche? *(al cine)*

⟨ MASTERY EXERCISES ⟩

EXERCISE P

Ricardo describes his neighbors to a friend. Fill in the appropriate form of the missing verbs.

Todos los días yo _____ a mi vecino, el señor Robles, cuando mi hermana y yo
        1. (ver)

_____ a la escuela. Él _____ en la calle con su perro Campeón.
    2. (ir)   *3.* (estar)

Campeón _____ muy fuerte y el señor Robles _____ al suelo a
          4. (ser)   *5.* (caer)

menudo. Nosotros _____ «Buenos días». Cuando yo _____ de la
                   6. (decir)   *7.* (venir)

escuela yo _____ los ladridos de Campeón que _____ en el jardín.
            8. (oír)   *9.* (estar)

Campeón y yo _____ buenos amigos y a veces yo _____ que cuidarlo
              10. (ser)   *11.* (tener)

cuando los señores Robles no _____ en casa. Los Robles _____
                              12. (estar)   *13.* (ser)

buenos vecinos y muchas veces Campeón _____ regalos a nuestra casa. Cuando
                                        14. (traer)

mi mamá _____ esto, mi hermana y yo _____ que devolver los regalos
          15. (ver)   *16.* (tener)

de Campeón.

EXERCISE Q

A classmate is conducting a survey to find out if people think alike. For each situation select the appropriate reaction from those given and write it.

caer en la misma fecha   decir «Buenos días»   traer mi estéreo

dar la cuenta al cliente   ir a la fiesta   ver el programa

dar un regalo a mi hermana   oír las noticias en la radio

EXAMPLE: Tú trabajas de mesero en un restaurante. *(Yo)*
          Yo **doy** la cuenta al cliente.

1. Hay una fiesta en casa de tu amigo Ricardo. *(Yo)*

2. Tú y tu hermano encuentran a un vecino en la calle. *(Nosotros)*

3. El tocadiscos de Ricardo no funciona. *(Yo)*

4. Tú y un amigo celebran sus cumpleaños el 2 de enero. *(Nuestro cumpleaños)*

5. Hay un programa bueno en la televisión. *(Yo)*

6. Es el cumpleaños de tu hermana. *(Yo)*

7. Estás en el auto y quieres saber qué pasa actualmente. *(Yo)*

<hr>

EXERCISE R

Answer these questions that a cousin asks you about school.

1. ¿A quién ves en la escuela todos los días?

2. ¿Oyes las respuestas de los otros alumnos?

3. ¿Traes tus libros a casa cada día?

4. ¿Tienes mucha tarea por lo general?

5. ¿De dónde es tu profesor de español?

6. ¿Vienen Uds. a casa después de las clases?

7. ¿Qué dice el maestro cuando contestas bien?

8. ¿Caen muchos exámenes en el mismo día?

9. ¿Vas al estadio para ver los partidos?

10. ¿Estás en tus clases a tiempo?

11. ¿Dan tus maestros notas altas?

<hr>

EXERCISE S

Write your impressions of your first day of classes in your journal. You may wish to include information on the following:

➤ the amount of work you are going to do

➤ the attendance record of your teachers

➤ their ability to see and hear everything

➤ the number of tests

➤ what you bring to class each day

➤ what you know about the school year

CHAPTER 7

Verbs with Spelling Changes in the Present Tense

♦ 1 ♦ Verbs Ending in *-CER* and *-CIR*

a. Most verbs whose infinitives end in *-cer* or *-cir* have the ending *-zco* in the first-person singular of the present tense. This pattern occurs only if a vowel precedes the *c* in the infinitive.

	ofrecer *to offer*	**conducir** *to drive*
yo	**ofrezco**	**conduzco**
tú	**ofreces**	**conduces**
Ud., él, ella	**ofrece**	**conduce**
nosotros, -as	**ofrecemos**	**conducimos**
vosotros, -as	**ofrecéis**	**conducís**
Uds., ellos, ellas	**ofrecen**	**conducen**

b. Common *-cer* verbs

aparecer *to appear*	ofrecer *to offer*
conocer *to know; to meet*	parecer *to seem*
desaparecer *to disappear*	reconocer *to recognize*
obedecer *to obey*	

c. Common *-cir* verbs

conducir *to drive; to lead*	traducir *to translate*
producir *to produce*	

NOTE:

The verbs *hacer* and *decir* are exceptions. (See Chapter 6.)

44

EXERCISE A

In an orientation session on community service, the students in your global studies class offer to perform service in various settings.

EXAMPLE: Gerardo / en el hospital
           Gerardo **ofrece servicio** en el hospital.

1. Rosita / en la escuela de párvulos

2. yo / en la oficina de un veterinario

3. Clara y Luz / en la biblioteca

4. tú / en la corte

5. Rogelio y yo / en la jefatura de la policía

6. Elena / en la enfermería

EXERCISE B

Gloria found an old box in the attic filled with a variety of documents written in English. You and other friends offer to help her translate them. Tell what each person translates.

EXAMPLE: Victoria / las cartas
           Victoria **traduce** las cartas.

1. Ana y yo / los poemas

2. Mariah / la canción

3. yo / el artículo del periódico

4. Kim y Adriana / las tarjetas

5. tú / este párrafo corto

EXERCISE C

Hugo is spending the summer on a farm. He quotes some of the farmer's comments in a letter to you. Fill in the missing verbs.

El sol _____ con el gallo pero _____ cuando hace mal tiempo. Yo
           1. (aparecer)   **2.** (desaparecer)

no _____ otra vida que la vida del campo. ¿_____ tú esos animales?
       3. (conocer)   **4.** (reconocer)

Los caballos siempre _____ a los campesinos. ¿Y esas flores? _____
                          5. (obedecer)   **6.** (parecer)

muy bonitas, ¿verdad? Nosotros _____ toda la comida que comemos en esta granja.
                                   7. (producir)

Además, los viernes yo _____ mi camión a un mercado en el pueblo. Muchos turistas
_____8. (conducir)

visitan ese pueblo y _____ que vienen solamente para comprar las legumbres. Dicen que
_____9. (parecer)

nosotros _____ legumbres a precios bajos. ¿_____ tú una vida mejor?
_____10. (ofrecer)_____11. (conocer)

EXERCISE D

**Answer the questions your younger brother asks you as you walk on the beach at night. In
your answers, use the cues in parentheses.**

1. ¿Dónde aparece el sol? *(en el este)*

2. ¿Cuándo desaparece la luna esta semana? *(por la mañana)*

3. ¿Cómo parecen las estrellas? *(muy pequeñas)*

4. ¿Reconoces esa estrella? *(no)*

5. ¿Dónde ofrecen cursos sobre las estrellas? *(en la escuela)*

6. ¿Conoces tú mucho del universo? *(un poco)*

◆ 2 ◆ *SABER* and *CONOCER*

a. The verbs *saber* and *conocer* both mean "to know." All of the present-tense forms of these two
verbs are regular except the *yo* form.

saber	*sé, sabes, sabe, sabemos, sabéis, saben*
conocer	*conozco, conoces, conoce, conocemos, conocéis, conocen*

b. *Saber* means "to know a fact, to have information about something, to know how to do something." *Saber* can be followed by a noun, a clause, or an infinitive.

Yo sé tu nombre.	*I know your name.*
María sabe dónde vivo.	*María knows where I live.*
Ellos no saben esquiar.	*They don't know how to ski.*

c. *Conocer* means "to know personally, to be acquainted with, to be familiar with." *Conocer* can
be followed by names of people, places, or things.

Conozco a Juan y María.	*I know Juan and María.*
Ella conoce Bogotá.	*She knows Bogotá.*
Él conoce un restaurante bueno.	*He's familiar with a good restaurant.*

d. Note the difference in meaning between the following sentences:

Él sabe el nombre del alcalde.	*He knows the mayor's name.*
Él conoce al alcalde.	*He knows the mayor.*

EXERCISE E

Mr. Moreno is proud of his family's many talents. Based on the drawings below, tell what he says they know how to do.

EXAMPLE: Alberto **sabe tocar el violín**.

1. Mi esposa y yo _____ .

2. Xavier _____ .

3. Mónica y Beatriz _____ .

4. Mis padres _____ .

5. Yo _____ .

EXERCISE F

Margarita has just moved to your city. She tells you the things with which she and her family are already acquainted.

EXAMPLE: mi mamá / el supermercado
          Mi mamá **ya conoce** el supermercado.

1. yo / el parque

2. mis hermanos / el cine

3. mi papá / a tu papá

4. mi hermana y yo / todas las tiendas

5. el perro / a nuestros vecinos

6. mi familia / a toda tu familia

EXERCISE G

As a party game, Dolores has prepared slips of paper with cues and the names of party guests. Whoever picks the slip must ask a question using *conocer* or *saber*, and the person(s) called upon must respond.

EXAMPLE: Rafael / jugar al boliche
          Rafael, ¿**sabes tú** jugar al boliche?
          Sí, **sé** jugar al boliche pero no muy bien.

1. Silvia y César / bailar el tango

2. Estela / el Parque Nacional

3. Isaac y Pedro / cocinar

4. Erika y Elena / la música del grupo «Los Amigos»

5. Ching / el presidente del país

6. Mirta / el número de teléfono de César

EXERCISE H

Pilar and her friend Rocío plan a shopping trip. Complete the dialogue below with the appropriate forms of *saber* or *conocer*.

ROCIO: Yo ya _____ lo que quieres hacer hoy. Ir de compras, ¿verdad?
1.

PILAR: Sí, tienes razón. Tú me _____ muy bien. ¿Vienes conmigo?
2.

ROCÍO: ¡Cómo no!

PILAR: Yo _____ una tienda que acaba de abrir en el centro. Tienen ropa bonita.
3.

ROCÍO: ¿_____ si es cara? No tengo mucho dinero.
4.

PILAR: Yo no _____ pero vamos. Mi mamá _____ la dirección
5.   6.

de la tienda. También ella _____ a una señora que trabaja ahí. Si la tienda es
7.

cara, solamente vamos a ver los diseños. Mi mamá y yo _____ coser.
8.

ROCÍO: Bueno, vamos. Quiero _____ la tienda.
9.

EXERCISE I

You're visiting a school while you are in Madrid. Answer the questions the students ask you.

1. ¿Conoces la ciudad de Madrid?

2. ¿Sabes conducir?

3. ¿Conoces a otros chicos españoles?

4. ¿Sabes tocar la guitarra?

5. ¿Conoces la música española?

6. ¿Sabes el nombre de un cantante español?

7. ¿Conoces la comida española?

8. ¿Sabes preparar un plato español?

9. ¿Sabes cómo se llama el Rey de España?

10. ¿Conoces la historia de España?

MASTERY EXERCISES

EXERCISE J

Raúl and Jaime talk about a concert. Fill in the missing verbs to complete the dialogue.

RAÚL: ¿_____ tú que hay un concierto en el parque esta noche?
          1. (saber)

JAIME: Sí, lo _____ . _____ que todo el mundo va a asistir.
              2. (saber)   **3.** (parecer)

RAÚL: ¿Qué grupos van a cantar y tocar?

JAIME: Yo _____ el nombre de uno de los grupos que anuncian, «The Zeros».
          4. (reconocer)

      ¿_____ tú su música?
        5. (conocer)

RAÚL: Sí, yo _____ su música y me gusta mucho, pero cantan en inglés.
           6. (conocer)

Ellos _____ muchos discos.
     7. (producir)

JAIME: ¿En inglés? Yo no _____ inglés. Si vamos al concierto,
               8. (saber)

      ¿_____ tú las canciones al español?
        9. (traducir)

RAÚL: Claro, pero hay un problema. Tengo que estar en casa a las once. Si yo no

      _____ a mis padres, no voy a poder salir por un mes. Tú ya
      10. (obedecer)

      _____ a mis padres.
      11. (conocer)

JAIME: ¿De veras? ¿Dices que si tú no les _____, tú _____ de
                    12. (obedecer)   **13.** (desaparecer)

      nuestra vida social?

RAÚL: Bueno. Yo pido permiso a mis padres, y si yo no _____, vas solo.
                          14. (aparecer)

JAIME: Está bien.

EXERCISE K

As an exchange student in Caracas, you're being interviewed for the school newspaper. Answer the reporter's questions.

1. ¿Ya conoces bien la ciudad de Caracas?

2. ¿Qué lugares conoces?

3. ¿Qué deportes sabes jugar?

4. ¿Qué clase de auto conduces?

5. ¿Obedeces a los maestros venezolanos?

6. ¿Sabes cuándo aparece esta entrevista en el periódico?

7. ¿Qué comentario ofreces a los estudiantes venezolanos?

8. ¿Qué proyecto produces durante este año?

EXERCISE L

You are writing to your Spanish key pal about the summer camp you are attending. You may wish to include the following in your letter:

> ► how the experience seems to you
>
> ► your familiarity with the different places in the camp, e.g., pool, dining room
>
> ► if the campers obey the camp's rules
>
> ► your impression of the counselors
>
> ► what special activities the camp offers
>
> ► what you now know how to do that you didn't know before

SER and ESTAR

Spanish has two different verbs, *ser* and *estar*, that both correspond to the English verb "to be." Which one you should use depends on the context.

◆ 1 ◆ Uses of SER

Ser is used:

a. to express a characteristic, a description, or an identification.

   (1) Characteristics

La sopa **es buena**.	*The soup is good.*
El profesor **es estricto**.	*The teacher is strict.*

   (2) Description

Martha **es alta**.	*Martha is tall.*
El señor Salas **es rico**.	*Mr. Salas is rich.*

   (3) Identification

¿Quién es?	*Who is it?*
Soy yo.	*It's me.*

b. to express occupation or nationality.

   (1) Occupation

Mi primo **es abogado**.	*My cousin is a lawyer.*
Ellos **son contadores**.	*They are accountants.*

   (2) Nationality

Pedro y Elenita **son españoles**.	*Pedro and Elenita are Spanish.*
Victoria **es peruana**.	*Victoria is Peruvian.*

c. to express time and dates.

   (1) Time

Son las dos.	*It's two o'clock.*
Es medianoche.	*It's midnight.*

(2) Dates

| **Es el tres de mayo.** | *It's May 3.* |
| **Es el primero de abril.** | *It's April 1.* |

d. with *de*, to express origin, possession, or material.

(1) Origin

| El muchacho **es de México.** | *The boy is from Mexico.* |
| Las naranjas **son de Valencia.** | *The oranges are from Valencia.* |

(2) Possession

| Ese reloj **es de Carmen.** | *That watch is Carmen's.* |
| La casa **es de mi tío.** | *The house is my uncle's.* |

(3) Material

| La blusa **es de seda.** | *The blouse is made of silk.* |
| El reloj **es de oro.** | *The watch is made of gold.* |

NOTE:

1. Adjectives used with *ser* must agree with the subject in number and gender.

| Miguel y Adalberto **son mexicanos.** | *Miguel and Adalberto are Mexican.* |
| Tía Clara **es puertorriqueña** también. | *Aunt Clara is Puerto Rican too.* |

2. In questions, the adjective usually follows the verb.

| ¿**Son viejos** los edificios? | *Are the buildings old?* |

3. The adjective *feliz* is generally used with *ser*.

| Ella **es feliz**. | *She is happy.* |

4. The forms of *ser* are summarized in the section on irregular verbs in the Appendix, page (385).

EXERCISE A

After a party at your home, your mother asks you about the friends who attended. Tell her about them using the correct forms of *ser* and the suggested adjectives below.

aburrido	bonito	guapo	responsable
amable	celoso	independiente	simpático
antipático	divertido	inteligente	tacaño

EXAMPLE: Adela es **amable y divertida**.

1. Stephen
2. Alicia y Sofía
3. Gerardo y Raúl
4. Diana
5. Hank
6. Marcos y Elsa

EXERCISE B

After introducing himself and some friends, Lorenzo tells their nationalities. Using the appropriate form of *ser*, tell what Lorenzo says.

EXAMPLE: Raquel / Chile
Raquel **es de** Chile. Ella **es chilena**.

1. yo / México

2. Beatriz / Argentina

3. Homero y Hugo / España

4. Gloria / Colombia

5. Inés y yo / México

6. tú (Juan) / Puerto Rico

7. ellas / Perú

EXERCISE C

You are helping a teacher clean out the school's lost and found at the end of the year. You identify the owners of many of the lost objects.

EXAMPLE: el suéter / Belinda
El suéter **es de** Belinda

1. los anteojos / Enrique

2. el reloj / Berta

3. las llaves / la señora Pérez

4. el diccionario / Roberto

5. los guantes de béisbol / Arturo y Víctor

6. las fotos / Pilar

EXERCISE D

Every student was asked to bring in an object or a picture of an object from another country. Write the question and the answer for each item listed.

EXAMPLE: estas monedas / Rusia
¿**De dónde son** estas monedas?
Son de Rusia.

1. estas castañuelas / España

2. estas maracas / Puerto Rico

3. esta cámara / Japón

4. estas galletas / Inglaterra

5. esta tortilla / México

<EXERCISE E>

Enrique goes to a watch repair shop. All the watches there show a different time. Tell what time it is on each clock.

EXAMPLE: **Son las cuatro y once**

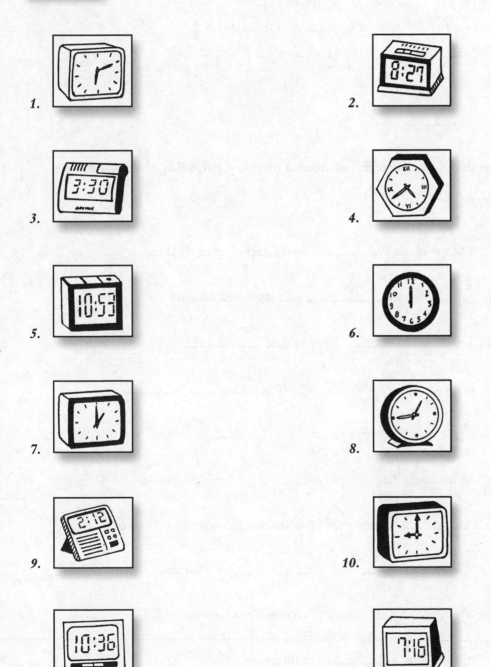

1.

2.

3.

4.

5.

6.

7.

8.

9.

10.

11.

12.

EXERCISE F

Answer your new friend's questions.

1. ¿Quién es Ud.?

2. ¿De dónde es Ud.?

3. ¿Cuál es su nacionalidad?

4. ¿Cómo es Ud.?

5. ¿De qué color es su casa?

6. ¿De qué material es su casa?

7. ¿Es Ud. un(a) alumno(a) diligente?

8. ¿Cómo son sus hermanos?

9. ¿Qué es su padre?

10. ¿Cómo son sus amigos?

11. ¿Quién es su mejor amigo(a)?

12. ¿De quién es esta cámara?

13. ¿Qué día es hoy?

14. ¿Cuál es la fecha de hoy?

15. ¿Qué hora es?

EXERCISE G

Complete this message that Carmen received from a new key pal, using the appropriate forms of the verb *ser*.

Querida Carmen:

Yo _____ Amelia Mariscal. _____ de un pueblo cerca de Buenos
       1.   2.

Aires. _____ argentina. Mi padre _____ ingeniero. Nuestra
       3.   4.

casa _____ muy bonita. _____ nueva y _____
       5.   6.   7.

de ladrillo. Mi dormitorio _____ muy grande porque yo _____ la
               8.   9.

hija mayor de la familia. _____ de color rosado y _____ muy
              10.   11.

lindo. Los dormitorios de mis hermanos (tengo tres) _____ más pequeños.
                               12.

La comida argentina _____ muy sabrosa. Comemos mucha carne. Yo sé cocinar y
               13.

a veces _____ la cocinera y mis hermanos _____ los meseros.
       14.   15.

_____ muy cómico cuando hacemos esto. Yo creo que mis hermanos
       16.

_____ guapos. También ellos _____ fuertes y
       17.   18.

_____ buenos futbolistas. Ya sabes que en mi país nosotros _____
19.   20.

aficionados al fútbol. Mis hermanos _____ miembros de un equipo y juegan
21.

bien. Ya _____ las cinco de la tarde y _____ la hora de mi clase de
22.   23.

baile. Escríbime pronto y cuéntame cómo tú _____ y cuáles _____ tus
24.   25.

pasatiempos favoritos. Hasta pronto.

Amelia

♦ 2 ♦ Uses of ESTAR

Estar is used:

a. to express location or position.

Madrid **está en España**.	*Madrid is in Spain.*
Mi tío **está en México**.	*My uncle is in Mexico.*
El libro **está en la mesa**.	*The book is on the table.*
¿Dónde **están los niños**?	*Where are the children?*

b. to express a condition or state.

La sopa **está caliente**.	*The soup is hot.*
María **está sentada**.	*María is seated.*
El señor Salas **está triste**.	*Mr. Salas is sad.*
¿Cómo **está Ud.**? **Estoy** muy bien.	*How are you? I'm very well.*
La ventana **está abierta**.	*The window is open.*

NOTE:

1. Adjectives used with *estar* agree with the subject in number and gender.

Ana **está ocupada**.	*Ana is busy.*
Los jóvenes **están ocupados**.	*The young people are busy.*

2. In questions, the adjective usually follows the verb.

¿Está ocupada Ana?	*Is Ana busy?*
¿Están ocupados los jóvenes?	*Are the young people busy?*

3. The forms of *estar* are summarized in the section on irregular verbs in the Appendix, page (384).

EXERCISE H

When Luisa comes home from school, she asks her mother where everyone and everything is. Write Luisa's questions and her mother's responses.

EXAMPLE: los refrescos / el refrigerador
¿**Dónde están** los refrescos?
Están en el refrigerador.

1. el pastel / el horno

2. el correo / la mesa del comedor

3. mis hermanos / el parque

4. mi blusa roja / el armario

5. la revista «Tú» / el sofá

6. tú / la cocina

7. mi diario / la cama

8. papá / la oficina

9. mis zapatos / el cuarto

EXERCISE I

The mathematics teacher is giving back a test. Tell how the students feel.

EXAMPLE: Marta / nervioso
Marta **está nerviosa**.

1. Gabriel / desilusionado

2. Rita y Linda / contento

3. yo / triste

4. Sergei y José / preocupado

5. Inés y Luigi / nervioso

6. Sofía / sorprendido

EXERCISE J

Alicia is working as a waitress. Write the complaints that she gets about what she serves. Use the suggestions below.

EXAMPLE: La ensalada **está vieja**.

el café	agrio
la ensalada	caliente
la hamburguesa	crudo
el helado	derretido
la leche	duro
el pan	frío
las papas fritas	horrible
el refresco	seco
la sopa	viejo

EXERCISE K

Your coach is upset and is delaying the start of practice because two teammates aren't there. Complete the dialogue with the appropriate forms of *estar*.

ENTRENADOR: ¿Quién _____ ausente hoy?
                                1.

TÚ: Creo que todos nosotros _____ presentes.
                                  2.

RAFAEL: No. José y Roberto no _____ aquí.
                                      3.

ENTRENADOR: ¿Y dónde _____ ellos? Yo _____ preocupado.
                           4.   5.

PABLO: Roberto y José _____ sentados debajo de un árbol.
                              6.

TÚ: ¿Por qué _____ ellos allí?
                   7.

PABLO: José _____ enfermo y Roberto _____ con él.
                   8.   9.

(Roberto llega.)

ENTRENADOR: Roberto, ¿cómo _____ José?
                                 10.

ROBERTO: Él _____ enfermo.
                   11.

(José llega.)

ENTRENADOR: ¿Cómo _____ tú?
                         12.

JOSÉ: Ahora yo _____ bien. Vamos a jugar.
                     13.

TÚ: Ahora nosotros _____ contentos porque podemos jugar.
                          14.

EXERCISE L

Susana is trying to understand how people feel in different circumstances. Answer her questions using the cues provided.

1. ¿Cómo estás cuando recibes una buena nota en un examen? *(contento)*
2. ¿Cómo estás cuando no puedes contestar la pregunta del profesor? *(preocupado)*
3. ¿Cómo estás cuando estás solo(a) en la casa? *(nervioso)*

4. ¿Cómo estás cuando el profesor da un examen de sorpresa? *(enojado)*

5. ¿Cómo estás cuando ganas un partido? *(emocionado)*

6. ¿Cómo estás cuando ves una telenovela? *(triste)*

7. ¿Cómo estás cuando comes demasiado chocolate? *(enfermo)*

8. ¿Cómo estás cuando tus padres te dan un coche nuevo? *(sorprendido)*

9. ¿Cómo estás cuando tu novio(a) sale con otra(o) chica(o)? *(celoso)*

10. ¿Cómo estás después de ayudar en casa? *(cansado)*

MASTERY EXERCISES

EXERCISE M

While standing in line for the movies, you hear these statements. Complete them with the appropriate form of *ser* or *estar*.

1. Guillermo _____ sentado porque _____ cansado.

2. En ese cuarto hace calor porque las ventanas _____ cerradas.

3. No comprendo. ¿Dices que Julio _____ peruano pero

   no _____ de Perú?

4. La madre de Elena _____ enfermera pero ella _____ en el hospital

   porque _____ enferma.

5. Los señores Arvida _____ ricos. Sus hijos siempre _____ en otras ciudades.

6. En el verano su ropa _____ de algodón, y en el invierno sus pantalones

   _____ de lana.

7. Tú _____ pálida hoy. ¿Cómo _____ tú?

8. El señor Pardos trabaja mucho. Siempre _____ muy cansado.

9. Los niños _____ preocupados porque no saben dónde _____

   su perro.

10. ¿_____ lunes hoy? ¿Y cuál _____ la fecha?

11. No traigo reloj. ¿Qué hora _____ ?

12. La motocicleta _____ nueva. _____ de mi hermana.

13. Mañana _____ día de fiesta. Yo _____ feliz.

14. Los colores vivos _____ más bonitos que los colores claros.

15. La película _____ aburrida. Nosotros _____ desilusionados.

(EXERCISE N)

You are working in a restaurant and all compliments and complaints are presented to you. List the compliments (*elogios*) and complaints (*quejas*) you received today about the service, food, and restaurant in general.

CHAPTER 9

Commands

◆ 1 ◆ Formal Commands of Regular Verbs

a. Formal or polite commands are formed by dropping the final -*o* from the first–person singular of the present tense and adding:

    1. -*e* for *Ud.* (singular) and -*en* for *Uds.* (plural) in the case of -*ar* verbs.

    2. -*a* for *Ud.* and -*an* for *Uds.* in the case of -*er* or -*ir* verbs.

Infinitive	Present Tense First Person Singular	Command Forms Singular	Plural	Meaning
abrir	**abro**	**abra**	**abran**	*open*
cerrar	**cierro**	**cierre**	**cierren**	*close*
decir	**digo**	**diga**	**digan**	*say, tell*
hablar	**hablo**	**hable**	**hablen**	*speak*
hacer	**hago**	**haga**	**hagan**	*do, make*
leer	**leo**	**lea**	**lean**	*read*
perder	**pierdo**	**pierda**	**pierdan**	*lose*
servir	**sirvo**	**sirva**	**sirvan**	*serve*
tener	**tengo**	**tenga**	**tengan**	*have*
traducir	**traduzco**	**traduzca**	**traduzcan**	*translate*
venir	**vengo**	**venga**	**vengan**	*come*
ver	**veo**	**vea**	**vean**	*see*
volver	**vuelvo**	**vuelva**	**vuelvan**	*return*

NOTE:

1. The vowel of the endings of the command forms is the "opposite" of the vowel endings of the third–person singular form of the present tense: -*e* for -*ar* verbs, and -*a* for -*er* and -*ir* verbs.

2. The subject pronoun (*Ud., Uds.*) follows the verb.

3. In Spanish America, *Uds.* can be either formal or informal.

b. To form the negative command, place *no* before the verb.

No hablen inglés.	*Don't speak English.*
No pierda las llaves.	*Don't lose the keys.*

c. Verbs that end in -*zar*, -*car*, and -*gar* have spelling changes in the command forms. The spelling change in -*zar* verbs occurs because in Spanish, *z* is rarely followed by *e* or *i*. The spelling change in -*car* and -*gar* verbs occurs to keep the original sounds of *c* and *g*.

Study the following examples:

Infinitive	Present Tense First Person Singular	Command Forms Singular	Plural	Meaning
empezar	**empiezo**	**empiece**	**empiecen**	*begin*
buscar	**busco**	**busque**	**busquen**	*seek*
jugar	**juego**	**juegue**	**jueguen**	*play*

EXERCISE A

The Santiago family just moved into a new house. Their neighbor invites Mrs. Santiago to her home. Write what she tells Mrs. Santiago to do.

EXAMPLE: venir a mi casa
        Venga a mi casa.

1. entrar en la casa

2. cerrar la puerta

3. pasar a la cocina

4. tomar un café

5. aprender a conducir

6. asistir a la reunión de la comunidad conmigo

7. subir al segundo piso

8. leer el periódico del barrio

9. pedir instrucciones a la policía

10. recordar nuestra cita mañana

EXERCISE B

Mrs. Ortega's grandchildren are leaving for camp. Write what she tells them to do.

EXAMPLE: prestar atención al consejero
        Presten atención al consejero.

1. no pelear con los otros chicos	6. leer muchos libros
2. decir la verdad siempre	7. escribir cada semana
3. llamar a casa los domingos	8. comer bien
4. no perder sus cosas	9. no correr mucho
5. tener paciencia	10. no beber muchos refrescos

EXERCISE C

You have been hired as a waiter (waitress). Write the instructions that the restaurant manager gives you.

EXAMPLE: saludar a los clientes
Salude a los clientes.

1. ofrecer los platos especiales del día

2. describir los platos si los clientes preguntan

3. contestar sus preguntas

4. preguntar qué van a tomar

5. poner pan y mantequilla en la mesa en seguida

6. traer la comida rápidamente

7. servir la ensalada primero

8. recordar los postres y el café

9. quitar los platos sucios de la mesa

10. dejar la cuenta en la mesa

11. volver a poner la mesa

EXERCISE D

You are moving into a new house, and the moving van has arrived. Tell the movers where to put your things.

1. Señor, *(subir)* _____ estos cartones al segundo piso.

2. Señores, *(colocar)* _____ el sofá contra esta pared.

3. Señor, *(sacar)* _____ las lámparas de la caja.

4. Señores, no *(maltratar)* _____ los cuadros.

5. Señores, *(poner)* _____ esa caja en la cocina.

6. Señor, no *(dejar)* _____ este sillón aquí.

7. Señores, *(leer)* _____ las etiquetas de las cajas.

8. Señor, *(cerrar)* _____ la puerta.

9. Señor, *(tener)* _____ mucho cuidado con esa mesa.

10. Señores, *(volver)* _____ a colocar el sofá contra la otra pared.

◆ 2 ◆ Formal Commands of Irregular Verbs

The following verbs have irregular formal command forms:

Infinitive	Present Tense First Person Singular	Command Forms		Meaning
		Singular	Plural	
dar	doy	dé	den	*give*
estar	estoy	esté	estén	*be*
ir	voy	vaya	vayan	*go*
ser	soy	sea	sean	*be*

NOTE:

1. *Dé* has an accent mark to distinguish it from *de* (of).

2. *Esté* and *estén* have accent marks to indicate that the stress falls on the last syllable.

EXERCISE E

Write the instructions your mother gave you when you and your brother stayed at a friend's house.

1. *(ser)* ¡_____ corteses!

2. *(hacer)* ¡_____ la cama por la mañana!

3. *(poner)* ¡_____ la ropa en el armario!

4. *(ir)* ¡_____ despacio!

5. *(dar)* ¡_____ las gracias después de comer!

6. *(tener)* ¡_____ mucho cuidado en la casa!

EXERCISE F

You and some friends are in *Sevilla* for *Carnaval*. Write the advice the hotel manager gives you as you tell him your plans.

EXAMPLE: Yo traigo mucho dinero. *(no)*
¡**No traiga** mucho dinero!

1. Nosotros buscamos un guía. *(sí)*

2. Llevamos máscaras en Carnaval. *(sí)*

3. Vamos despacio por las calles. *(sí)*

4. Estamos listos para salir del hotel a las diez. *(sí)*

5. Volvemos muy tarde. *(no)*

6. Conduzco mi coche. *(no)*

7. Hacemos caso de los anuncios. *(sí)*

8. Olvido la dirección del hotel. *(no)*

9. Doy una propina al guía. *(sí)*

10. Somos impacientes. *(no)*

♦ 3 ♦ Affirmative Familiar Commands (Singular)

a. The affirmative *tú* command of regular verbs and stem-changing verbs is the same as the *Ud.* form of the present tense.

Infinitive	Present Tense *UD.* Form	Meaning
abrir	**abre**	*open*
cerrar	**cierra**	*close*
dar	**da**	*give*
hablar	**habla**	*speak*
leer	**lee**	*read*
perder	**pierde**	*lose*
servir	**sirve**	*serve*
ver	**ve**	*see*
volver	**vuelve**	*return*

b. The following verbs have irregular affirmative *tú* commands:

Infinitive	Commands *Tú* Form	Meaning
decir	di	say, tell
hacer	haz	do, make
ir	ve	go
poner	pon	put
salir	sal	leave, go out
ser	sé	be
tener	ten	have
venir	ven	come

NOTE:

1. Subject pronouns are usually omitted.

2. The familiar commands are used: (1) between friends and classmates; (2) by parents and other adults when speaking to young children; (3) in other cases where there is a familiar (not a formal) relationship.

EXERCISE G

Write in Spanish the advice your father gave you on your first day of school.

EXAMPLE: llegar temprano a la escuela
¡**Llega** temprano a la escuela!

1. prestar atención en las clases

2. escuchar al maestro

3. preparar la tarea cada noche

4. comenzar la tarea al llegar a casa

5. asistir a la escuela todos los días

6. leer la tarea

7. pedir ayuda al maestro

8. escribir la tarea con cuidado

9. pensar antes de hablar

10. recibir buenas notas

EXERCISE H

You are in the kitchen while your mother hurries to finish preparing a special family meal. Write what she tells you to do.

EXAMPLE: tener paciencia conmigo
¡**Ten** paciencia conmigo!

1. ser bueno

2. hacer la ensalada

3. ir a la tienda

4. poner la mesa

5. salir de la cocina

6. venir acá

7. decir «buenas tardes» a los invitados

8. tener la bondad de ayudarme

EXERCISE I

Your friends always ask you for advice. What do you tell them to do in these circumstances?

EXAMPLE: La bicicleta de Roberto no funciona. *(pedir prestada la bicicleta de tu hermano)*
   ¡**Pide** prestada la bicicleta de tu hermano!

1. Gloria quiere resolver los problemas de la atmósfera. *(conservar energía, caminar más)*

2. La novia de Jorge no quiere ir al baile de la escuela. *(ir solo)*

3. Roberto pierde muchas cosas. *(tener más cuidado)*

4. Alicia no va a patinar porque sus amigos no quieren ir. *(ser más independiente)*

5. Sarita trabaja y acaba de recibir su primer cheque. *(poner el dinero en el banco)*

6. Felipe necesita un nuevo guante de béisbol. *(ahorrar el dinero)*

♦ 4 ♦ Negative Familiar Commands (Singular)

a. To form a negative *tú* command, use the stem of the *yo* form of the present tense and add *-es* for *-ar* verbs and *-as* for *-er* and *-ir* verbs.

Infinitive	Present Tense First Person Singular	Negative Familiar Command	Meaning
mirar	miro	no mir**es**	*don't look*
cerrar	cierro	no cierr**es**	*don't close*
decir	digo	no dig**as**	*don't say, tell*
leer	leo	no le**as**	*don't read*
perder	pierdo	no pierd**as**	*don't lose*
servir	sirvo	no sirv**as**	*don't serve*
tener	tengo	no teng**as**	*don't have*
ver	veo	no ve**as**	*don't see*

b. The following verbs have irregular *tú* commands:

dar	**no des**	*don't give*
estar	**no estés**	*don't be*
ir	**no vayas**	*don't go*
ser	**no seas**	*don't be*

c. Verbs that end in *-zar*, *-car*, and *-gar* have spelling changes in the negative familiar command forms. The spelling change in *-zar* verbs occurs because in Spanish, *z* is rarely followed by *e* or *i*. The spelling change in *-car* and *-gar* verbs occurs to keep the original sounds of *c* and *g*.

Infinitive	Present Tense First Person Singular	Negative Familiar Command	Meaning
almorzar	**almuerzo**	**no almuerces**	*don't have lunch*
buscar	**busco**	**no busques**	*don't look for*
llegar	**llego**	**no llegues**	*don't arrive*

EXERCISE J

While you're at the beach, you overhear a parent tell her small child not to do the following things. Write what she says.

EXAMPLE: no tomar el agua del mar
        ¡**No tomes** el agua del mar!

1. no poner arena en los zapatos

2. no comer arena

3. no estar en el mar solo

4. no caminar lejos

5. no perder los juguetes

6. no tener miedo del agua

7. no tirar arena

8. no me quitar el dinero

9. no molestar a las personas

10. no dejar la cubeta ahí

EXERCISE K

You are sitting in the dentist's waiting room with your younger brother. What do you tell him to do?

EXAMPLE: no gritar
        ¡**No grites!**

1. no romper la revista

2. no poner los pies en la silla

3. no ir ahí

4. no decir eso

5. no cerrar esa puerta

6. no salir de la oficina

7. no ser malo

⟨⟨ **MASTERY EXERCISES** ⟩⟩

EXERCISE L

You're visiting a botanical garden. As you enter the gate, you read the sign. Fill in the missing verbs.

1. *(pagar)* ¡ _____ la entrada en la caja!

2. *(entrar)* ¡No _____ sin pagar!

3. *(mirar)* ¡ _____ las flores!

4. *(tocar)* ¡No _____ las flores!

5. *(andar)* ¡ _____ en los caminos!

6. *(correr)* ¡No _____ en la hierba!

7. *(jugar)* ¡No _____ a la pelota en el jardín!

8. *(respetar)* ¡ _____ a las otras personas!

9. *(gritar)* ¡No _____ en el jardín!

10. *(comer)* ¡ _____ solamente en las mesas!

11. *(almorzar)* ¡No _____ en la hierba!

12. *(poner)* ¡ _____ los papeles en la basura!

13. *(tirar)* ¡No _____ papeles en el jardín!

14. *(gozar)* ¡ _____ de la naturaleza!

15. *(salir)* ¡Por favor, no _____ sin visitar nuestra tienda!

16. *(volver)* ¡Por favor, _____ al jardín pronto!

EXERCISE M

Several friends are helping you set up for a party. Tell them what to do.

1. *(colgar)* ¡Ricardo, _____ los globos ahí!

2. *(poner)* ¡Gladys, _____ los refrescos en esa mesa!

3. *(colocar)* ¡Arturo, no _____ las decoraciones en la puerta!

4. *(traer)* ¡Estela, no _____ el pastel ahora!

5. *(preparar)* ¡Mirta, _____ la limonada ahora!

6. *(sacar)* ¡Ricardo, no _____ los discos compactos todavía!

7. *(dejar)* ¡John, no _____ los platos ahí!

8. *(ir)* ¡Estela, _____ a la tienda para comprar hielo!

9. *(ayudar)* ¡Mirta, _____ a Arturo con las decoraciones!

10. *(abrir)* ¡Gladys, no _____ los regalos!

EXERCISE N

You're on a school trip, and the counselor gives the group the following instructions before leaving the airport in Caracas.

EXAMPLE: venir acá
¡**Vengan** acá!

1. poner las maletas en el autobús

2. subir al autobús rápidamente

3. no gritar en el autobús

4. respetar al chófer

5. bajar el equipaje del autobús

6. no perder el pasaporte

7. subir al cuarto en seguida

8. volver en quince minutos

9. no dejar nada de valor en el cuarto

10. no dar la llave a extraños

11. no perder la llave

12. cerrar bien la puerta del cuarto

13. recordar el número del cuarto

14. no olvidar el nombre del hotel

15. no pedir vino en el restaurante

16. no ser irresponsables

17. obedecer todas las reglas

18. no gastar todo el dinero

19. leer bien el itinerario

20. traer la cámara

EXERCISE O

You are going to play a game with a Spanish-speaking friend who is not familiar with the game. Prepare the instructions for playing the game. Include both affirmative and negative commands in the instructions.

CHAPTER
10

Preterit Tense of Regular Verbs

◆ 1 ◆ Regular -AR Verbs

a. The preterit tense of regular -ar verbs is formed by dropping the infinitive ending -ar and adding the personal endings -é, -aste, -ó, -amos, -asteis, -aron.

	hablar *to speak*	**cerrar** *to close*
yo	habl**é**	cerr**é**
tú	habl**aste**	cerr**aste**
Ud., él, ella	habl**ó**	cerr**ó**
nosotros, -as	habl**amos**	cerr**amos**
vosotros, -as	habl**asteis**	cerr**asteis**
Uds., ellos, ellas	habl**aron**	cerr**aron**

b. The first-person plural ending *(-amos)* is the same as in the present tense: *tomamos (we take, we took).*

c. Most verbs that are stem-changing (*o* to *ue*; *e* to *ie*) do not change the stem in the preterit tense: *(cerrar)* Present—*cierro*; Preterit—*cerré.*

d. The preterit tense has the following meanings in English:

Ud. habló   *you spoke, you did speak*

yo cerré   *I closed, I did close*

e. Verbs that end in *-car*, *-gar*, and *-zar* have a spelling change in the *yo* form. In *-car* and *-gar* verbs, this change occurs to keep the original sound of the *c* and *g*. The change occurs in *-zar* verbs because *z* rarely precedes *e* or *i* in Spanish.

sacar	**yo saqué**
jugar	**yo jugué**
empezar	**yo empecé**

Other verbs that have these changes are:

-car	**practicar, tocar, buscar**
-gar	**llegar, pagar**
-zar	**comenzar, almorzar**

◆ 2 ◆ Uses of the Preterit

a. The preterit tense is used to narrate an action or event in the past. It may indicate the beginning or end of the action, or the complete action or event begun and finished in the past.

(1) Beginning or End

Joe comenzó a trabajar.	*Joe began to work.*
Cerraron la tienda.	*They closed the store.*

(2) Complete Action

Visité a mi tía ayer.	*I visited my aunt yesterday.*
	(I went and returned.)

b. Some expressions that are often used with the preterit are:

anoche	*last night*	**el año pasado**	*last year*
anteayer	*the day before yesterday*	**el mes pasado**	*last month*
ayer	*yesterday*	**la semana pasada**	*last week*

EXERCISE A

Alejandro describes what he and his family did last night. Tell what he says.

EXAMPLE: mi padre / jugar al tenis
        Mi **padre** jugó al tenis.

1. yo / estudiar para un examen

2. mi mamá / preparar un pastel

3. mi hermana / limpiar su cuarto

4. Roberto y yo / mirar un programa de televisión

5. Marta y tú / trabajar en la tienda

6. mis hermanos / patinar

EXERCISE B

Laura spent last summer with her family on a farm. What does she say they did there?

EXAMPLE: mi tío / plantar maíz
        Mi tío **plantó** maíz.

1. yo / caminar en el bosque

2. Carlos / ayudar a mi tío

3. mi mamá y mi tía / cocinar mucho

4. mi papá / cortar la hierba

5. mi abuela / cuidar los pollos

6. Ernesto y yo / nadar en un lago

EXERCISE C

Alfonso has just returned from a trip to Spain. Using the words in parentheses, answer the questions Rafael asks him.

1. ¿Qué país visitaste? *(España)*

2. ¿Con quién viajaste? *(mi familia)*

3. ¿Cuánto tiempo pasaron Uds. allí? *(quince días)*

4. ¿Quién pagó el viaje? *(mi padre)*

5. ¿Cómo viajaron Uds.? *(en avión y en autobús)*

6. ¿Alquilaron Uds. un coche allí? *(no)*

7. ¿A qué ciudad llegaron Uds.? *(Madrid)*

8. ¿En qué ciudad terminaste el viaje? *(Málaga)*

9. ¿Entraste en muchos museos? *(sí)*

10. ¿Sacó tu hermano muchas fotos? *(sí)*

EXERCISE D

Complete this letter that Teresa writes to a friend by filling in the appropriate preterit form of the verbs indicated.

Querida Alicia:

Ayer yo _____ en ti varias veces. Yo _____ a escribir esta carta en
                    1. (pensar)   **2.** (comenzar)

muchas ocasiones pero nunca _____ a terminar la carta. Anoche la orquesta de
                                       3. (llegar)

la escuela _____ en una competencia. Yo _____ el violín y nosotros
                4. (tocar)   **5.** (tocar)

_____ el premio de segundo lugar. El coro _____ también pero
   6. (ganar)   **7.** (cantar)

no _____ ningún premio. Todavía me fascina la música y el mes pasado yo
       8. (ganar)

_____ a estudiar la guitarra. Como ves, _____ el violín por un
      9. (empezar)   **10.** (cambiar)

instrumento «menos serio».

La semana pasada yo _____ mi cumpleaños. Mis padres me _____
                            11. (celebrar)   **12.** (regalar)

muchos regalos bonitos. Mi familia me _____ a cenar a un restaurante elegante.
                                              13. (llevar)

Nosotros _____ un buen rato allí. Después, dos amigos me _____ a
　　　　14. (pasar)　　　　　　　　　　　　　　　　　　　　　　　　　　**15.** (invitar)

una discoteca y nosotros _____ hasta la medianoche. Yo _____ a
　　　　　　　　　　　　16. (bailar)　　　　　　　　　　　　　　　　　　**17.** (llegar)

casa cansada pero contenta. Al día siguiente yo _____ al tenis con mis
　　　　　　　　　　　　　　　　　　　　　　　18. (jugar)

hermanos pero ellos _____ .
　　　　　　　　　　19. (ganar)

¿Cómo _____ tú tu cumpleaños? ¿_____ tú algún lugar divertido?
　　　20. (pasar)　　　　　　　　　　　　　　　**21.** (visitar)

¿A quién _____ ? Yo _____ la foto que tu padre
　　　　　22. (invitar)　　　　　**23.** (buscar)

_____ de nosotras en la fiesta, pero no la _____ .
24. (sacar)　　　　　　　　　　　　　　　　　　　　**25.** (encontrar)

Hasta pronto. Teresa

EXERCISE E

Tell whether or not you and your friends did these things yesterday.

EXAMPLE:　escuchar discos compactos
　　　　　　Mi amigo Pedro **escuchó** discos compactos ayer.

OR:　　　　Yo **no escuché** discos compactos ayer.

1. practicar un deporte

2. trabajar mucho

3. descansar por la tarde

4. lavar el carro

5. usar la aspiradora

6. sacar fotografías

7. buscar un disco compacto nuevo

8. almorzar en el centro

EXERCISE F

Answer these questions that a friend asks while you're riding the school bus together one morning.

1. ¿Qué programa de televisión miraste anoche?

2. ¿Hablaste con tus amigos por teléfono anoche?

3. ¿Qué música tocaste?

4. ¿Estudiaron juntos tú y Alicia para el examen?

5. ¿Prepararon Uds. la escena para la clase de español?

6. ¿Terminaste el mensaje por correo electrónico a tu amigo?

7. ¿Preguntaste a tus padres si puedes cenar conmigo esta noche?

8. ¿Qué desayunaste hoy?

EXERCISE G

Gloria is showing her yearbook to a cousin. Write what the person in each picture did.

EXAMPLE: Lorenzo **sacó** fotografías.

1. Yo _____.

2. Gilberto y Anita _____.

3. Ricardo _____.

4. Juan y yo _____ .

5. Sarita _____ .

♦ 3 ♦ Regular *-ER* and *-IR* Verbs

a. The preterit tense of regular *-er* and *-ir* verbs is formed by dropping the infinitive ending *-er* or *-ir* and adding the personal endings *-í, -iste, -ió, -imos, -isteis, -ieron*.

	perder *to lose*	**abrir** *to open*
yo	perd**í**	abr**í**
tú	perd**iste**	abr**iste**
Ud., él, ella	perd**ió**	abr**ió**
nosotros, -as	perd**imos**	abr**imos**
vosotros, -as	perd**isteis**	abr**isteis**
Uds., ellos, ellas	perd**ieron**	abr**ieron**

b. The preterit endings are the same for *-er* and *-ir* verbs.

c. In *-ir* verbs, the first–person plural ending *(-imos)* is the same as in the present tense. In *-er* verbs, however, the endings are different.

viv*imos*	*we live*	**viv***imos*	*we lived*
beb*emos*	*we drink*	**beb***imos*	*we drank*

d. The accent mark is omitted over the following forms of *ver: vi, vio.*

e. Stem-changing verbs ending in *-er* do not change the stem vowel in the preterit tense. Stem-changing verbs ending in *-ir* have special stem changes in the preterit and are discussed in Chapter 11.

EXERCISE H

Raúl and some friends are telling what they had for dinner last night. Write what they say.

EXAMPLE: Rosa / arroz con frijoles
            Rosa **comió** arroz con frijoles.

1. Luis y Daniel / pescado

2. yo / arroz con pollo

3. Alicia / una ensalada

4. Bobby y yo / hamburguesas

5. tú / chuletas de cerdo

6. ellos / paella

EXERCISE I

The students are selecting their courses for the following year. What did they decide to study?

EXAMPLE: Tomás / francés
            Tomás **decidió estudiar** francés.

1. Lola / literatura

2. Carmen y Mary / baile

3. yo / biología

4. José y yo / música

5. tú / química

6. Jane / geografía

EXERCISE J

You're talking to a new friend who spent part of her life in the Dominican Republic. Write the questions you ask her about her background.

EXAMPLE: dónde / aprender el español
            ¿Dónde **aprendiste** el español?

1. cuándo / vivir en Santo Domingo

2. a qué escuela / asistir

3. cuándo / volver a los Estados Unidos

4. cuándo / decidir volver aquí

5. por qué / salir de Santo Domingo

EXERCISE K

Complete this letter that Ramona, who is visiting acquaintances in Mexico, writes to a friend back in her hometown.

Querida Gabriela:

Anoche yo _____ a una fiesta en casa de mi amiga Lourdes. Ellos _____
      1. (asistir)   **2.** (celebrar)

el cumpleaños de su hermana menor. Muchas personas _____ a la fiesta y la
                                                  3. (asistir)

hermana de Lourdes _____ muchos regalos.
                    4. (recibir)

La fiesta _____ a las nueve de la noche. Muchas personas no _____
          5. (comenzar)   **6.** (llegar)

hasta las diez. Un grupo de mariachis _____ «Las mañanitas» a la hermana de
                                    7. (cantar)

de Lourdes. Yo no _____ todas las palabras, pero me _____ mucho y
                 8. (entender)   **9.** (gustar)

_____ dos canciones más. Cuando _____ los mariachis, el padre
10. (aprender)   **11.** (terminar)

_____ una piñata y todos nosotros _____ de romperla.
12. (colgar)   **13.** (tratar)

Un joven guapo _____ la piñata.
              14. (romper)

Nosotros _____ y _____ muy bien. La mamá de Lourdes y sus
          15. (comer)   **16.** (beber)

tías _____ unos platillos muy sabrosos. Yo _____ tacos de pollo y
      17. (preparar)   **18.** (comer)

tamales. La mamá de Lourdes _____ enseñarme a preparar los tamales. Yo
                      19. (prometer)

_____ a casa a las doce y media de la noche.
20. (volver)

Hasta pronto.
Ramona

EXERCISE L

Answer these questions from your older sister. Use the cues provided.

1. ¿A qué hora saliste de la casa anoche? *(7:00)*

2. ¿Con quién asististe al concierto? *(Manuela)*

3. ¿Qué decidieron Uds. hacer después del concierto? *(ir a un restaurante)*

4. ¿Dónde comieron Uds.? *(el Café Colón)*

5. ¿Qué comiste? *(una hamburguesa)*

6. ¿A qué hora prometiste estar en la casa? *(11:00)*

7. ¿Cómo volviste a casa? *(en taxi)*

8. ¿A qué hora abriste la puerta de la casa? *(11:30)*

MASTERY EXERCISES

EXERCISE M

Describe what you and a friend did during a weekend trip to another city. Use the suggestions below.

asistir a un concierto

caminar por la ciudad

comer en un restaurante español

comprar unos discos compactos

correr en una carrera

gastar mucho dinero

jugar al tenis (boliche…)

perder la cartera

ver a unos amigos

visitar el museo

EXERCISE N

While visiting Costa Rica, you meet a girl who used to be an exchange student at your school. Tell her about yourself and the other people you both knew there.

EXAMPLE: el señor Álvarez / dejar de enseñar
       El señor Álvarez **dejó** de enseñar.

1. Miriam / volver a vivir en Puerto Rico

2. Jorge y Pedro / asistir a la misma universidad

3. Eddy / abrir una tienda de juguetes

4. tu profesor de inglés / escribir un libro de poemas

5. yo / ver a Daniel en España

6. Malika y yo / viajar a Europa

7. las hermanas Silva / correr en muchas carreras

8. Janet / recibir una beca

9. Alicia y Berta / aprender el japonés

10. la señora Oyama / salir de la escuela

EXERCISE O

You have to give an oral report about your trip abroad last summer. Prepare what you plan to say about the trip in Spanish. You may wish to include the following:

> ➤ where you traveled to
> ➤ with whom you traveled
> ➤ how you traveled
> ➤ the countries/cities you visited
> ➤ how long spent there
> ➤ what you saw
> ➤ whom you met there
> ➤ what you learned
> ➤ what you bought during the trip

CHAPTER 11

Verbs Irregular in the Preterit Tense

◆ 1 ◆ Preterit Tense of -IR Stem-Changing Verbs

a. Stem-changing verbs ending in *-ir* change the stem vowel *e* to *i* and *o* to *u* in the third-person singular and plural of the preterit tense.

	servir *to serve*	**dormir** *to sleep*
yo	serví	dormí
tú	serviste	dormiste
Ud., él, ella	s*i*rvió	d*u*rmió
nosotros, -as	servimos	dormimos
vosotros, -as	servisteis	dormisteis
Uds., ellos, ellas	s*i*rvieron	d*u*rmieron

b. Other verbs that change *e* to *i* are:

medir *to measure*	**referir** *to tell*	**sentir** *to feel*
pedir *to ask for*	**reñir** *to argue*	**vestir** *to dress*
preferir *to prefer*	**repetir** *to repeat*	

Other verbs that change *o* to *u* are:

morir *to die*	**podrir** *to rot*

c. Verbs ending in *-ar* or *-er* that are stem-changing don't change the stem vowel in the preterit tense.

pensar *to think*: **pensé, pensaste, pensó, pensamos, pensasteis, pensaron**

volver *to return*: **volví, volviste, volvió, volvimos, volvisteis, volvieron**

EXERCISE A

Luis tells what he and his friends preferred to do yesterday. Write what he says.

EXAMPLE: Paul y yo / ir al cine
Paul y yo **preferimos** ir al cine.

1. Enrique / ir a la piscina

2. tú / ver a tus amigos

3. Abdul y Mateo / montar en bicicleta

4. Jean y yo / ir a la playa

5. mi hermano / ver una película

6. Marta / mirar la televisión

7. ellos / jugar al fútbol

EXERCISE B

You overhear your mother on the phone telling a friend how late everyone slept. Write in Spanish what she says.

EXAMPLE: mi esposo y yo / 7:30
Mi esposo y yo **dormimos hasta** las siete y media.

1. Alejandro / 12:00

2. María y Elena / 10:30

3. tú / 8:15

4. Gregorio y Felipe / 11:00

5. yo / 7:00

6. mi padre / 5:00

EXERCISE C

Carmen is writing in her diary about the night she stayed at Raquel's house. Fill in the appropriate preterit forms of the verbs given.

Yo _____ pasar la noche en casa de Raquel porque nosotras _____
          1. (decidir)   **2.** (volver)

tarde del teatro. Antes de ir al teatro, nosotras _____ en un restaurante francés.
                                                                               3. (comer)

Yo _____ sopa de cebollas y me _____ mucho. Raquel
     4. (pedir)   **5.** (gustar)

_____ caracoles pero no le _____ . Ella _____
    6. (pedir)   **7.** (gustar)   **8.** (resolver)

no volver a ese restaurante. A veces Raquel es antipática. Ella _____ al
                                                          9. (reñir)

mesero una vez y luego le _____ su orden. Yo no _____ bien en su
                         10. (repetir)   **11.** (dormir)

casa pero Raquel _____ profundamente toda la noche.
                  12. (dormir)

♦ 2 ♦ Verbs That Change _I_ to _y_ in the Preterit

a. _-er_ and _-ir_ verbs whose stems end in a vowel change the endings of the preterit tense from _-ió_ to _-yó_ in the third-person singular and from _-ieron_ to _-yeron_ in the third-person plural. The endings for all other persons take an accent on the _-i_.

caer _to fall_			
yo	caí	nosotros, -as	caímos
tú	caíste	vostros, -as	caísteis
Ud., él, ella	ca**yó**	Uds., ellos, ellas	ca**yeron**

b. Verbs like caer:

construir _to build_	**leer** _to read_
creer _to believe_	**oír** _to hear_
distribuir _to distribute_	**poseer** _to possess; to own_
incluir _to include_	

EXERCISE D

Some friends are telling what they heard on the radio last night. Write what they say.

EXAMPLE: nosotros / las noticias
         Nosotros **oímos** las noticias.

_1._ tú / el tiempo

_2._ Tiffany / un debate

_3._ Felipe y Nicolás / un partido de fútbol

_4._ yo / música

_5._ ellos / un concierto

_6._ Beverly y yo / un concurso

EXERCISE E

The students in the woodworking class tell what they built. Write what they say.

EXAMPLE: Esteban / una mesa
Esteban **construyó** una mesa.

1. yo / una lámpara
2. ellos / un librero
3. Sarita / un marco
4. tú / un banco
5. Chun y Susan / una caja
6. Juan y yo / una silla

EXERCISE F

Some neighbors are discussing an incident that took place nearby. Write what they say.

EXAMPLE: yo / creer que mi hijo / cerrar la puerta
Yo **creí** que mi hijo **cerró** la puerta.

1. mi esposo / oír las noticias en el radio del carro
2. los señores Delgado / construir esa casa el año pasado
3. yo / leer las noticias en el periódico
4. la policía / incluir a mi hermano en la investigación
5. nosotros / creer / que un meteoro / caer en la casa
6. la explosión / destruir toda la casa de los señores Delgado y / romper las ventanas de mi casa

♦ 3 ♦ *I*-Stem Verbs in the Preterit

The following verbs have irregular stems and endings in the preterit:

	hacer *to do; to make*	**querer** *to want; to love*	**venir** *to come*
yo	hice	quise	vine
tú	hiciste	quisiste	viniste
Ud., él, ella	hizo	quiso	vino
nosotros, -as	hicimos	quisimos	vinimos
vosotros, -as	hicisteis	quisisteis	vinisteis
Uds., ellos, ellas	hicieron	quisieron	vinieron

NOTE:

The preterit endings of *i*-stem verbs do not have accent marks.

EXERCISE G

Mrs. Montes organized a potluck dinner. She tells who made each dish. Write what she says.

EXAMPLE: Silvia / el pastel de chocolate
        Silvia **hizo** el pastel de chocolate.

1. yo / la ensalada

2. los señores Rivas / la paella

3. Carmen / las legumbres

4. tú / el té helado

5. Rosa y yo / el arroz con pollo

6. Uds. / el flan

EXERCISE H

Roberto is not speaking to any of his friends because they didn't want to do what he wanted to do. Tell what his friends wanted to do.

EXAMPLE: Jaime / montar en bicicleta
        Jaime **quiso** montar en bicicleta.

1. Yolanda / ir al cine

2. Kenji / estudiar

3. tú / sacar fotografías

4. Eduardo y Patricia / mirar la televisión

5. Gabriel y yo / jugar al voleibol

6. Tony / descansar

EXERCISE I

Caterina tells her cousin how the members of her family came to her grandparents' anniversary party. Write what she says.

EXAMPLE: mi hermana / en taxi
        Mi hermana **vino** en taxi.

1. mis tíos / en autobús

2. el hermano de mi abuela / en tren

3. mis hermanos y yo / en coche

4. mi tía / en avión

5. mis padres / en coche

6. tú / a pie

7. mi madrina / en motocicleta

EXERCISE J

Answer these questions that a friend asks you. Use the words in parentheses.

1. ¿Hiciste la tarea anoche? *(sí)*

2. ¿Vinieron Carlos y Juanita a la escuela hoy? *(no)*

3. ¿Qué quiso hacer Alfredo el sábado pasado? *(ir de compras)*

4. ¿Cuándo vinieron tus primos a verte? *(el agosto pasado)*

5. ¿Cómo vino Berta a la escuela hoy? *(en taxi)*

6. ¿Por qué vino ella en taxi? *(perder el autobús)*

7. ¿Qué hizo tu mamá para cenar anoche? *(pollo)*

♦ 4 ♦ *U*-Stem Verbs in the Preterit

The following verbs have irregular stems and endings in the preterit:

Infinitive	Stem	Preterit Forms
andar	anduv	anduve, anduviste, anduvo, anduvimos, anduvisteis, anduvieron
estar	estuv	estuve, estuviste, estuvo, estuvimos, estuvisteis, estuvieron
poder	pud	pude, pudiste, pudo, pudimos, pudisteis, pudieron
poner	pus	puse, pusiste, puso, pusimos, pusisteis, pusieron
saber	sup	supe, supiste, supo, supimos, supisteis, supieron
tener	tuv	tuve, tuviste, tuvo, tuvimos, tuvisteis, tuvieron

NOTE:

The preterit endings of *u*–stem verbs do not have accent marks.

♦ 5 ♦ The Verbs *DAR, SER,* and *IR*

The verbs *dar, ser,* and *ir* are also irregular in the preterit. *Dar* takes the endings of regular *-er, -ir* verbs, but without a written accent in the first- and third-person singular forms. *Ser* and *ir* have the same forms in the preterit.

dar *to give*   **di, diste, dio, dimos, disteis, dieron**

ser *to be*
ir *to go*   **fui, fuiste, fue, fuimos, fuisteis, fueron**

EXERCISE K

Gerardo describes what he and a friend did last Saturday. Complete the statements with the correct forms of the preterit tense.

El sábado pasado Enrique y yo _____ al centro. Nosotros _____ allí
                                        1. (ir)   **2.** (estar)

porque yo _____ que comprar una nueva raqueta de tenis. Nosotros no
            3. (tener)

_____ encontrar la tienda que recomendó un amigo de Enrique. Este amigo le
  4. (poder)

_____ un papel con el nombre y la dirección de la tienda a Enrique, pero él no
  5. (dar)

_____ recordar dónde _____ ese papel. Enrique
  6. (poder)   **7.** (poner)

_____ que llamar por teléfono a su amigo y luego nosotros _____
  8. (tener)   **9.** (ir)

a la tienda. Yo le _____ las gracias a Enrique por su ayuda.
                      10. (dar)

EXERCISE L

Conchita and some friends are talking about what they did during the spring vacation. Tell what they say, using the preterit tense.

EXAMPLE: yo / hacer un viaje en autobús
          Yo **hice** un viaje en autobús.

1. Bonnie / andar en la playa

2. Paul y Eduardo / ir a Puerto Rico

3. nosotros / dar muchos paseos en el parque

4. tú / tener que trabajar

5. yo / estar en casa de una prima

6. Uds. / poder divertirse en casa

EXERCISE M

Answer the questions that a friend asks you about a party he didn't attend at Lorenzo's home.

1. ¿Con quién fuiste a la fiesta?

2. ¿Quiénes estuvieron allí?

3. ¿Supo Lorenzo por qué yo no fui a la fiesta?

4. ¿Cómo fuiste a casa de Lorenzo?

5. ¿Cómo fue la música?

6. ¿Pudiste bailar con Estela?

7. ¿Fueron Uds. al jardín de la casa?

8. ¿Tuviste que volver a casa temprano?

9. ¿Estuviste en casa a esa hora?

10. ¿Quién puso las decoraciones?

EXERCISE N

Your sister has just returned from an exchange program in Colombia. Answer the questions a friend asks you about her trip.

1. ¿Cuánto tiempo estuvo ella en Colombia?

2. ¿A quién pidió ella permiso para ir?

3. ¿Hizo ella el viaje sola?

4. ¿Con quién fue a Colombia?

5. ¿Cómo fue la familia con la que vivió?

6. ¿Pudiste pedirle muchos regalos?

7. ¿Pudo ella traer muchas cosas?

8. ¿Qué quiso ella hacer allí?

9. ¿Tuviste que ir al aeropuerto cuando llegó?

10. ¿Quién más fue a recibirla al aeropuerto?

11. ¿Cómo supiste la hora de su llegada?

12. ¿Durmió ella en el avión?

13. ¿Quién vino con ella?

14. ¿Tuvo ella alguna dificultad en Colombia?

15. ¿Qué ciudad de Colombia prefirió ella?

EXERCISE O

Complete the latest entry in Laura's diary, using the correct forms of the preterit tense.

Hoy por la mañana yo _____ en casa de mi amiga Gloria. Su padre
                        1. (estar)

_____ una casita de muñecas para su hermana menor, Teresa.
   2. (construir)

_____ una sorpresa para la niña. Teresa y yo _____ los muebles en
   3. (ser)   *4.* (poner)

la casa. Después nosotras _____ al centro para comprar otros muebles. Nosotras
                         5. (ir)

_____ por muchas tiendas hasta que nosotras _____ con unos
  6. (andar)   *7.* (dar)

muebles bonitos. Teresa _____ comprar todos los muebles pero nosotras no
                         8. (preferir)

_____ encontrar una mesita para el comedor. Ella _____ un
  9. (poder)   *10.* (leer)

catálogo de muebles y _____ una mesita bonita. Antes de salir de la casa,
                     11. (pedir)

Teresa y Gloria _____ las ventanitas de la casita. Ellas _____ tela
                    12. (medir)   **13.** (comprar)

e _____ cortinas para todos los cuartos de la casita. Yo quería comprar un
   14. (hacer)

regalito para Teresa pero no _____ encontrar nada. Cuando
                          15. (poder)

regresamos a casa, Teresa _____ a llorar. La casita de muñecas _____ de
                      16. (ponerse)   **17.** (caer)

la mesa al suelo. Yo _____ mucho lo que pasó. El perro _____ la casa
                  18.(sentir)   **19.** (destruir)

al correr a la puerta. La madre de Teresa _____ al perro y el perro
                                20. (reñir)

_____ que estar en el jardín. Yo _____ a casa a las ocho de la noche.
21. (tener)   **22.** (venir)

EXERCISE P

You went to the movies with a friend. Write an entry in you journal about the experience. You may wish to include the following:

> ➤ where you went

> ➤ with whom you went

> ➤ how you got there

> ➤ if you had to wait on line

> ➤ which film you saw

> ➤ where you sat in the theater

> ➤ what the ticket included, e.g., soda, popcorn

> ➤ if you liked or disliked the film

> ➤ where you went after the film

> ➤ at what time you arrived home

Imperfect Tense

♦ 1 ♦ Regular Verbs

a. The imperfect tense of regular verbs is formed by dropping the infinitive ending *(-ar, -er, -ir)*, and adding the following endings:

Infinitive	Stem	Imperfect Endings
mostrar	mostr	-aba, -abas, -aba, -ábamos, abais, -aban
volver	volv	-ía, -ías, -ía, íamos, íais, ían
abrir	abr	-ía, -ías, -ía, -íamos, -íais, ían

b. Verbs that are stem-changing in the present tense do not change the stem vowel in the imperfect.

c. The first- and third-person singular forms are the same. Subject pronouns are used if necessary to clarify the meaning of the verb.

> **EXERCISE A**

At a high-school reunion, some friends are remembering where they used to eat lunch when they were students. Write what they say.

EXAMPLE: Shaquille / la cafetería / siempre
Shaquille **almorzaba** en la cafetería siempre.

1. Luis y Yoko / el parque / a veces

2. tú / el restaurante / de vez en cuando

3. Jack y yo / casa / siempre

4. yo / la clase de arte / todos los días

5. ellos / el gimnasio / con frecuencia

6. nosotros / el patio de la escuela / a veces

7. mis primos / mi casa

EXERCISE B

David and some friends have given up eating sweets. What did they used to eat?

EXAMPLE: Pedro / helado todos los días
             Pedro **comía** helado todos los días.

1. Pascal / muchos chocolates

2. Yolanda / pastel en cada comida

3. Carol y yo / dulces todos los días

4. Arturo y Nick / flan con frecuencia

5. tú / helado después de las clases

6. María / jalea de guayaba

EXERCISE C

A group of friends are telling where they used to live. Write what they say.

EXAMPLE: Juan / Nevada
             Juan **vivía** en Nevada.

1. yo / Tejas

2. Ana / California

3. los hermanos Casero / Honduras

4. tú / la Florida

5. Fabiana y yo / San Juan

6. Uds. / Nueva York

EXERCISE D

Javier describes what life was like when he was younger. Write what he says.

EXAMPLE: nosotros / vivir en una casa grande
             Nosotros **vivíamos** en una casa grande.

1. yo / tener un perro

2. mis hermanos / jugar al fútbol conmigo

3. mi mamá / no trabajar

4. toda la familia / visitar a los abuelos los domingos

5. mi abuela / preparar comidas deliciosas

6. mis amigos y yo / correr en la calle

7. tú / hacer muchas bromas

8. mi papá / tener un automóvil convertible

9. mi hermano mayor / querer aprender a conducir

10. nosotros / salir de la ciudad con frecuencia

EXERCISE E

Your little brother asks your grandfather questions about his life. Answer his questions in the imperfect, using the cues provided.

1. ¿Dónde vivías cuando tenías mi edad? *(en un pueblo)*

2. ¿Con quién vivías? *(mis padres y hermanos)*

3. ¿Jugabas al béisbol a veces? *(sí)*

4. ¿Conocías a mi abuela cuando Uds. estaban en la escuela? *(no)*

5. ¿Asistían Uds. a la misma escuela? *(no)*

6. ¿Tenías una bicicleta? *(sí)*

7. ¿Cómo celebrabas tu cumpleaños? *(una fiesta)*

8. ¿Te daban muchos regalos? *(sí)*

9. ¿Nadaban tú y tus amigos en una piscina? *(un lago)*

10. ¿De qué tenías miedo? *(nada)*

♦ 2 ♦ Verbs Irregular in the Imperfect Tense

There are three irregular verbs in the imperfect tense: *ir*, *ser*, and *ver*.

Infinitive	Imperfect Endings
ir	iba, ibas, iba, íbamos, ibais, iban
ser	era, eras, era, éramos, erais, eran
ver	veía, veías, veía, veíamos, veíais, veían

EXERCISE F

Write where these people used to go in the summer.

EXAMPLE: José / a la playa
José **iba** a la playa.

1. tú / a las montañas

2. mi hermana y yo / al campamento

3. Hugo / a casa de sus abuelos

4. yo / al campo

5. Rodolfo y César / a la escuela

6. Ud. / al extranjero

EXERCISE G

Write what these people were like when they were younger.

EXAMPLE: Gladys / muy alta
          Gladys **era** muy alta.

1. yo / tímido
2. Patricia / bonita
3. los niños / traviesos
4. tú / cariñoso
5. Nilda y Victoria / muy enérgicas
6. Esteban y yo / consentidos

EXERCISE H

Write the types of programs these people used to watch.

EXAMPLE: mi mamá / telenovelas todos los días
          Mi mamá **veía** telenovelas todos los días.

1. Enrique / las películas policíacas los sábados
2. tú / los deportes los lunes
3. mi papá y yo / el reportaje deportivo cada noche
4. Kyoko y Pilar / las comedias
5. Pat y Mike / las noticias cada noche
6. Uds. / los programas de ciencia ficción cada semana

EXERCISE I

Tell who used to do these things. Write about each activity using the imperfect tense.

ayudar a mi madre siempre

ir al circo en la primavera

ir de compras con sus amigas los sábados

jugar al tenis cada sábado

practicar con el equipo por la tarde

vender limonada en el verano

ver los concursos cada noche

1. Mi abuela _____ .

2. Yo _____ .

3. Mis hermanos y yo _____ .

4. Mis amigos _____ .

5. Tú _____ .

6. Mi hermana _____ .

7. Mi prima _____ .

♦ 3 ♦ Uses of the Imperfect Tense

The imperfect tense is used:

a. to express what used to happen.

Íbamos a México todos los veranos.   *We would go (used to go) to Mexico every summer.*

Yo tocaba la guitarra.   *I played (used to play) the guitar.*

b. to express what happened repeatedly in the past.

Yo trabajaba a menudo durante las vacaciones.   *I often worked (used to work) during vacation.*

Pablo **me llamaba** mucho.   *Pablo called (used to call) me a lot.*

c. to describe what was going on at a particular time.

Leía el periódico durante el concierto.   *I read (was reading) the newspaper during the concert.*

d. to describe simultaneous actions in the past. *Mientras* is usually used to connect the two actions.

Yo **escribía** una **carta mientras escuchaba** la radio.   *I wrote a letter while I listened to the radio.*

e. to describe what was going on in the past (imperfect) when something else began or ended (preterit). *Cuando* usually links the two actions.

Yo **escribía** una carta **cuando** Carlos entró.   *I was writing a letter when Carlos entered.*

f. to describe persons or things in the past.

Jane **era** alta y bonita.   *Jane was tall and pretty.*

Los aviones **eran** muy grandes.   *The planes were very large.*

g. to express the time of day (hour) in the past.

Eran las once.   *It was eleven o'clock.*

EXERCISE J

The weather often affects what people do. Felipe's talking about the things he and his friends used to do in different kinds of weather. Write what he says, using the imperfect tense.

EXAMPLE: Yo **iba a la playa cuando hacía sol**.

1. Alicia y Melique _____.

2. Federico, John y yo _____.

3. Tú _____.

4. Yo _____.

5. El equipo _____.

EXERCISE K

Answer the questions that a new friend asks you about your childhood. Use the imperfect tense and the cues provided.

1. ¿Acompañabas a tu mamá a las tiendas? *(a veces)*

2. ¿Obedecías a tus padres? *(siempre)*

3. ¿Buscabas a tu mamá todos los días? *(sí)*

4. ¿Llorabas a menudo? *(sí)*

5. ¿Eras un niño (una niña) exigente? *(sí)*

6. ¿Poseían tú y tus hermanos muchos juguetes? *(no)*

7. ¿Gritabas mucho? *(no)*

8. ¿Dividían tus hermanos su dinero contigo? *(no)*

9. ¿Quitabas sus juguetes a los otros niños? *(sí)*

10. ¿Caías enfermo(a) a menudo? *(no)*

EXERCISE L

Someone played a prank in school, and the principal wants to know what everyone was doing at that time. Use the suggestions below to tell what these people were doing.

comer en la cafetería   hacer gimnasia
estar en la clase de biología   ir a la oficina
estudiar con Beto   leer en la biblioteca
hablar con el profesor de español   ver una película en la clase de historia

1. Juan _____ .

2. Peggy y yo _____ .

3. Eduardo y Mai-Li _____ .

4. Tú _____ .

5. Ellas _____ .

6. Yo _____ .

7. Adela _____ .

8. Tú y Yolanda _____ .

EXERCISE M

Something interrupted what various people were doing. Relate each pair of events in a complete sentence.

EXAMPLE: yo / hablar por teléfono / mi padre / llegar
Yo **hablaba** por teléfono **cuando** mi padre **llegó**.

1. Elena / bañarse / el teléfono / sonar

2. mi madre / cocinar / ella ver un ratoncito

3. yo / mirar la televisión / yo / oír un ruido

4. Gordon y yo / correr en el parque / empezar a llover

5. Ellos / dormir / el perro / ladrar

6. tú / leer un libro / la alarma / sonar

7. Janice y José / subir al árbol / una rama / caer

8. mi hermano / dormir profundamente / el despertador / sonar

EXERCISE N

Who was your hero (heroine) when you were younger? Use the imperfect tense in a series of sentences describing this person.

MASTERY EXERCISES

EXERCISE O

Rewrite this story in the imperfect tense.

Es la una de la mañana y todo el mundo duerme profundamente menos yo. Yo no puedo dormirme. No sé por qué. No estoy preocupado. No estoy enfermo.

Estoy ansioso porque pasado mañana voy a esquiar con mis amigos. Nosotros tenemos todo preparado y no me falta nada. Me gusta salir con ellos. Ya son las dos y media. Continúo despierto. Quiero tomar un vaso de leche caliente pero no tengo ganas de salir de la cama. Voy a contar ovejas—mi abuela dice que eso siempre la ayuda a dormir. Cuento ovejas pero después de quince minutos pierdo la cuenta.

Quiero gritar y llorar de la frustración. Ya son las cuatro. Trato de leer pero no puedo concentrarme en el cuento. Siempre soy así la noche antes de mi cumpleaños.

EXERCISE P

You have been asked to prepare a journal entry in which you describe what you were like five years ago. You may wish to include the following: your physical appearance, your personality, where you lived, your favorite and least favorite pastimes, your friends, places you enjoyed, etc.

Future Tense

◆ 1 ◆ *Ir A*+ Infinitive

An action in the future can be expressed in Spanish by the present tense of *ir* followed by the preposition *a* and the infinitive of the verb that indicates the future action.

Voy a estudiar más tarde.   *I'm going to study later.*

¿Qué **vas a hacer**?   *What are you going to do?*

EXERCISE A

Jorge can never guess what his friends are going to do. Write what Jorge guesses and what his friends are actually going to do.

EXAMPLE: Luis / jugar al tenis / trabajar
Luis **va a** jugar al tenis.
No, Luis **va a** trabajar.

1. Sergei / descansar / escuchar música

2. tú y Antonio / jugar al boliche / jugar al tenis

3. María / cocinar / tocar el piano

4. tú / ayudar a Felipe / leer un libro

5. Uds. / ver televisión / lavar los platos

6. Paco / dormir / estudiar

EXERCISE B

It's the end of the school year. Write six sentences in which you tell what you, your family, and your friends are going to do during the summer vacation.

EXERCISE C

The weather often affects our plans. Tell what you and your friends are going to do under these weather conditions.

EXAMPLE: si hace fresco
Si hace fresco, **vamos a montar** en bicicleta.

1. Si hace sol _____ .

2. Si hace frío _____ .

3. Si llueve _____ .

4. Si hace calor _____ .

5. Si nieva _____ .

♦ 2 ♦ Future Tense of Regular Verbs

a. The future tense of regular verbs is formed by adding the following personal endings to the infinitive form of the verb.

	hablar	comer	vivir
yo	hablar**é**	comer**é**	vivir**é**
tú	hablar**ás**	comer**ás**	vivir**ás**
Ud., él, ella	hablar**á**	comer**á**	vivir**á**
nosotros, -as	hablar**emos**	comer**emos**	vivir**emos**
vosotros, -as	hablar**éis**	comer**éis**	vivir**éis**
Uds., ellos, ellas	hablar**án**	comer**án**	vivir**án**

b. In English, the future tense is expressed by means of the helping verb *will* or *shall*.

Visitaré a mis primos el domingo.   *I shall visit my cousins on Sunday.*

¿**Viajarás** a México pronto?   *Will you visit Mexico soon?*

c. All the endings have an accent mark except *-emos.*

EXERCISE D

Write what these people will do next summer.

EXAMPLE: Bernardo / trabajar en una oficina
Bernardo **trabajará** en una oficina.

1. Eva / visitar a sus primos en el campo

2. mi hermana y yo / aprender a conducir

3. Fumi y Mario / jugar al tenis

4. mis padres / ir a Santo Domingo

5. yo / tomar una clase de baile

6. Elena y Teodoro / viajar a Costa Rica

7. tú / asistir a la universidad

8. Kim / ayudar a su padre en la tienda

9. Rosalía / participar en un concurso

10. nosotros / vivir cerca de la playa

EXERCISE E

Write when these people will do these things.

EXAMPLE: Elisa / volver a las montañas / el próximo invierno
Elisa **volverá** a las montañas el próximo invierno.

1. Alicia y yo / preparar la cena / esta noche

2. Simon / lavar el coche / pasado mañana

3. yo / ir a la biblioteca / mañana

4. los niños / jugar en un partido / el sábado que viene

5. tú / dar un paseo en el parque / por la tarde

6. Silvia y Amalia / correr en una carrera / en septiembre

7. el maestro / escribir una carta de recomendación / más tarde

EXERCISE F

You're saying good-bye to your best friend before going on vacation with your family to Mexico. Answer your friend's questions.

1. ¿Cuánto tiempo estarán Uds. en México? *(un mes)*

2. ¿Cuántas ciudades visitarás? *(tres)*

3. ¿Quién conducirá el coche? *(mis padres)*

4. ¿Qué cosas verás allí? *(monumentos y playas)*

5. ¿Me escribirás? *(sí)*

6. ¿Conocerán Uds. las playas de Acapulco también? *(sí)*

7. ¿Dormirás la siesta todos los días? *(sí)*

8. ¿Cuándo volverán Uds.? *(en agosto)*

♦ 3 ♦ Verbs Irregular in the Future Tense

Some verbs form the future tense by adding the future personal endings *(-é, -ás, -á, -emos, -éis, -án)* to an irregular stem.

a. Verbs like *poder* drop the *e* of the infinitive and then add the endings of the future tense.

poder: **podr –é, –ás, –á, –emos, –éis, –án**

Like **poder**: **haber, querer, saber**

b. In verbs like *poner*, the *e* (or *i*) of the infinitive is replaced by a *d*, and the endings of the future tense are added.

poner: **pondr –é, –ás, –á, –emos, –éis, –án**

Like **poner**: **salir, tener, venir**

c. The verbs *decir* and *hacer* drop two letters to form an irregular future stem.

decir: **dir –é, –ás, –á, –emos, –éis, –án**

hacer: **har –é, –ás, –á, –emos, –éis, –án**

EXERCISE G

Upon arrival in Buenos Aires, a group of students take a bus to their hotel. They're excited about what they'll be able to do in Argentina. Write what they say.

EXAMPLE: nosotros / poder conocer el barrio italiano
Nosotros **podremos** conocer el barrio italiano.

1. yo / poder conocer muchos lugares

2. Elena / poder ir de compras

3. Spiros y Estela / poder aprender a bailar el tango

4. tú / poder asistir a la ópera

5. Raúl / poder conocer las pampas argentinas

6. Diana y yo / poder ver a muchos gauchos

7. Uds./ poder tomar fotografías

EXERCISE H

Raquel writes to a friend and tells her about her plans. Complete her e-mail with the appropriate forms of the future tense of the verbs indicated.

Querida Elena:

¡Buenas noticias! Mi familia _____ un viaje a tu ciudad el mes que viene. Yo
                                    1. (hacer)

_____ el viaje con ellos. Yo no _____ la fecha exacta en que
2. (hacer)   *3.* (saber)

nosotros _____ hasta la próxima semana, pero yo _____ verte
      4. (salir)   *5.* (querer)

durante mi visita. ¿_____ tú ir a verme al hotel? Creo que Gloria y
                   6. (poder)

María _____ también. Nosotras _____ mucho que contar.
         7. (venir)   *8.* (tener)

Yo _____ el placer de invitarte a almorzar. Al saber la fecha de mi
    9. (tener)

llegada yo te la _____ en otro correo electrónico o te la _____
          10. (poner)   *11.* (decir)

por teléfono.

Hasta pronto.
Raquel

EXERCISE I

You and some friends are talking about the future. Where will you be in twenty years? Answer these questions.

1. ¿Tendrás un trabajo bueno?

2. ¿Ganarás mucho dinero?

3. ¿Saldrás todavía con tus amigos?

4. ¿Vendrás a ver a tus amigos de la juventud?

5. ¿Sabrás hablar español?

6. ¿Querrás vivir en otra ciudad?

7. ¿Harás muchos viajes a Europa?

8. ¿Pondrás mucho dinero en el banco?

9. ¿Qué dirás de tus amigos?

EXERCISE J

You're the stage manager for a school play. Using the verbs indicated, write what each of your crew members will do.

EXAMPLE: Yo no **podré** hacer todas las cosas.

1. Claude _____ la mesa al lado del sofá.
             (poner)

2. Miguel y Luz _____ que ayudar a Gerardo.
                  (tener)

3. El director _____ todo listo a las seis.
                (querer)

4. Todos nosotros _____ los adornos.
             (hacer)

5. Elena _____ dónde poner las flores.
   (saber)

6. Tú _____ a buscar una lámpara.
   (salir)

7. Los actores _____ aquí a las seis y cuarto.
   (venir)

8. Nosotros no _____ descansar hasta más tarde.
   (poder)

⟨ MASTERY EXERCISES ⟩

EXERCISE K

José is the youngest child in the family, and he loves to reaffirm what his parents say his brothers and sisters will do. Write what his parents say and then what José says.

EXAMPLE: Marcos / sacar la basura
            Marcos **va a sacar** la basura.
            Marcos **sacará** la basura.

1. Pablo / lavar el coche   5. José, tú / ayudar a Susana

2. Anita / hacer la ensalada   6. Gregory y Pablo / venir a casa temprano

3. Gregory / vender su bicicleta   7. Paul y yo / descansar

4. Susan / poner la mesa

EXERCISE L

On New Year's Eve, Mr. Moore is talking with you about what will happen during the coming year. Write what he says.

EXAMPLE: Gabriel / terminar sus estudios
            Gabriel **terminará** sus estudios.

1. Lorenzo / poder comprar un coche

2. Lorenzo y Gabriel / tener que buscar un trabajo

3. tú / hacer un viaje a Puerto Rico

4. Alicia y yo / salir a menudo

5. yo / venir a casa temprano

6. mis padres / vivir en otro estado

EXERCISE M

You will be an exchange student in Caracas and need to communicate with your host family. Prepare an electronic message to them in which you may wish to include the following:

➤ information regarding your travel plans (date of departure, flight information, arrival time)

➤ luggage you will bring

➤ questions about being met at airport

➤ questions about recognition in airport

➤ questions about getting around the city

➤ questions about currency exchange

➤ length of your stay

CHAPTER 14

Reflexive Verbs

♦ 1 ♦ Reflexive Verbs in Simple Tenses

a. A reflexive verb requires a reflexive pronoun *(me, te, se, nos, os, se)* that refers the action of the verb back to the subject.

Yo **me lavo**.   *I wash myself.*

Ellos **se visten**.   *They dress themselves. (They get dressed.)*

b. Reflexive pronouns generally precede the verb in the simple tenses.

Present Tense	
yo me lavo	nosotros (-as) nos lavamos
tú te lavas	vosotros (-as) os laváis
Ud., él, ella se lava	Uds., ellos, ellas se lavan

Preterit Tense	
yo me lavé	nosotros (-as) nos lavamos
tú te lavaste	vosotros (-as) os lavasteis
Ud., él, ella se lavó	Uds., ellos, ellas se lavaron

Imperfect Tense	
yo me lavaba	nosotros (-as) nos lavábamos
tú te lavabas	vosotros (-as) os lavasteis
Ud., él, ella se lavaba	Uds., ellos, ellas se lavaban

Future Tense	
yo me lavaré	nosotros (-as) nos lavaremos
tú te lavarás	vosotros (-as) os lavaréis
Ud., él, ella se lavará	Uds., ellos, ellas se lavarán

c. When a reflexive verb is used as an infinitive, the reflexive pronoun is attached to the end of the infinitive or placed before the conjugated verb. Both forms are accepted.

Voy a bañar**me**. ⎱
Me voy a bañar. ⎰ *I'm going to take a bath.*

Queremos levantar**nos** ahora. ⎱
Nos queremos levantar ahora. ⎰ *We want to get up now.*

d. Common reflexive verbs:

acostarse (ue)	*to go to bed*	lavarse	*to wash oneself*
afeitarse	*to shave*	levantarse	*to get up*
bañarse	*to take a bath, bathe*	llamarse	*to be named, be called*
cepillarse	*to brush (one's teeth, hair, or clothes)*	peinarse	*to comb one's hair*
desayunarse	*to have breakfast*	ponerse	*to put on (clothing)*
despertarse (ie)	*to wake up*	quedarse	*to stay, remain*
divertirse (ie)	*to enjoy oneself, have a good time*	quitarse	*to take off (clothing)*
dormirse (ue)	*to fall asleep*	sentarse (ie)	*to sit down*
irse	*to go away*	vestirse (i)	*to get dressed*

NOTE:

1. Some verbs that are reflexive in Spanish are translated nonreflexively in English.

nos quedamos *we remain*

él **se** va *he goes away*

2. Some reflexive verbs are stem-changing. In the end vocabulary, the stem change is indicated after the verb.

sentarse (ie) me s**ie**nto *I sit down*

vestirse (i) me v**i**sto *I get dressed*

EXERCISE A

Lola thinks that her family has many idiosyncrasies. Write what she says.

EXAMPLE: mi hermano / peinarse sin peine
Mi hermano **se peina** sin peine.

1. mi abuelo / lavarse las manos cincuenta veces al día

2. mi papá / afeitarse mientras bañarse

3. mis hermanas / bañarse por la mañana y por la noche

4. yo / ponerse perfume cinco veces al día

5. Berta y yo / ponerse la misma ropa

6. tú / vestirse en la oscuridad

EXERCISE B

Rita has been baby-sitting her neighbor's children. Answer the questions Rita is asked when the neighbor returns home.

EXAMPLE: ¿Se lavaron las manos? *(no)*
            No, **no se lavaron** las manos.

1. ¿Se puso Juan la pijama sin problema? *(sí)*

2. ¿Se bañaron Angela y Elena? *(no)*

3. ¿Se acostó Juan a las ocho? *(sí)*

4. ¿Se durmió delante de la televisión? *(no)*

5. ¿Se peinó Elena antes de acostarse? *(sí)*

6. ¿Te lavaste las manos? *(sí)*

7. ¿Se despertó Juan alguna vez? *(no)*

8. ¿Te dormiste cuando los niños se acostaron? *(no)*

EXERCISE C

Luis is at a camp reunion, reminiscing with his friends about the things they used to do. Write what he says, using the imperfect tense.

EXAMPLE: yo / levantarse temprano
            Yo **me levantaba** temprano.

1. Abraham y Sergio / despertarse a las seis

2. tú / vestirse rápidamente

3. el consejero / cepillarse los dientes después de cada comida

4. Paco y yo / nunca desayunarse

5. Alberto / dormirse en la cama y no quitarse la ropa

6. nosotros / divertirse en el lago

EXERCISE D

You are on vacation. Write five sentences in which you describe how you spend one day. Use the verbs suggested below.

acostarse	despertarse	dormirse	peinarse	quedarse
desayunarse	divertirse	lavarse	ponerse	vestirse

EXERCISE E

Using the cues provided, write what these people will do.

EXAMPLE: Esteban tiene hambre por la mañana. *(desayunarse)*
Él **se desayunará**.

1. La señora Singh está cansada. *(acostarse)*

2. Tú vas a ver un programa en la televisión. *(sentarse en el sillón)*

3. Los niños van a comer ahora. *(lavarse las manos)*

4. Richie acaba de jugar al béisbol. *(bañarse)*

5. Marta va a salir con sus amigas. *(peinarse bien)*

6. Yo tengo frío. *(ponerse un suéter)*

7. Llueve mucho y no queremos salir. *(quedarse en casa)*

8. Vemos un programa aburrido en la televisión. *(dormirse en el sofá)*

9. Luz oye el despertador. *(levantarse rápidamente)*

10. Tus tíos tienen un bebé recién nacido. *(llamarse Francisco)*

◆ 2 ◆ Reflexive Commands

In affirmative commands, reflexive pronouns follow the verb and are attached to it. In negative commands, reflexive pronouns precede the verb. Affirmative reflexive commands with more than two syllables have a written accent over the stressed vowel.

Affirmative Commands	Negative Commands
(tú) **¡Lávate!** (Uds.) **¡Lávense!**	(tú) **¡No te laves!** (Uds.) **¡No se laven!**
(Ud.) **¡Lávese!**	(Ud.) **¡No se lave!**

EXERCISE F

Your parents are away, and your older sister is in charge. Write in Spanish the commands she gives you.

EXAMPLE: bañarse ahora
¡Báñate ahora!

1. cepillarse los dientes

2. acostarse temprano

3. quitarse los zapatos

4. ponerse ropa limpia

5. quedarse en la casa

EXERCISE G

While you rehearse a school play, the teacher gives you directions. Write what she says you shouldn't do.

EXAMPLE: levantarse de la silla ahora
          ¡No te levantes de la silla ahora!

1. peinarse en este momento

2. sentarse en el sofá

3. ponerse el sombrero todavía

4. quitarse el suéter hasta más tarde

5. irse de la escena

EXERCISE H

A teacher walking through the school cafeteria tells a group of students to do the following things. Write what she says.

EXAMPLE: quedarse en la cafetería
          ¡Quédense en la cafetería!

1. desayunarse en silencio

2. quitarse los anteojos de sol

3. sentarse en las sillas

4. lavarse las manos

5. quedarse donde están ahora

EXERCISE I

What does she tell them they shouldn't do?

EXAMPLE: irse de la cafetería
          ¡No se vayan de la cafetería!

1. desayunarse en el piso

2. ponerse los anteojos de sol

3. peinarse aquí

4. quedarse cerca de la ventana

5. quitarse los zapatos

6. sentarse en la mesa

MASTERY EXERCISES

EXERCISE J

Rosa, Annette, Theresa, and Mary are sharing a hotel room on an overnight school trip. Complete their dialogue using the appropriate form of the reflexive verbs.

ROSA: _____, muchachas. Ya son las siete de la mañana.
   1. (despertarse)

MARY: ¿Quién _____ primero?
   2. (bañarse)

THERESA: La persona que _____ primero puede _____ primero.
   3. (levantarse)   *4.* (bañarse)

ROSA: Bueno, mientras yo _____, Uds. _____.
   5. (bañarse)   *6.* (peinarse)

MARY: Buena idea. Annette, _____. Vamos a llegar tarde.
   7. (levantarse)

ANNETE: Tengo mucho sueño. Vuelvo a _____ mientras Uds. _____.
   8. (dormirse)   *9.* (vestirse)

THERESA: ¡No _____ otra vez, Annette! Tenemos que _____ a las ocho.
   10. (dormirse)   *11.* (desayunarse)

ANNETTE: Bueno, ahora yo _____.
   12. (levantarse)

MARY: Theresa, ¿qué _____ hoy?
   13. (ponerse)

THERESA: Hace calor. Rosa y yo decidimos _____ pantalones cortos. ¿Y tú?
   14. (ponerse)

MARY: Yo _____ lo mismo.
   15. (ponerse)

ROSA: ¡Annette, no _____ aquí! _____ en el cuarto de baño, por favor.
   16. (peinarse)   *17.* (peinarse)

   Y mientras estás allí, _____ y _____ la cara.
   18. (bañarse)   *19.* (lavarse)

   Después yo _____ la cara y _____ también.
   20. (lavarse)   *21.* (peinarse)

THERESA: ¡Mary, _____ esa blusa! Es mía. ¡_____ otra blusa!
   22. (quitarse)   *23.* (ponerse)

MARY: Bueno, yo voy a _____ esta blusa blanca.
   24. (ponerse)

ROSA: Annette, no _____ en esa silla, por favor. Mi ropa está allí.
                 25. (sentarse)

ANNETTE: Yo no quiero salir. Prefiero _____ aquí. Todavía tengo sueño y hay
                                  26. (quedarse)

         buenos programas en la televisión por la mañana.

MARY: De ninguna manera, Annette. _____ ahora porque nosotras
                                 27. (vestirse)

estamos listas y _____ .
             28. (irse)

EXERCISE K

In your journal prepare an entry in which you describe a new friend. Using as many reflexive verbs as possible, you may wish to include the following:

> ➤ his/her name
> ➤ information concerning his/her daily routine
> ➤ information on how you and he/she enjoy yourselves
> ➤ things you tell him/her to do or not to do

Common Idiomatic Expressions with Verbs

Many Spanish verbs are used in idiomatic expressions. A list of common expressions follows:

♦ 1 ♦ Expressions with *HACER*

¿Qué tiempo hace? *How's the weather?*
¿Qué tiempo hace en julio? *How's the weather in July?*

hacer buen / mal tiempo *to be good / bad weather*
Hace mal tiempo hoy. *Today the weather is bad.*

hacer (mucho) frío / calor / fresco *to be (very) cold / warm / cool (weather)*
Hizo mucho frío anoche. *It was very cold last night.*

hacer (mucho) sol *to be (very) sunny*
Hace mucho sol por la tarde. *It's very sunny in the afternoon.*

hacer (mucho) viento *to be (very) windy*
Hace viento. *It's windy.*

hacer el favor de + infinitive *please …*
Haga el favor de abrir la ventana. *Please open the window.*

hacer un viaje *to take a trip*
Hacen un viaje cada año. *They take a trip each year.*

hacer una pregunta *to ask a question*
El niño hace muchas preguntas. *The boy asks many questions.*

hacer una visita *to pay a visit*
Ella hizo una visita a su abuela. *She paid a visit to her grandmother.*

EXERCISE A

Tell what you like to do in different kinds of weather. Use the suggestions below.

andar en el parque	ir al cine	mirar la televisión
correr en el parque	jugar al tenis	nadar en la piscina
ir a las montañas	leer un libro	quedarse en casa

EXAMPLE: hacer buen tiempo
        Cuando **hace** buen tiempo **me gusta andar en el parque**.

1. hacer sol

2. hacer mucho viento

3. hacer mal tiempo

4. hacer mucho calor

5. hacer fresco

6. hacer mucho frío

EXERCISE B

Describe the weather in each of the drawings below.

EXAMPLE: **Hace mucho viento.**

1. _____ .

2. _____ .

3. _____ .

4. _____ .

5. _____ .

Use an idiomatic expression with *hacer* to tell what these people do.

EXAMPLE: Moses no comprende un problema de la clase de matemáticas. *(Él)*
        Él **hace una pregunta**.

1. Alicia y Ramona se visten para ir a la escuela. *(Ellas preguntan)*

2. Los señores Ortiz quieren conocer Chile. *(Ellos)*

3. Yo estoy en la biblioteca y quiero estudiar, pero unos jóvenes hablan en voz alta. *(Yo digo)*

4. Tú tienes ganas de ver a tus primos. *(Tú)*

♦ 2 ♦ Expressions with *TENER*

¿Qué tiene Ud.?	*What's the matter with you?*
¿Qué tiene Ud. ahora?	*What's the matter with you now?*
tener... años	*to be . . . years old*
¿Cuántos años tiene Juan?	*How old is Juan?*
Juan tiene diez años.	*Juan is ten years old.*

tener (mucho) calor	*to be (very) warm (persons)*
¿Tiene Ud. calor?	*Are you warm?*
tener cuidado	*to be careful*
¡Ten cuidado en la playa!	*Be careful at the beach!*
tener dolor de cabeza	*to have a headache*
Ella tiene dolor de cabeza.	*She has a headache.*
tener dolor de muelas	*to have a toothache*
Él tiene dolor de muelas.	*He has a toothache.*
tener (mucho) frío	*to be (very) cold (persons)*
Los niños tienen frío.	*The children are cold.*
tener ganas de	*to feel like, want to*
Tengo ganas de gritar.	*I feel like screaming.*
tener (mucha) hambre	*to be (very) hungry*
No tengo hambre.	*I'm not hungry.*
tener la bondad de + infinitive	*to be kind enough to*
Tenga la bondad de cerrar la puerta.	*Be kind enough to close the door.*
tener miedo de	*to be afraid of*
Tienen miedo del mar.	*They're afraid of the sea.*
tener (mucha) sed	*to be (very) thirsty*
Tenemos sed ahora.	*We're thirsty now.*
tener (mucho) sueño	*to be (very) sleepy*
¿Tienen Uds. sueño?	*Are you sleepy?*
tener prisa	*to be in a hurry*
¡No tengas prisa!	*Don't be in a hurry!*
tener que + infinitive	*to have to, must*
Mi padre tiene que trabajar.	*My father has to work.*
tener razón / no tener razón	*to be right / to be wrong*
Mary siempre tiene razón.	*Mary is always right.*
Jamal no tiene razón.	*Jamal is wrong.*

EXERCISE D

Using an expression with *tener*, tell why these people do what they do.

EXAMPLE: Llevo pantalones cortos hoy.
          Yo **tengo calor**.

1. Pilar va al dentista.

2. Tú usas un suéter.

3. Yo busco otra respuesta a la pregunta.

4. Vamos a la playa.

5. Ellos comen una manzana.

6. Juan se acuesta.

7. El niño grita.

8. Ud. bebe una limonada.

9. Estudio ocho horas para un examen.

10. El señor corre.

11. Al no ver autos, el niño cruza la calle.

12. La madre toma dos aspirinas.

EXERCISE E

Use the expressions with *tener* in parentheses to complete Martín's dialogue with the school nurse.

ENFERMERA: Hola, Martín. ¿_____ ?
                                    1. (qué tener)

MARTÍN: _____ .
        2. (tener dolor de cabeza)

ENFERMERA: ¿_____ ?
             3. (tener fiebre)

MARTÍN: No creo. _____ y a veces _____ .
                 4. (tener frío)   **5.** (tener calor)

ENFERMERA: ¿Quieres comer algo?

MARTÍN: No, gracias. _____ .
               6. (no tener hambre)

ENFERMERA: ¿_____ beber algo?
            7. (tener ganas de)

MARTÍN: Sí, _____ .
         8. (tener sed)

ENFERMERA: Yo _____ llamar a tu mamá.
                9. (tener que)

MARTÍN: Ud. _____ . Yo _____ ir a casa.
            10. (tener razón)   **11.** (tener ganas de)

ENFERMERA: _____ darme tu número de teléfono.
              12. (tener la bondad de)

MARTÍN: Es el 555-0021.

ENFERMERA: Está bien. Tú _____ esperar a tu madre. Ella viene por ti.
                13. (tener que)

MARTÍN: Muchas gracias. Ahora yo _____ .
              14. (tener sueño)

♦ 3 ♦ Other Idiomatic Verbal Expressions

acabar de + infinitive   *to have just*
Él acaba de llegar.   *He has just arrived.*

dar la hora   *to strike the hour*
El reloj da las tres.   *The clock strikes three.*

dar las gracias   *to thank*
Damos las gracias al profesor.   *We thank the teacher.*

dar un paseo   *to take a walk*
Doy un paseo en el parque cada día.   *I take a walk in the park every day.*

darse la mano   *to shake hands*
Nos damos la mano.   *We shake hands.*

dejar caer   *to drop*
El niño deja caer la leche.   *The child drops the milk.*

dejar de + infinitive   *to fail to; to stop; to neglect to*
John deja de estudiar.   *John stops studying.*

echar al correo   *to mail*
Echo la carta al correo.   *I mail the letter.*

echar de menos   *to miss* (a person or thing)
Echo de menos a mis primos.   *I miss my cousins.*

estar de acuerdo	*to agree*
Estamos de acuerdo.	*We agree.*
guardar cama	*to stay in bed*
Él guarda cama por dos días.	*He's staying in bed for two days.*
llegar a ser	*to become; to get to be*
Quiero llegar a ser médico.	*I want to become a doctor.*
pensar + infinitive	*to intend to*
Pienso hacer un viaje.	*I intend to take a trip.*
ponerse + adjective	*to become; to turn*
El niño se puso triste.	*The child became sad.*
querer decir	
¿Qué quiere decir «dinero»?	*What does "dinero" mean?*
sacar una fotografía	*to take a picture*
Pedro saca muchas fotografías.	*Peter takes many pictures.*

EXERCISE F

Several friends are commenting on various topics. Select the expression from those listed below and write its appropriate form in the space provided.

dar	dejar caer	estar de acuerdo	ponerse
dar las gracias	dejar de	guardar cama	querer decir
dar un paseo	echar de menos	llegar a ser	sacar fotografías
darse la mano	echarla al correo	pensar	

1. Luis está enfermo. Él _____ por tres días.

2. Cuando mis padres no están en casa, mi hermana menor los _____ .

3. Estoy contento porque trabajo en un hospital. Quiero _____ médico.

4. Cuando conoces a una persona, es correcto _____ .

5. Escribí esta carta. Ahora voy a _____ .

6. Roy y yo tenemos las mismas ideas. Nosotros _____ .

7. Yo voy a jugar al tenis mañana. ¿Qué _____ tú hacer?

8. Jorge no quiere ponerse gordo. Él _____ comer dulces.

9. Mi tía me dio este reloj. Ahora tengo que _____ a ella.

10. Phyllis tiene una cámara nueva. Le fascina _____ .

11. Yo no pasé el examen de conducir y _____ furioso.

12. Felipe no comprende nada. Él siempre pregunta: «¿Qué _____ eso?»

13. Hace buen tiempo y necesito ejercicio. Voy a _____ en el parque.

14. ¡No le des ese vaso de cristal a Jaime! Él _____ todo.

15. ¿Qué hora es? El reloj _____ la una y media.

EXERCISE G

Answer these questions a friend asks you.

1. ¿Sacas muchas fotografías cuando haces un viaje?

2. ¿Guardas cama cuando estás enfermo(a)?

3. ¿Te pones nervioso(a) antes de un examen?

4. ¿Echas de menos a tus amigo(a)s durante las vacaciones?

5. ¿Acabas de comprar ese suéter?

6. ¿Dejas de estudiar cuando tus amigo(a)s te llaman por teléfono?

7. ¿Das un paseo cada noche?

8. ¿Das las gracias a tu madre cuando ella sirve la cena?

9. ¿Piensas trabajar durante el verano?

10. ¿Qué haces cuando conoces a una persona?

EXERCISE H

The teacher asks the class to rewrite these sentences using an expression with *dar*, *hacer*, *tener*, or *querer*.

EXAMPLE: **Le duele** el estómago.
         Tiene dolor de estómago.

1. **Desea** ir al cine esta noche.

2. Tú **debes** estudiar.

3. Abra la puerta, **por favor**.

4. ¿Qué **significa** esta palabra?

5. Ellos **caminan** por el parque.

6. ¿**Qué edad tienes**?

7. **Me duele** la cabeza.

EXERCISE I

Carmen is spending a few weeks at a nature camp. Complete this letter with the appropriate idiomatic expressions.

Querida Susana:

Yo _____ volver de un paseo formidable. Casi todos los días hacemos lo mismo.
    1. (to have just)

El grupo _____ en el bosque y vemos muchas cosas interesantes. Cuando _____
    2. (to take a walk)   **3.** (the weather is good)

salimos muy temprano y no volvemos hasta muy tarde. Yo _____ usar un sombrero,
                                                          4. (to have to)

especialmente cuando _____ . Tengo mi cámara conmigo y yo _____ .
                        5. (it's very sunny)   **6.** (to take many pictures)

Un día una chica _____ mi cámara y yo _____ furiosa. La cámara está
                    7. (to drop)   **8.** (to become)

bien y ella y yo _____ en que fue un accidente. Nosotras _____ y ahora somos
                  9. (to agree)   **10.** (to shake hands)

buenas amigas. Por lo general, _____ aquí. Por la mañana y por la tarde _____ .
                                11. (the weather is good)   **12.** (it's cold)

Nosotras _____ llevar un suéter con nosotras cuando salimos. También cuando
          13. (to have to)

nosotras _____ a otro sitio llevamos comida y bebidas para no _____ ni
          14. (to take a trip)   **15.** (to be hungry)

_____ . Las actividades son fuertes y a las ocho de la noche yo ya _____ .
  16. (to be thirsty)   **17.** (to be sleepy)

Yo _____ a mis amigas pero Uds. pueden _____ a este campamento.
    18. (to miss)   **19.** (to pay a visit)

Ahora yo _____ porque quiero _____ esta carta. _____
          20. (to be in a hurry)   **21.** (to mail)   **22.** (please)

contestar esta carta.

Cariñosamente.
Carmen

EXERCISE J

A friend is helping you study for a Spanish test. He asks you what would you ask to learn the following:

1. qué ropa usar hoy

2. el efecto de la temperatura en una persona

3. por qué una persona va al dentista

4. si un amigo quiere ir a un restaurante

5. la edad de una persona

6. si quieres beber agua

7. por qué un amigo va al médico

8. el significado de una palabra

9. por qué un amigo está triste

Negation

♦ 1 ♦ Negatives

a. The most common negative is *no*, which always precedes the conjugated verb.

Yo **no leo** el libro.   *I don't read the book.*

¿**No escribiste** la carta?   *Didn't you write the letter?*

EXERCISE A

Pablo is answering a friend's questions about where the students in his class are from. Write what he says.

EXAMPLE: ¿Es Marta de México? *(Venezuela)*
              No, Marta **no es** de México. Ella es de Venezuela.

1. ¿Son Juan y Xavier de Puerto Rico? *(España)*

2. ¿Es Alberto de la República Dominicana? *(Colombia)*

3. ¿Es Laura de Guatemala? *(Costa Rica)*

4. ¿Son Rafael y Linda de la Argentina? *(Chile)*

5. ¿Eres tú de los Estados Unidos? *(Nicaragua)*

EXERCISE B

You and your friends are in your basement. Your mother wants to know what you're doing. Answer her questions.

EXAMPLE: ¿Miran Uds. la televisión?
              No, no miramos la televisión.

1. ¿Juegan Uds. al ajedrez?

2. ¿Leen Uds. el periódico?

3. ¿Come Enrique helado?

4. ¿Hablas tú por teléfono?

5. ¿Preparas tú la tarea para mañana?

6. ¿Arreglan Uds. el cuarto?

7. ¿Practicas tú el diálogo con Luis?

(EXERCISE C)

From the list below, tell five things you are not going to do this weekend.

caminar en el parque   jugar al fútbol   ver una película

estudiar en la biblioteca   lavar el coche   visitar a los abuelos

ir a la playa   nadar

EXAMPLE: **No voy a ir a la playa.**

b. Other negatives are:

nada   *nothing, (not) anything*

nadie   *no one, nobody, (not) anyone*

ni… ni   *neither… nor; not…either…or…*

ninguno (–a)   *no, none, (not) any*

no   *no, not*

nunca   *never, (not) ever*

tampoco   *neither, not either*

c. A double negative is acceptable in Spanish. In fact, this construction occurs frequently. If one of the negatives is *no*, it precedes the verb. If *no* is omitted, the other negative must precede the verb.

No veo **nada**.
Nada veo. } *I don't see anything.*

Él **no** juega **nunca**.
El **nunca** juega. } *He never plays.*

d. *Nadie* can be used as the subject or the object of the verb. When it is the object of the verb, it is preceded by the preposition *a*.

Nadie entra.
No entra **nadie**. } No one enters.

BUT

No veo **a nadie**.   *I don't see anyone (anybody).*

A nadie veo.   *I see no one (nobody).*

e. Ninguno drops the final -*o* and takes a written accent over the *u* if it comes immediately before a masculine singular noun. If a preposition comes between *ninguno* and the noun, the full form is used.

Ningún alumno está ausente. *No pupil is absent.*

Ninguno de los alumnos está ausente. *None of the pupils is absent.*

Ninguna casa tiene ascensor. *No house has an elevator.*

EXERCISE D

Sarita's telling her mother the chores that her friends never do. Tell what she says.

EXAMPLE: ayudar en casa *(Juanita)*
Juanita nunca ayuda en casa.

1. sacar la basura *(Raquel)*

2. ir de compras *(Jorge y Pedro)*

3. lavar el coche *(Alejandro)*

4. preparar la ensalada *(Beatriz y Alex)*

5. pasar la aspiradora *(Tomás y Víctor)*

6. sacar al perro *(Oyuki)*

7. poner la mesa *(Esteban)*

8. secar los platos *(Lola y Emilio)*

EXERCISE E

During a camping trip, your friend tries your patience with her questions. Answer them in Spanish, using a form of *ninguno*, if possible, or *nada*.

EXAMPLE: ¿Cuántos videojuegos tienes?
No tengo **ninguno**.

1. ¿Ves los pájaros?

2. ¿Tienes una lamparita?

3. ¿Lees el mapa?

4. ¿Llevas la mochila?

5. ¿Preparas la cena?

6. ¿Necesitas mi ayuda?

EXERCISE F

Mr. Perales is complaining to his wife about his day at work. Tell what he says.

EXAMPLE: saludar a los jefes
Nadie saluda a los jefes.

1. contestar el teléfono

2. ayudar a la secretaria

3. llegar a tiempo

4. tomar una hora de almuerzo

5. arreglar su escritorio

6. recibir a los clientes

7. hablar en voz baja

EXERCISE G

During a date, Theresa finds Juan very distracted. Give Juan's answers to her questions.

EXAMPLE: ¿A quién miras?
No miro a nadie.

1. ¿A quién hablas?
2. ¿A quiénes buscas?
3. ¿A quién esperas?
4. ¿A quién admiras?
5. ¿A quiénes respondes?

EXERCISE H

Maria's helping her mother prepare a shopping list. Tell what she says to her mother.

EXAMPLE: pan
No tenemos ningún pan.

1. fruta
2. chocolate
3. helado
4. queso
5. cebolla
6. mantequilla
7. pastel

EXERCISE I

Lupe is comparing herself to a popular actress she just saw on a talk show. Tell what she says.

EXAMPLE: No le gusta el color rojo.
No me gusta el color rojo **tampoco**.

1. Nunca se levanta temprano.
2. No come carne.
3. No le gusta decir adiós.
4. Nunca usa paraguas.
5. No fuma.

EXERCISE J

César is describing a new neighbor. Tell what he says about him.

EXAMPLE: jugar al béisbol o al fútbol
Él **no juega ni** al béisbol **ni** al fútbol.

1. leer periódicos o revistas
2. jugar a las damas o al ajedrez
3. ver películas o documentales
4. correr o caminar a la escuela
5. coleccionar estampillas o monedas
6. dibujar o pintar

EXERCISE K

Pedro describes a dream he had. Complete his description with the appropriate negative expressions.

Roberto y yo estamos en una fiesta. Estamos sentados en el sofá porque _____
                                                                                        1.

conocemos _____ . _____ nos habla. La fiesta es muy aburrida.
                    2.   3.

Tenemos hambre pero _____ hay _____ de comer. Por fin una chica sale de
                              4.   5.

la cocina con unos platos en la mano pero ella _____ nos ofrece _____ .
                                                        6.   7.

Roberto y yo vamos a la mesa y vemos que _____ hay _____ plato bueno.
                                                    8.   9.

A nosotros _____ nos gustan _____ los tacos _____
                    10.   11.   12.

los frijoles. Queremos salir pero _____ encontramos _____ puerta.
                                          13.   14.

_____ contesta nuestras preguntas. _____ chico quiere ayudarnos.
        15.   16.

Yo _____ puedo salir de allí y Roberto _____ puede salir
        17.   18.

_____ . Le digo a Roberto que _____ voy a aceptar una invitación
        19.   20.

a una fiesta donde _____ conozco _____ . En ese momento oigo una
                          21.   22.

voz que me pregunta: —Pedro, ¿_____ vas a comer con tus compañeros en la cafetería?
                                        23.

Entonces me despierto y digo: —_____ vuelvo a dormirme en la clase otra vez.
                                          24.

♦ 2 ♦ NEGATIVE EXPRESSIONS

Some useful negative expressions are:

Creo que no.	*I don't think so.*
De nada.	*You're welcome.*

en ningún lado
en ninguna parte } *nowhere*

Mejor no.	*Better not.*
Ni yo tampoco.	*Me neither.*
No es así.	*It's not so.*
No es para tanto.	*It's not such a big deal.*
No hay más remedio.	*It can't be helped.*
No importa.	*It doesn't matter.*
No lo creo.	*I don't believe it.*
¡No me digas!	*Don't tell me! (You don't say!)*
No me gusta nada.	*I don't like it at all.*
No puede ser.	*It can't be.*
No puedo más.	*I can't take it anymore.*
¿No te parece?	*Don't you think so?*
¿Por qué no?	*Why not?*

EXERCISE L

Several friends are sitting around and making plans. Using the following expressions, react to their statements.

De nada.   No lo creo.   No puede ser.

Ni yo tampoco.   No me gusta nada.   ¿Por qué no?

No es para tanto.

EXAMPLE: Juan dice: —Cuando mis primos dicen «gracias» yo nunca sé qué contestar.
         Tú dices: **—Debes decir «de nada».**

1. Roberto dice: —Yo no tengo clases mañana.

Tú dices: _____

2. Luis dice: —Después de estos días de lluvia, dicen que va a hacer buen tiempo mañana.

Tú dices: _____

3. Laura dice: —Si vamos a la playa podemos practicar el esquí acuático.

Tú dices: _____

4. Esteban dice: —Mañana es el cumpleaños de Lázaro.

Tú dices: _____

5. Anita dice: —Lázaro tiene un coche de último modelo.

Tú dices: _____

6. Tomás dice: Vamos a llamar a Lázaro por teléfono.

Tú dices: _____

(**EXERCISE M**)

Poor Enrique spent the summer working while his friends went to Mexico. Using the expressions given, write appropriate responses that Enrique would make as his friends tell him about their trip.

Creo que no	No hay más remedio.	No me gusta nada.
En ningún lado	No lo creo.	No puedo más.
No es para tanto.	No me digas.	

EXAMPLE: Raúl dice: —¡En el avión nos sentamos en primera clase!
Enrique dice: —**No es para tanto.**

1. Joaquín dice: —Encontramos a tu maestra de español en un restaurante.

Enrique dice: _____

2. Felipe dice: —Cuando fuimos a pescar, yo pesqué un pez de cien libras.

Enrique dice: _____

3. Laura dice: —Visitamos muchos museos.

Enrique dice: _____

4. Alfredo dice: —Vamos a volver a México el verano que viene. ¿Vas con nosotros?

Enrique dice: _____

5. Héctor dice: —¿Vas a trabajar otra vez durante el verano?

Enrique dice: _____

6. Alicia dice: —Me encanta la música de los mariachis. ¿Sabes dónde venden discos compactos de esta música?

Enrique dice: _____

7. Ofelia dice: —Tienes que ver las fotos que sacamos durante el viaje.

Enrique dice: _____

⟨ MASTERY EXERCISES ⟩

EXERCISE N

An exchange student asks you some questions in Spanish. Answer using a negative word or expression.

1. ¿Están cerradas las tiendas hoy?

   No, _____ de las tiendas está cerrada hoy.

2. ¿Visitaste el museo de arte?

   No visité _____ museo de arte.

3. ¿Vas al concierto o al cine?

   No voy _____ al concierto _____ al cine.

4. ¿Cuándo juegas al tenis?

   _____ juego al tenis.

5. ¿Quién habla español en tu casa?

   _____ habla español en mi casa.

6. ¿A quién acompañas después de las clases?

   No acompaño _____ después de las clases.

7. ¿Qué haces por la noche?

   No hago _____ por la noche.

8. ¿Lees algún libro interesante?

   No leo _____ libro interesante.

9. ¿Te gustan las películas de ciencia ficción?

   No, _____ veo esas películas.

EXERCISE O

While visiting Mexico City, you have a frustrating bank-related experience. Relate the experience to a friend in an e-mail message. You may wish to include the following:

- ➤ no bank is open today
- ➤ you never use the automatic teller machine
- ➤ you have no money in your wallet
- ➤ there is no one to speak to at the bank
- ➤ no one offers to help you
- ➤ you don't like to borrow money from friends

Noun and Pronoun Structures

Noun and Articles

♦ 1 ♦ Gender of Nouns

a. All nouns in Spanish are either masculine or feminine. Nouns ending in *-o* and nouns refer-ring to male beings are generally masculine. Nouns ending in *-a*, *-d*, or *-ión* and nouns referring to female beings are generally feminine.

Masculine	Feminine	
el libro *the book*	**la pluma** *the pen*	**la ciudad** *the city*
el padre *the father*	**la madre** *the mother*	**la lección** *the lesson*

b. The gender of other nouns must be learned individually.

Masculine	Feminine
el lápiz *the pencil*	**la flor** *the flower*
el papel *the paper*	**la sal** *the salt*

c. The articles used before masculine singular nouns are *el* (the) and *un* (a, an). The articles used before feminine singular nouns are *la* (the) and *una* (a, an).

Masculine	Feminine
el hombre *the man*	**la mujer** *the woman*
un cuadro *a picture*	**una silla** *a chair*

d. The article is generally repeated before each noun in a series.

| Come **una** naranja y **un** huevo. | *He eats an orange and an egg.* |
| Compra **la** leche y **el** pan. | *He buys the milk and the bread.* |

EXERCISE A

Enrique tells his little cousin the names of the kinds of food they see at the supermarket. Write what Enrique says.

EXAMPLE: **la leche**

1.

2.

3.

4.

5.

6.

7.

8.

9.

10.

11.

12.

13.

14.

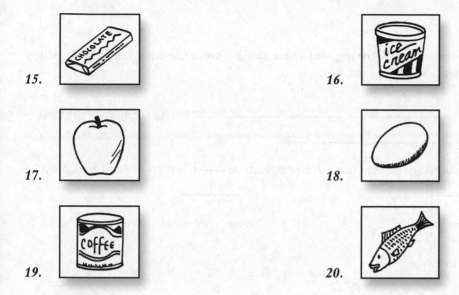

15.

16.

17.

18.

19.

20.

 EXERCISE B

School has begun, and Carolina is preparing a shopping list of the school supplies she will need. Help her prepare the list.

EXAMPLE: **un bolígrafo**

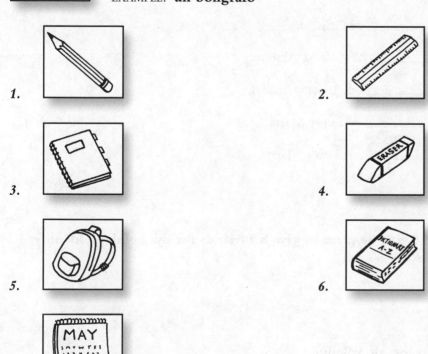

1.

2.

3.

4.

5.

6.

7.

EXERCISE C

Jorge and his cousin Javier have been figuring out their family tree. Identify the relationships among the following members of their families.

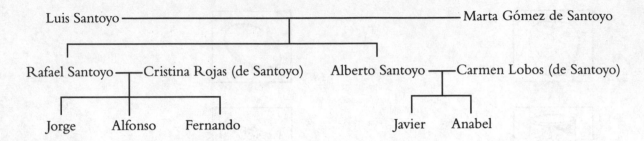

EXAMPLE: Jorge es **el primo** de Javier

1. Alfonso es _____ de Rafael.

2. Alberto es _____ de Jorge.

3. Anabel es _____ de Carmen.

4. Fernando es _____ de Jorge.

5. Alberto es _____ de Anabel y Javier.

6. Anabel es _____ de Javier.

7. Luis es _____ de Javier.

8. Rafael es _____ de Cristina.

9. Marta es _____ de Rafael y Alberto.

10. Cristina es _____ de Javier y Anabel.

11. Anabel es _____ de Luis y Marta.

12. Alfonso es _____ de Luis y Marta.

EXERCISE D

Alejandro is thinking about the gifts he plans to give his friends for the holidays. Identify the items he includes on his list.

EXAMPLE: **una pelota de voleibol**

1.

2.

3.

4.

5.

6.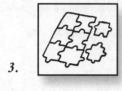

7.

8.

◆ 2 ◆ Plural of Nouns

a. Nouns ending in a vowel form the plural by adding -*s*.

Singular	Plural
el libro *the book*	**los libros** *the books*
la pluma *the pen*	**las plumas** *the pens*
un amigo *a friend*	**unos amigos** *some friends*
una clase *a class*	**unas clases** *some classes*

b. Nouns ending in a consonant form the plural by adding -*es*.

Singular	Plural
el profesor *the teacher*	**los profesores** *the teachers*
la ciudad *the city*	**las ciudades** *the cities*

c. Nouns ending in -*z* change *z* to *c* before adding -*es*.

Singular	Plural
el lápiz *the pencil*	**los lápices** *the pencils*
la actriz *the actress*	**las actrices** *the actresses*

d. An accent mark is added or dropped in nouns ending in *n* or *s* to keep the original stress.

Singular	Plural
el joven	**los jóvenes**
el examen	**los exámenes**
el inglés	**los ingleses**
la lección	**las lecciones**

NOTE:

1. The articles *el* and *la* become *los* and *las* when used with plural nouns.

2. The plural forms of the indefinite articles are *unos* and *unas*; they mean some, a few, several.

EXERCISE E

Before going to summer camp, Rose studies a list of recommended articles of clothing. Tell how many of each item she should pack.

EXAMPLE: blusa (2)
     dos blusas

1. falda *(2)*

2. pantalón largo *(5)*

3. camiseta *(6)*

4. pañuelo *(10)*

5. traje de baño *(3)*

6. calcetín blanco *(8)*

7. pantalón corto *(7)*

8. suéter *(2)*

9. chaqueta *(2)*

10. juego de ropa interior *(6)*

EXERCISE F

You're helping your Spanish teacher review a writing exercise submitted by students in another class. Read each one and then indicate what that person likes or dislikes.

EXAMPLE: Me gusta el tenis. También me gusta nadar.
     A Roberto **le gustan los deportes**.

1. Me gusta ver las noticias. También me gusta ver las telenovelas.

A Sue le _____.

2. Me gusta el inglés. También me gusta pasar muchas horas en la biblioteca.

A Iván le _____.

3. Me gusta el gato de Jorge. También me gusta el perro de mi abuelo.

A Clara le _____.

4. Me gustan los videojuegos. También me gustan los juegos computarizados.

A Lorenzo le _____.

5. Me gusta «Tom Sawyer». También me gusta «Jane Eyre».

A Laurie le _____.

6. Me gusta escuchar la radio. También me gustan mucho los conciertos.

A Gabriel le _____.

♦ 3 ♦ Forms of the Articles

   a. There are four definite articles in Spanish corresponding to English *the*.

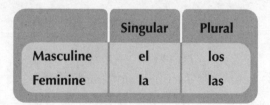

	Singular	Plural
Masculine	el	los
Feminine	la	las

NOTE:

Feminine nouns that begin with a stressed *a* sound (*a-* or *ha-*) take the articles *el* and *un* in the singular. In the plural, the articles are *las* and *unas*.

el agua	*water*	**las a**guas	*waters*
un agua		**unas a**guas	
el aula	*classroom*	**las a**ulas	*classrooms*
un aula		**unas a**ulas	
el hacha	*ax*	**las ha**chas	*axes*
un hacha		**unas ha**chas	

BUT

la **amiga**
la **alum**na } (initial *a* is not stressed)

b. There are four indefinite articles in Spanish corresponding to English *a (an)*, *some*, *several*, *a few*.

	Singular	Plural
Masculine	un	unos
Feminine	una	unas

un amigo   *a friend*   **unos** amigos   *some friends*

una blusa   *a blouse*   **unas** blusas   *several blouses*

♦ 4 ♦ Uses of the Articles

The definite article is used:

a. before the names of languages and other subjects of study *(asignaturas)*, unless the subjects of study follow *hablar*, *en*, or *de*.

El inglés es una lengua.   *English is a language.*

Estudio **el** español.   *I study Spanish.*

La química es difícil.   *Chemistry is difficult.*

BUT

Él **habla** español.   *He speaks Spanish.*

Escriben **en** alemán.   *They write in German.*

Mi libro **de** historia está en el escritorio.   *My history book is on the desk.*

b. before titles (except when speaking directly to a person).

El señor Gómez no está aquí.   *Mr. Gómez is not here.*

La doctora Álvarez sabe mucho.   *Dr. Álvarez knows a lot.*

BUT

Buenos días, señora Molina.   *Good morning, Mrs. Molina.*

c. before the words *escuela*, *clase*, and *iglesia* when they follow a preposition.

Voy **a la** escuela.   *I'm going to school.*

Están **en la** iglesia.   *They are in church.*

d. before certain geographic names.

la América Central	*Central America*
la América del Norte	*North America*
la América del Sur	*South America*
la Argentina	*Argentina*
la Florida	*Florida*
el Canadá	*Canada*
los Estados Unidos	*the United States*
el Perú	*Peru*

BUT

Alemania	*Germany*
España	*Spain*
Europa	*Europe*
Francia	*France*
Inglaterra	*England*
Italia	*Italy*
México	*Mexico*
Rusia	*Russia*

NOTE:

Current informal usage tends to omit the definite article before the names of countries.

Vivo en Estados Unidos.	*I live in the United States.*

e. before the days of the week, to express the English word *on.*

No voy a la escuela los domingos.	*I don't go to school on Sundays.*

f. The indefinite article is used to express the English word *a (an).*

Tengo **un** hermano.	*I have a brother.*

g. The indefinite article is omitted before a noun expressing nationality, profession, or occupation when it follows the verb *ser.*

Pablo **es** francés.	*Paul is a Frenchman (is French).*
Ese hombre **es** zapatero.	*That man is a shoemaker.*
Ella va a **ser** médico.	*She's going to be a doctor.*

BUT

If the noun is modified, the indefinite article is used.

Deseo ser **un** médico bueno.	*I want to be a good doctor.*

EXERCISE G

Answer the questions a new student asks you. Use the cues provided.

1. ¿Eres francés (francesa)? *(español / española)*

2. ¿Qué asignaturas estudias? *(inglés, biología, historia)*

3. ¿Cómo se llama tu profesora de inglés? *(Miss McCarthy)*

4. ¿En qué aula tienes la clase de historia? *(210)*

5. ¿Qué deportes te gustan? *(tenis, natación)*

6. ¿En que día vas al laboratorio en la clase de biología? *(jueves)*

7. ¿A qué hora de la noche te acuestas? *(10:30)*

8. ¿Qué país de la América del Sur deseas visitar? *(Perú, Argentina)*

9. ¿Sabes escribir en español? *(no)*

10. ¿Qué es tu padre? *(ingeniero)*

EXERCISE H

Use the correct form of the articles to complete this e-mail that Jorge received from a friend living in Mexico. Some sentences may not need an article.

Mientras estamos en _____ escuela prestamos atención al maestro y contestamos
                            1.

en _____ español. _____ miércoles tomé una lección de _____ música.
        2.   3.   4.

Aprendo a tocar _____ guitarra. El profesor es _____ argentino y es
                        5.   6.

_____ guitarrista profesional. Durante las vacaciones él viaja por _____
        7.   8.

México, _____ Venezuela y _____ Estados Unidos. Se llama
                9.   10.

_____ señor Rivas. Su padre es _____ guitarrista. La clase es difícil
        11.   12.

porque _____ señor Rivas prefiere hablar en _____ español, pero aprendo
                13.   14.

así _____ español mientras asisto a la clase de _____ música.
            15.   16.

_____ sábado vamos a un concierto de _____ música flamenca.
        17.   18.

⟨ MASTERY EXERCISES ⟩

EXERCISE I

Describe the contents of a time capsule that you and a friend are preparing.

EXAMPLE: **una pelota de béisbol**

EXERCISE J

Roberto is telling a friend about his Spanish teacher. Tell what he says.

EXAMPLE: ella / vivir / Estados Unidos
Ella **vive en los** Estados Unidos.

1. ella / ser / señora Flores

2. ella / ser / América del Sur

3. Buenos Aires / estar / Argentina

4. ser / argentina

5. ser / profesora buena

6. hablar / italiano y español

7. su esposo / ser / médico

8. ellos / pasar el verano / Canadá

9. ella / dar un examen / viernes

10. corregir los exámenes / pluma verde

(**EXERCISE K**)

Prepare a short autobiographical statement that will be placed on your Spanish class' Web page. Do not identify yourself by name as your classmates will have to identify you from the descriptive clues you provide. You may wish to include the following: nationality, place of birth, parents/grandparents' background, what you do, where you study, what you study, favorite subjects, what you want to be, your Saturday activities, where you go, etc.

CHAPTER

18

Pronouns

◆ 1 ◆ Subject Pronouns

Singular	Plural
yo *I*	**nosotros, -as** *we*
tú *you (familiar)*	**vosotros, -as** *you (familiar)*
usted (Ud.) *you*	**ustedes (Uds.)** *they (masculine)*
él *he*	**ellos** *they (masculine)*
ella *she*	**ellas** *they (feminine)*

Subject pronouns are not used in Spanish as often as in English. Normally the verb ending indicates the subject. Spanish subject pronouns are used for clarity, emphasis, and politeness.

Él dibuja mientras **ella** escribe cartas.	*He draws while she writes letters.*
No entres: **yo** debo entrar primero.	*Don't enter: I should enter first.*
Pase. Tome asiento.	*Enter. Have a seat.*

NOTE:

1. Even though subject pronouns are usually omitted, *usted, (Ud.),* and *ustedes (Uds.)* are regularly used.

2. The *vosotros* (familiar plural) form is used in Spain but rarely in Spanish America, where the *ustedes* form is preferred.

3. The English pronoun *it* is not expressed as a subject in Spanish.

¿Dónde está? Está allí.	*Where is it? It's over there.*
¿Qué es? Es un libro.	*What is it? It's a book.*

EXERCISE A

Arturo is asking you the nationalities of some of his new classmates. Write your answers in Spanish, using the correct subject pronouns.

EXAMPLE: Enrique / Guatemala
           Él es de Guatemala.

1. Rosa / Puerto Rico

2. Jacques y Pierre / Francia

3. David / España

4. Kyung Mi y Mi Soo / Corea

5. Arturo / Chile

6. Arturo y Miriam / Colombia

7. Pietro / Italia

EXERCISE B

A new student asks you the following questions. Use the correct subject pronouns in your answers.

1. ¿Cómo te llamas?

2. ¿Dónde vives?

3. ¿Quién es ese chico?

4. ¿Adónde van tú y tus amigos por la tarde?

5. ¿Qué hacen Uds. allí?

6. ¿Quiénes son esos señores?

7. ¿Podemos tú y yo estudiar juntos?

8. ¿Dónde juegan al tenis tus amigos?

9. ¿Quieres ver una película esta noche?

10. ¿Qué clases vas a tomar el año próximo?

◆ 2 ◆ Prepositional Pronouns

Prepositions, which will be more fully explained in the next chapter, are words that define a relationship to a person, place, or thing. When a personal pronoun follows a preposition, it takes the following forms:

Singular	Plural
mí *me*	**nosotros, -as** *us*
ti *you (familiar)*	**vosotros, -as** *you (familiar)*
usted (Ud.) *you*	**ustedes (Uds.)** *you*
él *him, it*	**ellos** *them (masculine)*
ella *her, it*	**ellas** *them (feminine)*

a. Prepositional pronouns are used as the objects of a preposition and always follow the preposition.

No es para **mí**; es para **ella**.   *It's not for me; it's for her.*

b. The pronouns *mí* and *ti* combine with the preposition *con* as follows:

conmigo *with me*   contigo *with you*

NOTE:

1. Prepositional pronouns are identical to subject pronouns, except for *mí* and *ti*.

2. The forms *conmigo* and *contigo* do not change in gender and number.

3. The familiar plural form *vosotros, -as* is used in Spain but rarely in Spanish America, where the form *ustedes (Uds.)* is preferred.

c. Common prepositions

a *to, at*	**entre** *between, among*
cerca de *near*	**hacia** *toward*
con *with*	**para** *for*
contra *against*	**por** *for*
de *of, from*	**sin** *without*
en *in, on*	**sobre** *on top of, over*

EXERCISE C

While visiting Mexico, you and a friend are in a department store. Your friend wants to know for whom you're buying gifts. Answer her questions, using prepositional pronouns in your responses.

EXAMPLE: ¿Es el cinturón para tu papá?
    Sí, el cinturón **es** para **él**.

1. ¿Es la bolsa para tu mamá?

2. ¿Son los guantes para tus tías?

3. Los zapatos son para ti, ¿verdad?

4. ¿Son las botas para tu hermano?

5. ¿Es la estatua para Jaime?

6. ¿Son los libros para César y Arturo?

7. Los aretes son para mí, ¿verdad?

8. ¿Son los discos compactos para nosotros?

EXERCISE D

Before Alfredo goes to the movies, he wants to know what his younger brother is going to do. Answer Alfredo's questions, using the appropriate prepositional pronoun and the cue provided.

EXAMPLE: ¿Vas al parque con Luis? *(no)*
    No, no voy al parque con **él**.

1. ¿Vas al centro con mamá? *(no)*

2. ¿Vas a la piscina con Beto y Anita? *(no)*

3. ¿Vas al estadio con Víctor? *(no)*

4. ¿Vas al museo con Gloria y Antonia? *(no)*

5. ¿Vas al supermercado con papá? *(no)*

6. ¿Vas a la biblioteca con tus amigos? *(no)*

7. ¿Vas al cine conmigo? *(sí)*

EXERCISE E

Your little cousin is asking you a lot of questions while you're baby-sitting her in the park. Answer her questions, using the correct pronoun.

EXAMPLE: ¿Viven muchos animales en el parque?
    Sí, muchos animales viven en **él**.

OR: **No**, muchos animales **no** viven en **él**.

1. ¿Reman muchas personas en el lago?

2. ¿Juegan muchos niños cerca de la piscina?

3. ¿Andan tus amigos por el parque?

4. ¿Estamos lejos del carrusel ahora?

5. ¿Te gusta sentarte en los bancos?

6. ¿Te subes a las atracciones conmigo?

7. ¿Venden globos en la entrada?

8. ¿Crecen flores debajo de las piedras?

9. ¿Mueren las plantas sin agua?

10. ¿Vuelan los pájaros sobre las nubes?

11. ¿Viven muchas personas en el edificio?

♦ 3 ♦ Direct Object Pronouns

a. Direct object pronouns tell who or what receives the action of the verb. Direct object pronouns replace direct objects and agree with them in gender and number.

Singular		Plural	
me	*me*	**nos**	*us*
te	*you (fam.)*	**os**	*you (fam.)*
le	*him, you*	**los**	*them, you (m.)*
lo	*him, you (formal, m.); it (m.)*	**las**	*them, you (f.)*
la	*her, you (formal, f.); it (f.)*		

NOTE:

1. Either *le* or *lo* may be used to express *him*.

2. The plural form of both *le* and *lo* is *los*.

b. The direct object pronoun is usually placed directly before the verb.

¿Quién pronuncia **las palabras**?   *Who pronounces the words?*

El profesor **las** pronuncia.   *The teacher pronounces them.*

¿Tiene **el libro** Albert?   *Does Albert have the book?*

Albert no **lo** tiene.   *Albert doesn't have it.*

c. The direct object pronoun precedes the main verb or is attached to an infinitive.

Nos van a visitar.
Van a visitar**nos**. ⎱ *They're going to visit us.*

Ella no **la** desea ver.
Ella no desea ver**la**. ⎱ *She doesn't want to see it/her/you (formal).*

d. Direct object pronouns follow the affirmative command, but they come immediately before the verb in the negative command.

Bórre**la**.   *Erase it.*

BUT

No **la** borre.   *Don't erase it.*

NOTE:

When the direct object pronoun follows the affirmative command, an accent mark is normally required on the stressed vowel of the verb in order to keep the original stress. If the affirmative command has only one syllable *(pon)*, no accent mark is required *(ponlo)*.

(EXERCISE F)

Julio describes to his mother what happens in his Spanish class. His little brother repeats everything he says, with a slight variation. Tell what his brother says.

EXAMPLE: La maestra enseña la lección.
        La maestra **la** enseña.

1. La clase saluda a la profesora.

2. Ella tiene un periódico español.

3. La maestra muestra los anuncios a la clase.

4. Teresa lee un anuncio en voz alta.

5. Roberto mira las fotos.

6. La profesora ayuda a Ahmed.

7. Beatriz y Lorenzo no comprenden un párrafo.

8. Fernando explica unas palabras.

EXERCISE G

Answer your friend's questions in Spanish, using the correct direct object pronoun.

EXAMPLE: ¿Lees el periódico todos los días?
Sí, **lo leo** todos los días.

OR: **No, no lo leo** todos los días.

1. ¿Vas a ayudar a Peter?

2. ¿Quieres esta hamburguesa?

3. ¿Compró las flores Sarita?

4. ¿Van a vender la casa tus abuelos?

5. ¿Lavas tu ropa los sábados?

6. ¿Escribes tus cartas en español?

EXERCISE H

The Spanish Club is planning a party. Tell what one of the co-presidents tells the members to do.

EXAMPLE: Jorge / poner las banderas allí.
Jorge, **ponlas** allí.

1. Sarita / preparar la limonada

2. Rafael y Emma / comprar los refrescos

3. Gabriel / quitar las sillas

4. Simón e Hilda / traer los vasos

5. Estela / invitar a los profesores

6. Gustavo / mandar las invitaciones

7. Alejandro / revisar la música

EXERCISE I

Using the statements in Exercise H, tell what the other co-president tells the members not to do.

EXAMPLE: Jorge, ponlas allí.
Jorge, **no las pongas** allí.

EXERCISE J

Answer the questions that a new friend asks you. Use a direct object pronoun in your responses.

EXAMPLE: ¿Usas un diccionario en tu clase?
Sí, **lo uso** en mi clase.

OR: No, **no lo uso** en mi clase.

1. ¿Tienes el dinero?

2. ¿Contestas las preguntas correctamente?

3. ¿Me comprendes cuando hablo rápidamente?

4. ¿Esperas recibir regalos para la Navidad?

5. ¿Recibes buenas notas en todas tus clases?

6. ¿Piensas celebrar tu cumpleaños este mes?

7. ¿Lees el periódico todos los días?

8. ¿Perdiste tu cartera recientemente?

9. ¿Llevas un abrigo en el invierno?

10. ¿Aprendes a bailar el tango?

11. ¿Vas a comer la hamburguesa?

12. ¿Preparas las tareas por la noche?

13. ¿Estudias la química este año?

14. ¿Ayudan los profesores a los alumnos?

15. ¿Escuchas a la profesora?

♦ 4 ♦ Indirect Object Pronouns

a. Indirect objects tell to whom or for whom the action of the verb is performed. Indirect object pronouns replace indirect objects and agree with them in gender and number.

Singular		Plural	
me	*to me*	**nos**	*to us*
te	*to you (fam.)*	**os**	*to you (fam.)*
le	*to you (formal)*	**les**	*to you (formal)*
	to him, to her		*to them (m. and f.)*

NOTE:

1. The forms *le* and *les* are used as both masculine and feminine indirect object pronouns.

2. If the meaning is not clear or if we wish to add emphasis, a phrase with *a + a prepositional* pronoun may be used in addition to the indirect object pronouns.

(Clarity) Yo les hablo **a ellos**.   *I speak to them.*

(Emphasis) **A mí** me gusta comer.   *I like to eat.*

Sentences with both indirect object and indirect object pronoun are very common in Spanish.

3. The forms *me, te, nos,* and *os* are also used for direct object pronouns and for reflexive pronouns.

4. The indirect object pronoun may be identified in English by the preposition *to + a person.* The *to* may be expressed or implied.

Les da el dinero.   *He gives the money to them.*

                              (He gives them the money.)

b. The indirect object pronoun is usually placed before the verb.

Ana **le** habla.   *Ana speaks to him/her/you (formal).*

Ella **me** escribe una carta.   *She writes a letter to me.*

                              (She writes me a letter.)

c. When a verb is followed by an infinitive, indirect object pronouns precede the verb or are attached to the infinitive.

¿**Me** quieres decir la verdad? ⎫
                              ⎬ *Do you want to tell me the truth?*
¿Quieres decir**me** la verdad? ⎭

d. The indirect object pronoun is attached to the end of an affirmative command, but is placed before a negative command.

Escríbe**me** una carta.   *Write a letter to me. (Write me a letter.)*

BUT

No **me** escribas una carta.   *Don't write a letter to me. (Don't write me a letter.)*

NOTE:

When the indirect object pronoun follows and is attached to the affirmative command, an accent mark is normally required on the stressed vowel of the verb in order to keep the original stress.

(EXERCISE K)

Rogelio is telling a friend what gifts he is giving to various people. Tell what he says.

EXAMPLE: a mi abuela / flores
          Le doy flores a mi abuela.

1. a mis tíos / dulces

2. a Luisa / un pañuelo

3. a Pablo / un disco compacto

4. a mis primas / una muñeca

5. a Martín / un juego electrónico

6. a ti / un cartel

EXERCISE L

Tomás's father is very proud of the trophy his son won and wants to show it to everyone, but Tomás already did that. Tell what Tomás tells his father.

EXAMPLE: Quiero mostrarle el trofeo a tu abuelo.
                   Ya le mostré el trofeo a **mi** abuelo.

1. Quiero mostrarles el trofeo a tus hermanos.

2. Quiero mostrarle el trofeo a tu tío.

3. Quiero mostrarles el trofeo a tus padrinos.

4. Quiero mostrarle el trofeo al profesor.

5. Quiero mostrarle el trofeo a tu mamá.

6. Quiero mostrarles el trofeo a todos mis amigos.

EXERCISE M

Phil is telling a friend what to do for various people before leaving for camp.

EXAMPLE: a Alejandro / devolver la raqueta de tenis
                   Debes devolverle la raqueta de tenis a Alejandro.

1. a mí / comprar otro disco compacto

2. a Billy / prestar los patines

3. a Sarita y a Pilar / pedir una disculpa

4. a la profesora / escribir una carta

5. a Miguel y a mí / invitar a comer

6. a tu hermana / pagar los diez dólares

7. a Vicente y a Dan / hablar

8. a tus padres / pedir dinero

EXERCISE N

Using an indirect object pronoun, express your boss's instructions to you on your first day of work as a waiter.

EXAMPLE: dar el menú a los clientes
¡**Dales** el menú!

1. llevar agua a la señora

2. dar otra cuchara al niño

3. pedir la orden a los jóvenes

4. quitar el menú a los niños

5. llevar la hamburguesa al señor

6. servir el postre a las señoras

7. ofrecer más café a esa señorita

8. dar la cuenta a los hombres

9. traer el dinero a mí

EXERCISE O

Sarita and her sister are preparing to leave for a study-abroad program. Write what their father tells them.

EXAMPLES: a mí / llamar cada domingo
Llámenme cada domingo.

a sus amigas / no hablar por teléfono
No les hablen a sus amigas por teléfono.

1. a mí / escribir todos los días

2. a nosotros / no comprar regalos

3. a Gloria / no buscar revistas de telenovelas

4. a su profesora / mandar una tarjeta

5. a Arturo y a Felipe / no traer recuerdos

6. a mí / no llamar todos los días

7. a tus hermanos / no prometer nada

8. a su abuela / comprar un regalo

EXERCISE P

Answer the questions that an exchange student asks you. Use the appropriate indirect object pronoun in each of your answers.

1. ¿Pides dinero a tu abuelo?

2. ¿Quién te presta dinero?

3. ¿Quién enseña a los alumnos?

4. ¿Haces tú muchas preguntas al profesor?

5. ¿Escribes a tus primos que viven lejos?

6. ¿Haces favores a tus compañeros?

7. ¿Prometen Uds. a sus padres estudiar diligentemente?

8. ¿Contestas tú al maestro correctamente?

9. ¿Pides muchos regalos a tu tío?

10. ¿Ofreces tu ayuda a tu papá cuando él conduce el carro?

11. ¿Das regalos a tu mamá con frecuencia?

12. ¿Te hablan tus amigos por la mañana?

13. ¿Muestras tus buenas notas a tus amigos?

14. ¿El maestro les da a Uds. muchos exámenes?

15. ¿Siempre dices la verdad a tus padres?

◆ 5 ◆ The Verb *GUSTAR*

a. *Gustar* (to please) is used to express "to like."

Me gusta la comida.	*I like the food.*
	(Literally: The food pleases me.)
Te **gustan** las manzanas.	*You like the apples.*
	(Literally: The apples please you.)
Nos gusta jugar a las damas.	*We like to play checkers.*
	(Literally: To play checkers pleases us.)

b. *Gustar* is preceded by an indirect object pronoun. The form of *gustar* agrees with the subject, which generally follows it.

Te **gusta el libro**.	*You like the book.*
Te **gustan los libros**.	*You like the books.*
Nos **gusta la revista**.	*We like the magazine.*
Nos **gustan las revistas**.	*We like the magazines.*
Les **gusta** leer.	*They like to read.*

NOTE:

If the thing liked is not a noun but an action (expressed by a verb in the infinitive), *gustar* is used in the third person singular.

Me gusta leer y escribir.	*I like to read and write.*

c. To clarify the indirect object pronouns *le* and *les*, or to give emphasis, the indirect object normally precedes the indirect object pronoun.

A Josefa no le gusta cantar.	*Josefa doesn't like to sing.*
A los niños les gusta correr.	*The children like to run.*
A José le gusta el helado.	*Joseph likes the ice cream.*
A mí no me gusta saltar.	*I don't like to jump.*

♦ 6 ♦ Other Verbs Like *GUSTAR*

encantar
fascinar } *to delight* (Used for things that someone likes a lot or loves.)

Me encantan las películas.	*I love movies.*
parecer	*to seem*
La comida **me parece** buena.	*The food seems good to me.*
doler	*to be painful, to cause sorrow*
faltar	*to be lacking, to need*
tocar (a uno)	*to be one's turn*

NOTE:

Since *parecer* is usually followed by an adjective, the adjective must agree in number and gender with the item described.

La blusa me parece **bonita.**	*The blouse seems pretty to me.*
Las noches me parecen **largas.**	*The nights seem long to me.*

EXERCISE Q

Tell whether you like or dislike each of the following activities.

EXAMPLE: **Me gusta bailar.**

OR: **No me gusta bailar.**

1.

2.

3.

4.

5.

6.

7.

8.

9.

10.

EXERCISE R

You've taken a young cousin to an amusement park, and it's now time to eat. Based on the illustrations, ask him what he likes and write his responses as indicated.

EXAMPLE: **¿Te gusta el helado?**
Sí, me gusta el helado.

1. _____ ?

No, _____ .

2. _____ ?

No, _____ .

3. _____ ?

Sí, _____ .

4. _____ ?

Sí, _____ .

5. _____ ?

Sí, _____ .

6. _____ ?

Sí, _____ .

EXERCISE S

You and your friends are talking about your likes and dislikes. Tell what is said.

EXAMPLE: a Gloria / gustar / ir al cine
         A Gloria **le gusta** ir al cine.

1. a ti / no gustar / los dibujos animados

2. a ustedes / gustar / las comedias

3. a mí / no gustar / los documentales

4. a Estela / gustar / comer en un restaurante

5. a Felipe y a mí / encantar / los tacos de pollo

6. a ellas / encantar / las telenovelas

7. a Gonzalo / no gustar / las noticias

8. a ellos / encantar / mirar los partidos de fútbol

9. a nosotros / no gustar / las novelas largas

10. a ella / encantar / cocinar

EXERCISE T

After your school's varsity soccer practice, you and your friends are describing what hurts. Tell what you and they say.

EXAMPLE: a Ramón / las piernas
         A Ramón **le duelen** las piernas.

1. a mí / los ojos

2. a Vinnie / la espalda

3. a Juan y a mí / la cabeza

4. a Gunther / los oídos

5. a Clara y a Antonia / las manos

6. a Esteban / la garganta

EXERCISE U

As the Pérez family sits down to dinner with their guests, Mrs. Pérez notices that certain things are missing from the table. Tell what she says.

EXAMPLE: a tu papá / un cuchillo
A tu papá **le falta** un cuchillo.

1. a tus abuelos / la ensalada

2. a mí / una cucharita

3. a Eduardo y a Lourdes / un vaso

4. a ti / un plato

5. a nosotros / la sal y la pimienta

6. a Carlos / un tenedor y una cuchara

7. a Uds. / la servilleta

EXERCISE V

Marisol is telling her mother what she and various classmates think of their math class. Tell what she says.

EXAMPLE: a mí / Beto / muy inteligente
A mí, Beto **me parece** muy inteligente.

1. al profesor / la clase / perezoso

2. a Griselda y a Gladys / el maestro / estricto

3. a Tomás / las tareas / difícil

4. a Luz y a mí / los exámenes / justo

5. a Angel / los alumnos / simpático

6. a mí / la clase / aburrido

◁§ MASTERY EXERCISES §▷

EXERCISE W

Complete the e-mail message that Roberto writes to a new key pal with the appropriate pronoun or expression.

Querido amigo:

_____ me llamo Roberto Casares. Mi familia y _____ vivimos en Chicago, una
     1.   *2.*

ciudad grande de los Estados Unidos. _____ practicar los deportes, especialmente el béisbol.
                                                   3.

Yo _____ practico casi todos los días. Soy miembro de un equipo que se llama «Los cuervos».
    4.

Tengo muchos amigos en el equipo a quienes _____ ganar partidos. Mi familia no es grande.
                                          5.

Vivimos en una casa pequeña. Mi hermano Alfredo comparte el cuarto _____.
                                                       6.

_____ es un chico bueno, pero nunca puedo estar solo en el cuarto _____. Hay un
    7.   *8.*

televisor en nuestro cuarto, pero _____ los dibujos animados. _____ muy cómicos y
                                  9.   *10.*

_____ mira todos los sábados por la mañana cuando a mí _____ dormir. Muchas
    11.   *12.*

veces yo dejo de hablar _____ porque él no _____ respeta. Es difícil salir con mis
                                 13.   *14.*

amigos sin _____. Siempre quiere acompañar _____ cuando salgo con
                 15.   *16.*

_____. Tengo una amiga especial. _____ se llama Connie. Yo _____
    17.   *18.*   *19.*

admiro mucho. Pasamos mucho tiempo juntos: _____ caminar en el parque y sacar fotografías.
                                                      20.

Ella _____ guarda en un álbum. Ella hizo copias para _____ de todas las fotos que
         21.   *22.*

sacamos. Ella _____ pone en otro álbum y _____ dio el álbum como regalo.
               23.   *24.*

¡_____ pronto! La foto del equipo es para _____ . ¡No _____ enseñes a
   25.   *26.*   *27.*

tus amigos!

                                                    Hasta pronto.

                                                    Roberto

EXERCISE X

You found an old board game. In your journal, write a summary of your discovery. Use as many pronouns as possible. You may wish to include the following: what you found, where you found it, to whom you showed it, what you did with it, the rules of the game, who loves to win/not lose, their impression of the game.

Prepositions

Prepositions are words that relate a noun or pronoun to some other word in the sentence.

Yo voy **a** la tienda.	*I'm going to the store.*
Ella estudia **con** George.	*She studies with George.*
Trabajo **en** la biblioteca.	*I work in the library.*

♦ 1 ♦ Uses of the Preposition *A*

a. The preposition *a* is used to indicate destination or direction.

Vamos **a** la fiesta.	*We're going to the party.*
Llegamos temprano **a** la escuela.	*We arrived at school early.*
El café está **a** la derecha.	*The café is to the right.*

NOTE:

1. The preposition *a* (to) combines with *el* (the) to form the contraction *al* (to the).

María va **al** mercado.	*María goes to the market.*
El profesor habla **al** alumno.	*The teacher speaks to the student.*

2. The preposition *a* never combines with the other articles *(la, los, las)* to form a single word.

Rosa va **a la** tienda.	*Rosa goes to the store.*
El profesor habla **a los** alumnos.	*The teacher speaks to the students.*

3. In some expressions, *a* plus the definite article is used where there's no equivalent in English.

Juegan **al** béisbol.	*They play baseball.*

EXERCISE A

Tell where you're going, based on the drawings below.

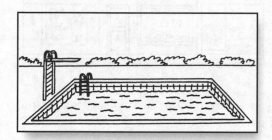

EXAMPLE: **Voy a la piscina.**

1.

2.

3.

4.

5.

6.

7.

8.

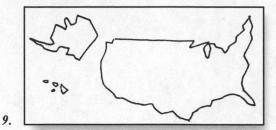

9.

10.

b. The preposition *a* is required before the direct object of a verb if the direct object is a person, a personalized group, a pet, or something personified.

Ana visita **a** Peter.	*Ana visits Peter.*
El niño ve **al** hombre.	*The boy sees the man.*
Pablo invita **a** sus amigos.	*Pablo invites his friends.*
Lola saca **al** perro.	*Lola takes the dog out.*

BUT

Ana visita la escuela.	*Ana visits the school.*
El niño ve la pelota.	*The boy sees the ball.*

c. The preposition *a* is required before the pronouns *¿quién?, ¿quiénes?, nadie,* and *alguien,* when they refer to a person.

No conoce **a** nadie.	*He doesn't know anyone.*
Vio **a** alguien en la calle.	*He saw someone in the street.*
¿**A** quién defendemos?	*Whom do we defend?*

NOTE:

1. When used before a direct object, the preposition *a* (personal *a*) has no equivalent in English. When used before an indirect object, it is translated as "to."

Veo **a** mi prima.	*I see my cousin.*
Hablo **a** mi prima.	*I speak to my cousin.*

2. The personal *a* is not used after the verb tener (to have).

Tiene una hermana bonita.	*He has a pretty sister.*
Tengo muchos amigos.	*I have many friends.*

EXERCISE B

You and a friend are attending a civic function. Tell your friend who's talking to whom.

EXAMPLE: el alcalde / los ciudadanos
El alcalde **habla a** los ciudadanos

1. el médico / la enfermera

2. el profesor / los alumnos

3. el zapatero / el cliente

4. la señorita Vargas / los señores Polaski

5. Veronique / las amigas

6. Luis y Fernando / la chica

7. tú y yo / el alcalde

8. mi madre / la profesora

EXERCISE C

Complete this letter that Cristina writes to her friend while visiting Spain. Insert the personal *a* or the contraction *al* only when needed.

Querida Gloria:

Mientras espero _____ mozo para bajar la maleta, te escribo estas pocas palabras. Durante
              1.

mi viaje vi _____ muchos lugares bonitos e interesantes. También tuve la oportunidad de
           2.

conocer _____ muchos jóvenes españoles. Un día visité _____ mi familia en
        3.   4.

Sevilla. Mi prima invitó _____ otros parientes y _____ unos amigos a una cena
                         5.   6.

en su casa. Me divertí mucho. Ahora salgo para Barcelona donde quiero ver _____ Enrique.
                                                                           7.

Él estudió en mi escuela el año pasado. Tiene _____ muchos amigos. Pienso llamar
                                               8.

_____ mis padres esta noche. Oigo _____ alguien en la puerta.
9.   10.

Adiós por ahora.

Cristina

EXERCISE D

Tell your plans for this evening. Use *a* or *al* when needed.

EXAMPLE: ver la televisión
        Pienso ver la televisión.

1. escuchar / el grupo «Coquí»

2. hablar / el vecino

3. jugar / las damas

4. llamar / Elsa

5. esperar / mis padres

6. oír / música

7. acompañar / mi madre

EXERCISE E

Use complete sentences and the cues in parentheses to answer the questions that your new friend asks you.

1. ¿A quiénes saludas por la mañana? *(los vecinos)*

2. ¿A quién ayudas tú? *(mis amigos)*

3. ¿Respetan los jóvenes a sus padres? *(sí)*

4. ¿A quién admiras más? *(el presidente)*

5. ¿Tienes muchos primos y amigos? *(sí)*

6. ¿A quién esperas tú al salir de la escuela? *(nadie)*

7. ¿Cuándo visitas al dentista? *(cada año)*

8. ¿Escuchas a los maestros en tu escuela? *(sí)*

9. ¿A quién buscas cuando tienes un problema? *(mi hermana)*

10. ¿Amas tú a toda tu familia? *(sí)*

> **d.** The preposition *a* is used in time expressions to indicate "at."
>
> ¿**A** qué hora es la fiesta?   *At what time is the party?*
>
> Es **a** las ocho.   *It's at 8 o'clock.*
>
> Llego **a** la una.   *I arrive at one o'clock.*

EXERCISE F

While vacationing in Puerto Rico, Javier wants to know at what time different activities will take place. Using the cues provided, answer his questions.

EXAMPLE: ¿A qué hora es la excursión en barco? *(2:00)*
　　　　　Es **a las dos**.

1. ¿A qué hora es el desayuno? *(7:30)*

2. ¿A qué hora es la clase de natación? *(9:00)*

3. ¿A qué hora vamos a comer el almuerzo? *(1:00)*

4. ¿A qué hora vamos al Viejo San Juan? *(4:00)*

5. ¿A qué hora quieres cenar? *(8:00)*

6. ¿A qué hora comienza el baile? *(10:30)*

◆ 2 ◆ Uses of the preposition *DE*

a. The preposition *de* corresponds to *of*, *from*, or *about* in English.

¿**De** qué hablas?	*What are you speaking about?*
Hablo **de** la fiesta.	*I'm speaking about the party.*
Recibo cartas **de** Juan.	*I receive letters from Juan.*
Sacan fotos **de** los niños.	*They take photos of the children.*

NOTE:

1. The preposition *de* (of, from) combines with *el* (the) to form *del* (of the, from the, about).

El Sr. Pérez es el presidente **del** país.	*Mr. Pérez is the president of the country.*
Ana recibe dinero **del** jefe.	*Ana receives money from the boss.*

2. The preposition *de* never combines with the other articles (*la, los, las*) to form a single word.

¿Recibe Ud. cartas **de las** muchachas?	*Do you receive letters from the girls?*

EXERCISE G

A group of friends went to see a movie. Say what they're talking about afterwards.

EXAMPLE: Alejandro / la película
　　　　　Alejandro **habla de** la película.

1. Elena / los actores

2. Esteban y Flor / el cuento

3. Ernie / el reparto

4. Beto y Antonio / los carros antiguos

5. Aisha y Marcel / la ropa

6. Alicia / el fin

7. Hiroshi y Pedro / las escenas cómicas

8. yo / la actriz principal

EXERCISE H

You and a friend are visiting his grandmother. Say what she tells you to do.

EXAMPLE: cerrar las ventanas / el comedor
       ¡**Cierren** las ventanas **del** comedor!

1. traer flores / el jardín

2. sacar las fotos / los nietos

3. oír el ruido / la calle

4. abrir la puerta / la sala

5. salir / la casa

b. In Spanish, possession is expressed as follows: *noun* (thing possessed) followed by *de* plus noun (possessor). This is equivalent to the English possessive expressed with *of*. In Spanish, there is no apostrophe to show possession.

el libro **de** Alberto $\begin{cases} \textit{the book of Alberto} \\ \\ \textit{Alberto's book} \end{cases}$

la cámara **de** la muchacha $\begin{cases} \textit{the camera of the girl} \\ \\ \textit{the girl's camera} \end{cases}$

los lápices **de** los alumnos $\begin{cases} \textit{the pencils of the students} \\ \\ \textit{the student's pencils} \end{cases}$

c. *¿De quién?, ¿De quiénes?* (Whose?) are used to ask *to whom* something belongs.

¿**De quién** son las plumas?   *Whose (sing.) pens are they?*

¿**De quiénes** son las fotos?   *To whom (pl.) do the photos belong?*

EXERCISE I

Tell whom the following items belong to.

EXAMPLE: los anteojos / el maestro
　　　　　Son los anteojos **del** maestro.

1. la mochila / la alumna

2. el diccionario / Isaac

3. los tenis / los chicos

4. el reloj / el director

5. la cámara / mi hermano

6. la bandera / la escuela

7. las tarjetas / Beatriz y Charlotte

8. la calculadora / el señor Rivas

9. las fotos / Javier

10. las estampillas / la secretaria

EXERCISE J

A friend is helping you clean up the living room. Tell her who owns the various things she finds.

EXAMPLE: ¿De quién son las historietas? *(mi hermano menor)*
　　　　　Son de mi hermano menor.

1. ¿De quién son las llaves? *(mi mamá)*

2. ¿De quién es el pasaporte? *(el novio de mi hermana)*

3. ¿De quién son las revistas? *(la amiga de mi mamá)*

4. ¿De quién es el suéter? *(el primo de Juan)*

5. ¿De quién es la novela? *(el profesor de inglés)*

6. ¿De quién es el bolígrafo? *(mi papá)*

> **d.** A *de* phrase may also function as an adjective.
>
> la clase **de** biología　　　*the biology class*
>
> un reloj **de** oro　　　*a gold watch*

EXERCISE K

Juanita is playing a game with her little cousin. He has to identify an object or person based on the clues Juanita gives him. Help him get the correct answers.

EXAMPLES: Juan Pardo / el padre
el padre **de** Juan
un examen / matemática
un examen **de** matemática

1. un reloj bueno y caro / oro

2. un libro de palabras en inglés y español / diccionario

3. una bandera roja, blanca y azul / los Estados Unidos

4. julio y agosto / meses

5. martes y jueves / días

6. la primavera y el otoño / estaciones

7. a, be, ce, de / letras

8. Beto Suárez Olmeda / Tomás Ramos Olmeda (primo)

> **e.** The phrase *de* + *la mañana (la tarde, la noche)* is used following a specific hour to indicate A.M. or P.M.
>
> Son las diez **de la mañana**.   *It's 10:00 A.M.*
>
> Te veo a las dos **de la tarde**.   *I'll see you at 2:00 P.M.*

EXERCISE L

Tell at what time you usually do the following activities. Be sure to include the Spanish equivalent of A.M. or P.M. in your response.

EXAMPLE: desayunarte
Me desayuno a las siete de la mañana.

1. despertarte

2. almorzar

3. entrar en la escuela

4. salir del colegio

5. cenar con tu familia

6. lavar los platos

7. jugar con tus amigos

8. acostarte

9. apagar la luz

f. *De* is also used together with other prepositions to indicate location.

El jardín está **detrás de** la casa.   *The garden is behind the house.*

Las flores están **dentro del** florero.   *The flowers are in the vase.*

EXERCISE M

Use the expressions below to tell where the buildings in the pictures are located.

a la derecha de	dentro de	enfrente de
al lado de	detrás de	a la izquierda de
cerca de		

EXAMPLE: El teatro está **al lado de la iglesia**.

1. El museo está _____.

2. La escuela está _____.

3. El supermercado está _____.

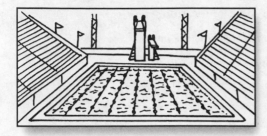

4. La piscina está _____.

5. El hotel está _____.

6. La estatua está _____.

◆ 3 ◆ Prepositions with Infinitives

a. In Spanish, the infinitive is the only verb form that may follow a preposition. The following prepositions and prepositional phrases are commonly used before an infinitive:

a *to, at*	después de *after*
al *upon, on*	en vez de *instead of*
antes de *before*	sin *without*
de *of, to*	

Al salir de la casa, él cerró la puerta.	*Upon leaving the house, he closed the door.*
Ella corrió **en vez de caminar**.	*She ran instead of walking.*
Pensó **antes de contestar**.	*She thought before answering.*

EXERCISE N

Combine a suggestion from each of the columns below and tell what you and your friends do in various situations.

al	cenar	mi amiga	contar el secreto
antes de	estudiar	mi amigo	decir gracias
después de	ir al cine	mis amigos	hablar por teléfono
en vez de	pedir permiso	mis amigos y yo	mirar la televisión
sin	pensar	yo	salir de la casa
	recibir un regalo		tomar un refresco

EXAMPLE: **Sin pensar, mi amigo contó el secreto.**

b. The preposition *a* is required before any infinitive that follows a verb of (1) beginning, (2) movement, (3) teaching/learning, or (4) helping.

(1) Beginning

comenzar a + *infinitive*
empezar a + *infinitive* } *to begin to + verb*

Comienzan a cantar.   *They begin to sing.*

Empezamos a correr.   *We began to run.*

(2) Movement

ir a + *infinitive*   *to go to + verb*
Va a tocar el piano.   *She's going to play the piano.*

correr a + *infinitive*   *to run to + verb*
Corren a cerrar las ventanas.   *They run to close the windows.*

venir a + *infinitive*   *to come to + verb*
Vengo a verte.   *I'm coming to see you.*

(3) Teaching/Learning

enseñar a + *infinitive*   *to teach to + verb*
El maestro nos **enseña a leer.**   *The teacher teaches us to read.*

aprender a + *infinitive*   *to learn to + verb*
Aprendemos a hablar español.   *We're learning to speak Spanish.*

(4) Helping

ayudar a + *infinitive*   *to help (to) + verb*
Ella me **ayuda a bailar.**   *She helps me dance.*

EXERCISE O

Gladys describes an afternoon with some friends. Put what she says in complete sentences. Be sure to include the preposition.

EXAMPLE: dos jóvenes españoles / venir / almorzar conmigo
Dos jóvenes españoles **vienen a almorzar** conmigo.

1. yo / ir / esperarlos en el restaurante

2. yo / correr / llegar temprano al restaurante

3. el mesero / correr / poner la mesa

4. nosotros / empezar / comer en seguida

5. mis amigos / aprender / hablar inglés

6. yo / ir / hacer un viaje a España

7. ellos / ayudarme / pronunciar las palabras

8. yo / enseñarles / cantar en inglés

EXERCISE P

Using a verb from column A and an expression from column B, tell what these people are doing.

_A_	_B_
aprender	contar el dinero
ayudar	decirme las noticias
comenzar	lavar el carro
correr	limpiar la casa
empezar	patinar en hielo
enseñar	pronunciar bien
ir	trabajar por la tarde
venir	ver el accidente

EXAMPLE: **Tú comienzas a trabajar por la tarde**.

1. Yo _____ .

2. Mi hermano _____ .

3. Mis padres _____ .

4. Mi hermana _____ .

5. Mis amigos _____ .

6. Mi madre _____ .

7. Mi profesor _____ .

c. The preposition *de* is required before any infinitive that comes after one of the following four verbs:

acabar de + *infinitive*	*to have just*
Acaban de cenar.	*They've just eaten dinner.*
cesar de + *infinitive*	*to stop*
Cesó de llover.	*It stopped raining.*
dejar de + *infinitive*	*to quit, stop*
Juan **dejó de darme** el dinero.	*Juan stopped giving me the money.*
tratar de + *infinitive*	*to try to*
Trataron de llamarme.	*They tried to call me.*

EXERCISE Q

Tell what these people have just done.

EXAMPLE: yo / ver un partido de fútbol
      Yo **acabo de ver** un partido de fútbol.

1. Gerardo / jugar al tenis

2. mi mamá / ir de compras

3. mis hermanas / salir con sus amigas

4. Tommy y Enrique / lavar el carro

5. Alicia y yo / hablar por teléfono

EXERCISE R

You're working as a counselor in a day camp. Using the cues, tell the children to stop doing the following.

EXAMPLE: correr *(Uds.)*
      ¡Dejen de correr!

1. gritar *(tú)*

2. pelear *(Ana y Kyoko)*

3. hablar *(tú—Carlos)*

4. tirar la pelota *(Bárbara y Juan)*

5. silbar *(tú—Isabel)*

EXERCISE S

Help Ricardo write a note to a friend in Venezuela.

EXAMPLE: las clases / acabar / terminar
Las clases **acaban de** terminar.

1. yo / acabar / recibir mi licencia de conducir

2. Jorge / dejar / tomar clases de conducir

3. él / tratar / pasar el examen varias veces

4. Jorge y yo / cesar / ser amigos

5. Jorge / no tratar / llamarme

> **d.** The following verbs are used without a preposition before an infinitive:
>
> | | | | |
> |---|---|---|---|
> | deber | *ought to, must* | pensar | *to intend* |
> | dejar | *to let, allow* | poder | *to be able, can* |
> | desear | *to wish, desire* | preferir | *to prefer* |
> | esperar | *to hope, expect to* | prometer | *to promise* |
> | necesitar | *to need* | querer | *to want, wish to* |
> | oír | *to hear* | saber | *to know how to* |
>
> **Debo ir** a la escuela hoy.   *I ought to go to school today.*
> No **pueden salir** ahora.   *They can't go out now.*
> Él **promete ser** bueno.   *He promises to be good.*
> Ella **sabe jugar** al ajedrez.   *She knows how to play chess.*
>
> NOTE:
> Remember that the verb *dejar* changes meaning when it's followed by the preposition *de*.
>
> ¡Déjenme entrar!   *Let me in!*
> Ya **dejó de** llover.   *It already stopped raining.*

EXERCISE T

Answer these questions that a new friend asks you.

1. ¿Qué prefieres, caminar en el parque o ir de compras?

2. ¿Qué debes hacer para mañana?

3. ¿Necesitas pedirles permiso a tus padres antes de salir?

4. ¿Qué esperas hacer este fin de semana?

5. ¿Puedes acompañarme a un concierto el sábado?

6. ¿Deseas comer en un restaurante argentino?

7. ¿Sabes tocar la guitarra?

8. ¿Prometes llamarme por teléfono mañana?

9. ¿Piensas ir a la fiesta de Marisol?

10. ¿Con quién esperas ir a la fiesta?

EXERCISE U

Your teacher is telling your class what should happen when she's absent. Write what she says, using the suggestions provided in the three columns below.

EXAMPLE: **Yo debo dejar una lección interesante.**

la clase	deber	aprender la lección
todos	desear	cooperar con el maestro
Uds.	esperar	dejar una lección interesante
yo	necesitar	estudiar mucho
	pensar	prestar atención
	poder	repasar la lección
	preferir	sentarse en su propio asiento
	prometer	ser amables
	querer	trabajar en grupos
		traer los libros a la clase
		volver al día siguiente

◆ 4 ◆ Common Expressions with Prepositions

al aire libre	*outdoors, in the open air*
A los niños les gusta jugar **al aire libre**.	*The children like to play outdoors.*
a menudo	*often*
Veo a mis primos **a menudo**.	*I see my cousins often.*
a pie	*on foot*
Él va a la escuela **a pie**.	*He goes to school on foot.*
a tiempo	*on time*
El tren llega **a tiempo**.	*The train arrives on time.*
a veces	*sometimes*
A veces me gusta dormir la siesta.	*Sometimes I like to take a nap.*
con cuidado	*carefully*
Escribo la tarea **con cuidado**.	*I write the assignment carefully.*

de memoria	*by heart*
Él sabe la dirección **de memoria**.	*He knows the address by heart.*
De nada.	*You're welcome.*
Muchas gracias. **De nada.**	*Thanks a lot. You're welcome.*
de nuevo	*again*
Escribí la oración **de nuevo**.	*I wrote the sentence again.*
de pie	*standing*
Todos están **de pie**.	*Everyone is standing.*

de pronto ⎫
de repente ⎬ *suddenly*

De repente empezó a llover.	*Sudddenly, it started to rain.*
en punto	*sharp*
Es la una **en punto**.	*It's one o'clock sharp.*
en serio	*seriously*
Él toma todo **en serio**.	*He takes everything seriously.*
en venta	*for sale*
El coche de mi tío está **en venta**.	*My uncle's car is for sale.*
en vez de	*instead of*
Ella descansó **en vez de** trabajar.	*She rested instead of working.*

EXERCISE V

Norma is describing a camping trip in her diary. Write the expressions that are needed to complete the entry in her diary.

El club de la escuela va a acampar _____. _____ van a la playa _____
                                    1. (often)   **2.** (sometimes)   **3.** (instead of)

ir a las montañas. No importa, porque a mí me gusta estar _____. El autobús siempre
                                                            4. (outdoors)

sale de la escuela _____ : a las siete de la mañana _____. En el autobús
                    5. (on time)   **6.** (sharp)

la consejera del club explicó _____ las reglas _____. Ya las sé
                               7. (again)   **8.** (carefully)

_____. Ella toma _____ su responsabilidad. Ella viajó _____
 9. (by heart)   **10.** (seriously)   **11.** (standing)

_____ sentarse. Cuando llegamos a la playa, fuimos al campamento _____ .
   12. (instead of)   **13.** (on foot)

_____ comenzó a hacer mucho frío. Gladys me prestó un suéter. Le di las gracias y ella
   14. (suddenly)

contestó:—_____ .
          15. (you're welcome)

⇔ MASTERY EXERCISES ⇔

EXERCISE W

Read this story. Select the preposition that should be used in each sentence. Note that in some cases a preposition may not be needed.

A una señora le gusta andar _____ pie cuando va _____ mercado
                               1. (a/de)   **2.** (al/a la)

todos los días. _____ menudo lleva _____ su hija _____ ella.
                3. (A/De)   **4.** (a/)   **5.** (a/con)

Prefiere _____ estar _____ aire libre, especialmente cuando cesa _____
         6. (a/)   **7.** (en el/al)   **8.** (a/de)

llover. _____ veces pasa por el parque en vez _____ tomar una ruta más
        9. (De/A)   **10.** (a/de)

directa _____ centro. Un día _____ salir de su casa _____ ocho y
         11. (al/a la)   **12.** (al/a)   **13.** (a los/a las)

media _____ mañana, ella comenzó _____ andar por el parque. Cerca
        14. (del/de la)   **15.** (a/de)

_____ entrada vio _____ la niña _____ vecino.
  16. (del/de la)   **17.** (a/)   **18.** (del/de la)

Corrió _____ ayudarla. Trató _____ hablarle _____ niña pero
        19. (a/)   **20.** (/de)   **21.** (al/a la)

la niña empezó _____ llorar. _____ fin la niña dijo: —Yo no debo
            22. (a/de)   **23.** (Al/A la)

_____ hablarle _____ usted porque no la conozco _____ usted—.
  24. (a/)   **25.** (/a)   **26.** (a/)

La señora prometió _____ ayudar _____ niña _____ encontrar la casa
               27. (a/)   **28.** (al/a la)   **29.** (a/)

_____ tía. Después _____ andar por unos minutos la señora le preguntó:

    30. (del/ de la)   **31.** (de/)

—¿Qué hora es?— La niña contestó: —Yo no sé _____ decir la hora—. La señora prometió

                                                 32. (/a)

_____ enseñarle _____ decir la hora. _____ repente la niña dejó

    33. (de/)   **34.** (/a)   **35.** (De/A)

_____ andar. Vio _____ un perro.

    36. (/de)   **37.** (a/)

EXERCISE X

Simón is a new neighbor who has just moved to your area from Colombia. Answer his questions.

1. ¿Hace calor en los meses del verano?

2. ¿A qué hora salen los niños a jugar?

3. ¿De qué color es tu motocicleta?

4. ¿A qué hora del día tienes la lección de tenis?

5. ¿Escuchas los discos compactos de tus amigos?

6. ¿Cuál es el periódico más popular de la ciudad?

7. ¿Viven tus compañeros de escuela cerca de aquí?

8. ¿Cuáles son los colores de la escuela?

9. ¿A qué hora empiezas a trabajar?

10. ¿Quién es el profesor de historia?

EXERCISE Y

A friend has accepted your invitation to visit you soon. Write your friend an e-mail message in which you describe your plans for the visit. You may wish to include the places you will visit together, their location, a reason for visiting each site, and what you intend to do at each one.

Adjective/Adverb and Related Structures

CHAPTER

20

Adjectives

♦ 1 ♦ Agreement of Adjectives

Adjectives describe nouns and agree in number (singular or plural) and gender (masculine or feminine) with the nouns they modify.

a. Adjectives ending in *-o* change *-o* to *-a* when describing a feminine singular noun.

Carlos es alt**o**.	*Carlos is tall.*
María es alt**a**.	*María is tall.*

b. Adjectives ending in *-e* remain the same when describing a feminine singular noun.

Él es valient**e**.	*He's brave.*
Ella es valient**e**.	*She's brave.*
El muchacho es inteligent**e**.	*The boy is intelligent.*
La muchacha es inteligent**e**.	*The girl is intelligent.*

c. Adjectives of nationality that end in a consonant add an *-a* when describing a feminine singular noun.

Paul es francés.	*Paul is French.*
Claire es frances**a**.	*Claire is French.*

d. The plural of adjectives, like the plural of nouns, is formed by adding *-s* if the adjective ends in a vowel, or *-es* or *-as* if the adjective ends in a consonant.

Singular	Plural
Carlos es alt*o*.	**Carlos y Pedro son alt*os*.**
María es alt*a*.	**María y Anita son alt*as*.**
El muchacho es inteligent*e*.	**Los muchachos son inteligent*es*.**
La muchacha es inteligent*e*.	**Las muchachas son inteligent*es*.**
Paul es francés.	**Paul y Pascal son frances*es*.**
Claire es frances*a*.	**Claire y Paulette son frances*as*.**

NOTE:

1. Adjectives ending in -o have four forms. ric**o**, ric**a**, ric**os**, ric**as**

2. Adjectives ending in -e (or a consonant) have two forms, one for the singular and one for the plural.

Singular	Plural	Meaning
cortés	corteses	*courteous*
débil	débiles	*weak*
fuerte	fuertes	*strong*

3. Adjectives of nationality ending in a consonant have four forms.

   español, español**a**, español**es**, español**as**

4. Adjectives of nationality with an accent mark on the last syllable drop the accent mark in the feminine singular and in both plural forms.

   alem**á**n, alemana, alemanes, alemanas *German*

   franc**é**s, francesa, franceses, francesas *French*

   ingl**é**s, inglesa, ingleses, inglesas *English*

5. Adjectives that modify two or more nouns of different gender use the masculine plural.

   Yassir y Alice son altos.   *Yassir and Alice are tall.*
   Yassir y Alice son españoles.   *Yassir and Alice are Spanish.*

EXERCISE A

Gregorio, an exchange student in your school, is describing his new friends to you. Tell what he says about them.

EXAMPLE: Javier / interesante
          Javier **es interesante**.

1. Jeffrey / fuerte

2. Cathy / bonito

3. Gloria y Claudia / colombiano

4. Inés / cortés

5. Marco / simpático

6. Pauline / francés

7. Enrique y Lourdes / alto

8. Omar / responsable

9. Las hermanas Dini / popular

10. Kyoko y Mei Ling / divertido

EXERCISE B

At a regional meeting of new exchange students in your area, you introduce them and tell their nationalities.

EXAMPLE: Fritz / alemán
          Fritz **es alemán**.

1. Salvador / español

2. Gina / italiano

3. Edson y Milton / brasileño

4. Yoko / japonés

5. Claudine y Marie / francés

6. Sara / inglés

7. José y Pilar / puertorriqueño

8. Brigitte y Eva / alemán

EXERCISE C

How would you describe your friends? Using the adjectives below, write six sentences about your friends or classmates.

alto	cortés	guapo	responsable
bajo	diligente	independiente	serio
cómico	divertido	inteligente	simpático

EXAMPLE: Elena y Migdalia son **guapas** y **responsables**.

EXERCISE D

Describe the differences between you and your siblings or best friend. Use the adjectives below.

alegre	diligente	gordo	perezoso
cómico	divertido	independiente	quieto
delgado	generoso	melancólico	serio

EXAMPLE: Yo soy **cómico** y mi hermana es **seria**.

◆ 2 ◆ Position of Adjectives

a. Descriptive adjectives generally follow the noun they describe.

una chica **guapa**	*a pretty girl*
un niño **bueno**	*a good boy*
un señor **mexicano**	*a Mexican man*

b. Adjectives expressing number or quantity generally come before the noun.

algunos chicos	*some boys*
cada año	*each year*
mucho dinero	*much money*
tres muchachas	*three girls*

EXERCISE E

You're talking to a blind date on the telephone. Answer his or her questions.

1. ¿Eres alto(a) o bajo(a)?

2. ¿De qué color tienes los ojos?

3. ¿Y el pelo?

4. ¿Tienes el pelo largo o corto?

5. ¿Eres divertido(a) o serio(a)?

6. ¿Eres paciente?

7. ¿Tienes muchos amigos?

8. ¿Cuántas clases tomas?

9. ¿Son aburridas las clases?

10. ¿Es grande tu familia?

11. ¿Cuántos hermanos y hermanas tienes?

EXERCISE F

Prepare a list of things you need to redecorate your bedroom.

EXAMPLE: una cama / doble
una cama **doble**

1. un escritorio / grande

2. una silla / cómodo

3. butaca / rojo, dos

4. una alfombra / negro

5. unas cortinas / bonito

6. lámpara / tres, bueno

7. un estante / fuerte

8. una mesa / pequeño, redondo

9. almohada / duro, tres

10. un televisor / nuevo

EXERCISE G

Make a list of things you see in the beautiful garden outside your window.

EXAMPLE: jardín / uno, bonito
un jardín **bonito**

1. rosa / tres, rojo

2. geranio / alguno, rosado, rojo

3. planta / mucho, verde

4. árbol / dos, viejo

5. pájaro / uno, alegre

6. clavel / mucho, blanco

7. insecto / mucho, feo

EXERCISE H

While vacationing in Germany, Lisa wrote to her key pal in Costa Rica. Complete Lisa's
e-mail by choosing the appropriate adjectives from the list of choices for each paragraph.
Notice that adjectives in each group are listed alphabetically.

nos. 1–8

bello
bonito
colombiano
dos
grande
idéntico
moderno
nuevo

nos. 9–16

antiguo
cómico
formidable
interesante
libre
mucho
serio
simpático

nos. 17–22

alemán
divertido
nuevo
otro
sincero
tres

Querida Lucía:

Hay _____ alumnos _____ en mi clase de matemáticas. Ellos tienen quince años
　　　　1.　　　　　　　　　　2.

y son hermanos, pero no son gemelos _____. Se llaman Lola y Luis. Vienen de Bogotá,
　　　　　　　　　　　　　　　　3.

Colombia, y son _____. Ahora viven en un _____ apartamento
　　　　　　　　4.　　　　　　　　　　　　　　　　5.

_____ y _____ cerca de un jardín _____. Lola es muy
　　6.　　　　　　　7.　　　　　　　　　　　　　8.

_____, pero Luis es más _____. Lola dice que los deportes son
　　9.　　　　　　　　　　　　　10.

_____, pero Luis prefiere pasar su tiempo _____ en la biblioteca porque
　11.　　　　　　　　　　　　　　　　　　12.

le gustan las novelas _____. A mí me gusta pasar _____ horas con ellos
　　　　　　　　　　13.　　　　　　　　　　　　14.

porque son muy _____ y _____. Mañana vamos a ver una película
　　　　　　　15.　　　　　16.

_____. En _____ correo electrónico te escribo más de mis amigos
　　17.　　　　　　18.

_____ y de sus _____ perros _____.
　19.　　　　　　　20.　　　　　21.

Tu amiga _____,
　　　　　　　　22.

Luisa

♦ 3 ♦ Shortening of Adjectives

a. The following adjectives drop the final *-o* when used before a masculine singular noun:

uno	*one, a, an*	un amigo	*one (a) friend*
bueno	*good*	un buen amigo	*a good friend*
malo	*bad*	un mal año	*a bad year*
primero	*first*	el primer día	*the first day*
tercero	*third*	el tercer piso	*the third floor*
alguno	*some*	algún día	*some day*
ninguno	*no, not any*	ningún dinero	*no money*

NOTE:

1. The complete form of the adjective is used when:

   (a) it follows a masculine singular noun.

un muchacho **malo**	*a bad boy*

   (b) it modifies a feminine or plural noun.

una muchacha **buena**	*a good girl*
algunos libros	*some books*

   (c) a preposition comes between the adjective and the noun.

el **primero** de junio	*June 1*

2. The adjectives *alguno* and *ninguno* require an accent mark when the *-o* is dropped: *algún, ningún.*

   b. *Ciento* becomes *cien* before any plural noun and before the numbers *mil* (thousand) and *millón* (million). The short form is not used with multiples of *ciento* (*doscientos, trescientos, etc.*) or in combination with any other number (*ciento diez*):

cien libros (muchachas)	*one (a) hundred books (girls)*
cien mil años	*one (a) hundred thousand years*
cien millones de dólares	*one (a) hundred million dollars*

   BUT

cuatrocientos alumnos	*four hundred students*
cuatrocientas personas	*four hundred people*
ciento veintiséis dólares	*one (a) hundred twenty-six dollars*

   c. *Santo* becomes *San* before the name of a male saint, unless the name begins with *To-* or *Do-*.

San Francisco	*Saint Francis*
San José	*Saint Joseph*

   BUT

Santo Tomás	*Saint Thomas*
Santo Domingo	*Saint Dominic*

NOTE:

The feminine form of *santo* is *santa*.

Santa María   *Saint Mary*

d. *Grande* becomes *gran* before a singular noun and means "great." When *grande* follows the noun, it means "large" or "big."

un **gran** hombre   *a great man*

una **gran** mujer   *a great woman*

BUT

una casa **grande**   *a large house*

EXERCISE I

Select the correct form of each adjective in parentheses to complete Adriana's description of her cousin Esteban.

Esteban es mi primo, pero somos _____ amigos también. Él es el _____
                                    1. (buen / buenos)   **2.** (primer / primero)

hijo de mis tíos Pedro y Beatriz. Yo soy la _____ hija de mis padres. Vivimos en
                                              3. (primer / primera)

el mismo edificio: yo vivo en el _____ piso y mis tíos viven en el _____ .
                                      4. (primer / primera)   **5.** (tercer / tercero)

_____ amigos creen que Esteban y yo somos hermanos. Cuando yo
6. (Algún / Algunos)

tengo _____ _____ día, Esteban es la _____ persona con quien hablo.
          7. (un / uno)   **8.** (mal / malo)   **9.** (primer / primera)

Este verano pensamos hacer un viaje juntos a _____ Francisco y a _____
                                                10. (San / Santo)   **11.** (San / Santa)

Monica. Yo tengo _____ dinero ahorrado, pero Esteban no tiene _____
                    12. (algún / alguno)   **13.** (ningún / ninguno)

dinero todavía. Necesitamos _____ setenta y cinco dólares. Yo tengo ya
                              14. (cien / ciento)

_____ dólares en el banco. Mi tía dice que Esteban no puede ahorrar
15. (cien / ciento)

ni _____ centavo. Su cumpleaños es el _____ de julio. Siempre recibe
    16. (un / uno)   **17.** (primer / primero)

_____ regalos de dinero. Va a ser _____ verano _____
18. (algún / algunos)   **19.** (un / uno)   **20.** (mal / malo)

si no hago _____ excursión.
              21. (ningún / ninguna)

EXERCISE J

Roberto has just learned that many Spanish speakers are named after a saint. Write the name of the saint after whom Roberto's friends were named.

1. Guillermo   *4.* Luis   *7.* Tomás   *9.* María

2. Cecilia   *5.* Domingo   *8.* Teresa   *10.* Alfonso

3. Fernando   *6.* Juan

MASTERY EXERCISES

EXERCISE K

Gloria shows you her closet. Describe some of the things you see, using the adjectives below.

cien   largo   pequeño

grande   negro   sucio

japonés   nuevo   viejo

EXAMPLE: nuevo
un sombrero nuevo

1.

2.

3.

4.

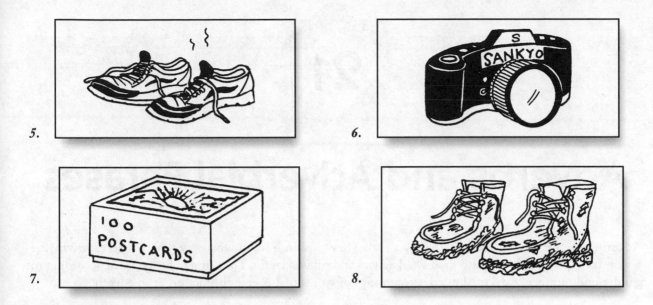

5.

6.

7.

8.

EXERCISE L

Research a vacation destination on the Internet. Then prepare 7 statements you would write in a postcard to a friend that express why you like this place.

21

Adverbs and Adverbial Phrases

Adverbs describe the action expressed by a verb. They explain how, in what way, when, where, or why the action takes place. Adverbs also modify adjectives and other adverbs. They don't change form according to gender and number. Adverbial phrases are groups of words that together function as an adverb.

♦ 1 ♦ Adverbs and Adverbial Phrases of Mode

a. Adverbs of mode (those answering the question how? or in what way?) are generally formed by adding -*mente* to the feminine singular form of an adjective.

Adjective		Adverb	
correcta	*correct*	**correctamente**	*correctly*
fácil	*easy*	**fácilmente**	*easily*

NOTE:

1. Adjectives that have an accent mark keep the accent mark when they are changed to adverbs.

rápida   rápidamente

2. The adjectives *bueno* and *malo* form adverbs irregularly.

bueno   *good*   bien   *well*
mal   *bad*   mal   *badly*

Es un carro **bueno**,   *It's a good car,*
pero Pedro conduce **mal**.   *but Pedro drives badly.*

b. Adverbial phrases of mode are usually formed as follows:

de manera + *adjective*
Él habla **de manera extraña**.   *He talks in a strange way.*

de modo + *adjective*
Él habla **de modo extraño**.   *He talks in a strange way.*

EXERCISE A

After Migdalia's first singing recital, people commented on her talent. Complete each comment by writing the appropriate form of the adverb.

EXAMPLE: su profesor de música: correcto
Ella canta **correctamente**.

1. sus padres: divino

Ella canta _____ .

2. su hermano: malo

Ella canta _____ .

3. sus abuelos: alegre

Ella canta _____ .

4. su novio: dulce

Ella canta _____ .

5. una amiga: suave

Ella canta _____ .

6. otro cantante: bueno

Ella canta _____ .

EXERCISE B

A classmate asks how you do different things. Answer his or her questions using the cue given in parentheses.

EXAMPLE: ¿Cómo completas tus tareas? *(diligente)*
Yo completo mis tareas **diligentemente**.

1. ¿Cómo almuerzas? *(rápido)*

2. ¿Cómo hablas a tu novio(a)? *(dulce)*

3. ¿Cómo patinas? *(malo)*

4. ¿Cómo caminas a las clases? *(lento)*

5. ¿Cómo saludas a tus amigos? *(cordial)*

6. ¿Cómo comprendes a la maestra de español? *(fácil)*

◆ 2 ◆ Adverbs and Adverbial Phrases of Time or Frequency

a. Adverbs of time or frequency

ahora	*now*	nunca	*never*
anoche	*last night*	¿cuándo?	*when?*
ayer	*yesterday*	pronto	*soon*
entonces	*then*	siempre	*always*
hoy	*today*	tarde	*late*
luego	*then, next*	temprano	*early*
mañana	*tomorrow*	todavía	*still, yet*

b. Adverbial phrases of time or frequency

algún día	*some day*	muchas veces	*often*
a veces	*sometimes*	pocas veces	*seldom*
esta noche	*tonight*	primero	*first*
este fin de semana	*this weekend*	todos los días	*every day*
más tarde	*later*		

EXERCISE C

Tell when, or how frequently, you do or are going to do the following things. For each statement, use the suggested adverb or adverbial phrase.

EXAMPLES: bañarse / todos los días.
Yo me baño todos los días.
descansar / mañana
Yo voy a descansar mañana.

1. ir de compras / este fin de semana

2. estudiar para un examen / esta noche

3. llegar a tiempo a la escuela / siempre

4. ser rico / algún día

5. escribir el ejercicio / ahora

6. visitar a los abuelos / pronto

7. recibir malas notas / pocas veces

8. pelear con los padres / nunca

EXERCISE D

Using the expressions given, tell how frequently you do these things.

a veces   nunca   siempre

muchas veces   pocas veces   todas los días

EXAMPLE: lavar los platos
          Nunca lavo los platos.

1. preparar la tarea

2. ir al supermercado

3. cocinar

4. arreglar su cuarto

5. pasar la aspiradora

6. lavar el carro

7. trabajar en el jardín

♦ 3 ♦ Adverbs and Adverbial Phrases of Place

a. Common adverbs of place (answering the question *where?*)

abajo	*below, downstairs*	derecho	*straight ahead*
¿adónde?	*(to) where?*	detrás	*behind*
allí	*there*	¿dónde?	*where?*
aquí	*here*	enfrente	*in front of, opposite*
arriba	*above, upstairs*		

b. Common adverbial phrases of place

a la derecha	*to the right*	delante de	*in front of, ahead of*
a la izquierda	*to the left*	detrás de	*behind*
debajo de	*beneath*	frente a	*facing, in front of*

EXERCISE E

You are helping a new friend become familiar with the downtown area of your city. Use the map below to tell him the location of the buildings listed. Express the location using an adverbial phrase.

EXAMPLE: el banco

El banco **está detrás del cine**.

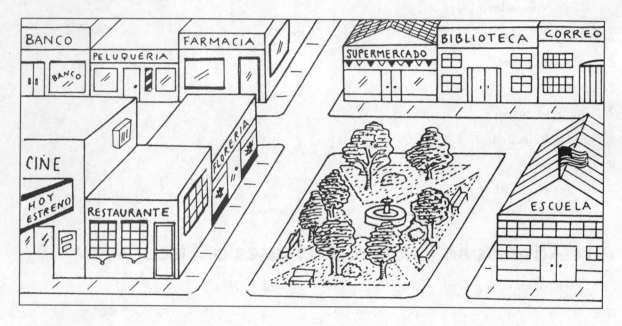

1. la florería	*4.* el correo	*6.* la escuela
2. la biblioteca	*5.* el parque	*7.* el cine
3. el restaurante		

EXERCISE F

In each group, select the adverb that is in a different category (mode, time, or place) from the other three.

EXAMPLE: alegremente, libremente, **temprano**, lentamente

1. ayer, siempre, correctamente, entonces

2. débilmente, ahora, luego, nunca

3. ¿adónde?, dulcemente, bien, rápidamente

4. ¿cuándo?, hoy, nunca, tristemente

5. diligentemente, tarde, sinceramente, perezosamente

6. pronto, aquí, abajo, ¿dónde?

7. allí, arriba, ¿dónde?, fácilmente

8. ¿por qué?, anoche, todavía, mañana

9. felizmente, mal, rápidamente, ¿cuándo?

10. difícilmente, a la derecha, allí, derecho

EXERCISE G

You're talking about your language class. Complete each sentence with the appropriate adverb.

EXAMPLE: No comprendemos a Jorge cuando habla.
         Él habla **rápidamente**.

1. Yo hago la tarea sin errores.

   Yo hago la tarea _____ .

2. Yo estudio siete días a la semana.

   Yo estudio _____ .

3. La maestra dice «por favor» y «gracias» a los alumnos.

   Ella habla _____ .

4. Nosotros comprendemos todo lo que dice la profesora.

   Nosotros comprendemos _____ .

5. La maestra tiene una voz bonita.

   Ella canta _____ .

6. A Roberto le gusta hablar.

   Él habla _____ en la clase.

7. Mi amigo no recibe buenas notas.

   Él sale _____ en todos los exámenes.

EXERCISE H

Tell where the objects in the picture below are located. Use adverbial phrases of place in your sentences.

EXAMPLE: **El vaso está al lado de la leche.**

1. El guante de béisbol _____ .

2. Los gatos _____ .

3. La niña _____ .

4. Las papitas _____ .

5. El automóvil _____ .

EXERCISE I

Your Spanish teacher met with each student individually to discuss their work and how they do it. Write a summary of what the teacher told you. Be sure to include adverbs of mode, time or frequency, and place in your summary.

Numbers

◆ 1 ◆ Cardinal Numbers

a. 0 to 99

0 cero	13 trece	26 veintiséis (veinte y seis)
1 uno	14 catorce	27 veintisiete (veinte y siete)
2 dos	15 quince	28 veintiocho (veinte y ocho)
3 tres	16 dieciséis (diez y seis)	29 veintinueve (veinte y nueve)
4 cuatro	17 diecisiete (diez y siete)	30 treinta
5 cinco	18 dieciocho (diez y ocho)	31 treinta y uno *(and so on)*
6 seis	19 diecinueve (diez y nueve)	40 cuarenta
7 siete	20 veinte	50 cincuenta
8 ocho	21 veintiuno (veinte y uno)	60 sesenta
9 nueve	22 veintidós (veinte y dos)	70 setenta
10 diez	23 veintitrés (veinte y tres)	80 ochenta
11 once	24 veinticuatro (veinte y cuatro)	90 noventa
12 doce	25 veinticinco (veinte y cinco)	99 noventa y nueve

NOTE:

1. Compound numbers 16 to 99 are connected by *y*.

2. Although numbers 16 to 19 and 21 to 29 may be connected by *y*, they are usually written as one word. Note the spelling changes that occur when these numbers are written as one word.

   die**z**   die**ci**séis

   veint**e**   veint**i**uno

3. *Uno* and combinations of *uno* (like *veintiuno* and *treinta y uno*) become *un* before masculine nouns and *una* before feminine nouns.

   un libro   *one (a) book*

vein**tiún** asientos	*twenty-one seats*
treinta y **un** profesores	*thirty-one teachers*
una mesa	*one (a) a table*
veinti**una** camisas	*twenty-one shirts*
treinta y **una** sillas	*thirty-one chairs*

EXERCISE A

As you leave a summer camp in Mexico, your friends give you their telephone numbers. Rewrite them using Spanish words.

EXAMPLE: Silvia 5-47-08-23
cinco-cuarenta y siete–cero ocho–veintitrés

1. Arturo 6-31-74-92

2. Raquel 3-65-22-81

3. Emilio 7-27-00-48

4. Graciela 2-59-11-17

5. Humberto 9-13-36-14

6. Raúl 8-72-12-41

7. Linda 9-97-16-67

8. Pedro 5-33-21-86

EXERCISE B

While touring Spain, you help the tour guide give out the room assignments at the hotel.

EXAMPLE: Enrique y José, 57
Para Enrique y José, el cincuenta y siete.

1. Louise y Estela, 38

2. Elisa y Jane, 71

3. Billy y Tomás, 43

4. Javier y Antonio, 15

5. Rita y María, 64

6. Clara y Marcela, 86

7. Felipe y Hugo, 29

EXERCISE C

Use the following map to tell your Spanish-speaking friend the expected high and low temperatures in some major cities of the United States. All temperatures are in degrees Fahrenheit.

EXAMPLE: Los Angeles

      La temperatura alta será setenta y seis grados y la baja sesenta y dos grados.

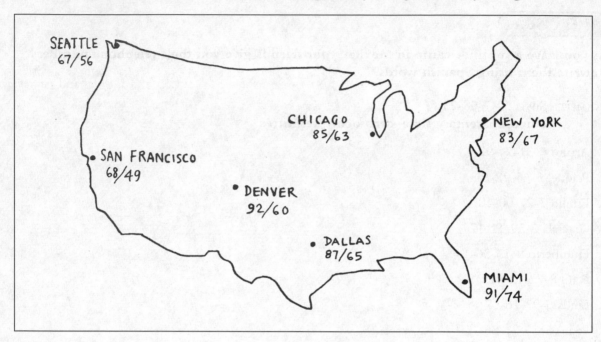

1. Miami	*4.* Denver	*6.* Dallas
2. Chicago	*5.* New York	*7.* San Francisco
3. Seattle		

b. 100 to 1,000,000

100	cien	800	ochocientos (–as)
101	ciento uno (–a)	900	novecientos (–as)
200	doscientos (–as)	1,000	mil
300	trescientos (–as)	2,000	dos mil
400	cuatrocientos (–as)	2,500	dos mil quinientos
500	quinientos (–as)	100,000	cien mil
600	seiscientos (–as)	1,000,000	un millón (de)
700	setecientos (–as)		

NOTE:

1. *Cien* becomes *ciento* when it's followed by another number from one to ninety-nine.

cien libros	*one hundred books*
cien casas	*one hundred houses*
cien mil habitantes	*one hundred thousand inhabitants*
cien millones	*one hundred million*

   BUT

cien**to** veinte libros	*one hundred twenty books*

2. Numbers that express hundreds, like *doscientos* and *trescientos*, become *doscientas* and *trescientas* before a feminine noun.

doscientas páginas	*two hundred pages*
trescientas plumas	*three hundred pens*

3. In Spanish, compound numbers higher than a thousand (such as 1, 110) are expressed with *mil*. Words like *twelve hundred* have no equivalent in Spanish.

mil doscientos	*twelve hundred (one thousand two hundred)*
mil novecientos noventa	*nineteen hundred ninety (one thousand nine hundred ninety)*
dos mil quinientos	*twenty-five hundred (two thousand five hundred)*

4. No equivalent to the English word *a* or *one* is expressed before *ciento* or *mil*, but the equivalent *un* must be used before *millón*. *Millón* (pl. *millones*) also requires *de* when a noun follows.

ciento diez alumnos	*a (one) hundred ten students*
mil dólares	*a (one) thousand dollars*

   BUT

un millón de dólares	*a (one) million dollars*
dos millones de habitantes	*two million inhabitants*

5. In many Spanish-speaking countries, the commas in large numbers change to periods:

   1,000 becomes 1.000 and 1,000,000 becomes 1.000.000. The periods in decimal numbers change to commas: 1.10 becomes 1, 10.

EXERCISE D

You and a friend are comparing the population of cities around the world. Express the approximate population of these cities, using Spanish words.

EXAMPLE: Madrid / 3,228,000
tres millones doscientos veintiocho mil

1. México, D.F / 8,463,906
2. París / 2,154,000
3. Tokio / 12,677,917
4. Chicago / 2,833,321
5. San Francisco / 744,041
6. Barcelona / 1,605,602
7. Buenos Aires / 2,776,138
8. New Orleans / 223,388
9. Atlanta / 486,411
10. Seattle 582,454

EXERCISE E

You're using Mexico City as your base for several side trips to other cities. Express in Spanish the approximate distance by car between Mexico City and each of the other cities you plan to visit.

EXAMPLE: Cuernavaca / 82 kilómetros
Cuernavaca está a **ochenta y dos** kilómetros

1. Acapulco / 305 kilómetros
2. Puebla / 120 kilómetros
3. Veracruz / 424 kilómetros
4. Oaxaca / 516 kilómetros
5. Toluca / 56 kilómetros
6. Guadalajara / 450 kilómetros
7. Querétaro / 257 kilómetros

EXERCISE F

Tell the year in which these family members were born.

EXAMPLE: tu prima favorita
Mi prima favorita **nació en mil novecientos setenta y ocho**.

1. tu padre
2. tu madre
3. tu hermano(a)
4. tu abuelo
5. tu abuela
6. tu tío favorito
7. tú

EXERCISE G

The airlines have just lowered their fares. Tell how much each of these flights will cost one-way *(ida)* and round-trip *(ida y vuelta)*.

AEROLINEAS INTERNACIONALES
BOLETOS DE IDA
SAN JUAN $139   COSTA RICA $209
CANCÚN $159   BARCELONA $299
BUENOS AIRES $499   CARACAS $299

EXAMPLE: Caracas *(ida / ida y vuelta)*
Ida: **doscientos noventa y nueve dólares**.
Ida y vuelta: **quinientos noventa y ocho dólares**.

1. Barcelona *(ida / ida y vuelta)*   4. Cancún *(ida / ida y vuelta)*

2. Costa Rica *(ida / ida y vuelta)*   5. Buenos Aires *(ida / ida y vuelta)*

3. San Juan *(ida / ida y vuelta)*

EXERCISE H

Mr. Jiménez is planning his summer vacation and wants to find out the foreign currency exchange rate for $50 (US) for various countries. Write down what he finds out in the newspaper and on the Internet.

EXAMPLE: Francia / 37.50 euros
Cincuenta dólares es igual a **treinta** y **siete euros y cincuenta centavos**.

1. Argentina / 185.62 pesos argentinos

2. Chile / 29,420 pesos chilenos

3. Colombia / 125,920 pesos colombianos

4. Costa Rica / 28,666.50 colones

5. España / 37.50 euros

6. México / 693 nuevos pesos mexicanos

7. Nicaragua / 1,014 córdobas

8. Paraguay / 260,590 guaraníes

9. República Dominicana / 1,816 pesos dominicanos

10. Venezuela / 107, 594 bolívares

EXERCISE I

You're preparing a surprise party for a friend and you're writing the details in Spanish in your diary. Complete the sentences using the correct form of *uno*.

1. Mañana Federico cumple treinta y _____ años.

2. Invitamos a cincuenta y _____ personas.

3. Hay cuarenta y _____ globos.

4. Necesitamos treinta y _____ velas para el pastel.

5. Vamos a necesitar _____ silla más.

6. Podemos comer el pastel con _____ cuchara.

EXERCISE J

You're working at a hotel that is going to be refurbished. Complete the following sentences with *cien* or *ciento*.

1. Hay _____ cuartos en el hotel.

2. _____ cincuenta y cinco personas van a pasar la noche en el hotel.

3. Unos cuartos cuestan _____ dólares la noche.

4. Otros cuartos cuestan _____ veinte y cinco dólares.

5. La reparación va a durar _____ días.

◆ 2 ◆ Arithmetic Expressions

The following expressions are used in arithmetic problems in Spanish:

y, más	*plus (+)*
menos	*minus (−)*
por	*(multiplied) by, "times" (×)*
dividido por	*divided by (÷)*
son, es igual a	*equals (=)*

(EXERCISE K)

Express the following in Spanish.

1. 35 + 70 = 105
2. 187 + 542 = 729
3. 691 − 255 = 436
4. 1,323 − 1,022 = 301
5. 1,968 + 2,741 = 4,709
6. 636 × 25 = 15,900
7. 338 ÷ 26 = 13
8. 700 + 300 = 1,000
9. 500 + 400 = 900
10. 900 − 350 = 550
11. 900 + 800 = 1,700
12. 110 + 115 = 225
13. 743 − 243 = 500
14. 20,000 ÷ 100 = 200
15. 800,000 + 200,000 = 1,000,000
16. 1,400,000,000 + 600,000 = 2,000,000
17. 2,400 ÷ 12 = 200
18. 5,000 ÷ 500 = 10
19. 930 × 17 = 15,810
20. 359 × 26 = 9,334

♦ 3 ♦ Ordinal Numbers

1°	primero (-a), primer	1st	*first*
2°	segundo (-a)	2nd	*second*
3°	tercero (-a), tercer	3rd	*third*
4°	cuarto (-a)	4th	*fourth*
5°	quinto (-a)	5th	*fifth*
6°	sexto (-a)	6th	*sixth*
7°	séptimo (-a)	7th	*seventh*
8°	octavo (-a)	8th	*eighth*
9°	noveno (-a)	9th	*ninth*
10°	décimo (-a)	10th	*tenth*

NOTE:

1. All ordinal numbers agree in gender *(m. /f.)* and number *(sing. /pl.)* with the nouns to which they refer.

   el séptimo mes   *the seventh month*
   la séptima semana   *the seventh week*

2. The numbers *primero* and *tercero* drop the final −*o* when they come before a masculine singular noun.

   el primer hombre   *the first man*
   el tercer mes   *the third month*

BUT

la primera semana	*the first week*
la tercera vez	*the third time*

3. If a preposition comes between *primero* or *tercero* and the noun, the full form is used.

el primero de mayo	*May 1*

4. Ordinal numbers are generally used to express rank order only from the first to the tenth in a series. Numbers above ten have ordinal forms, too, but they are seldom used. Instead, a cardinal number is placed after the noun, and the word *número* is understood.

la sexta lección	*the sixth lesson*
Felipe Segundo	*Felipe II (Felipe the Second)*

BUT

la lección catorce	*the fourteenth lesson or lesson (number) fourteen*
Alfonso Doce	*Alfonso XII (Alfonso the Twelfth)*

EXERCISE L

You step into a hotel elevator. Tell on which floor each of the following places is located. Use the word *piso* in your response.★

EXAMPLE: El bar **está en el tercer piso.**

1. la piscina
2. las tiendas
3. las oficinas
4. la peluquería

5. el restaurante
6. el salón de banquetes
7. el salón Martel

8. el teatro
9. la discoteca
10. los periódicos

★In most Spanish-speaking countries, the first floor (or ground floor) is called **planta baja** (PB); the second floor, **primer piso**; and so forth.

EXERCISE M

You're helping a younger brother learn the order of the months. Tell what position each month occupies in the calendar year.

EXAMPLE: abril
     el cuarto mes

1. junio
2. septiembre
3. enero
4. diciembre
5. febrero
6. octubre
7. julio
8. marzo
9. agosto
10. mayo
11. noviembre

EXERCISE N

Write the sentences, changing the number in parentheses into a Spanish word.

1. Siéntate en el *(3°)* asiento.
2. Saliste mal en la *(5°)* prueba.
3. Naciste en junio, el *(6°)* mes del año.
4. Acabas de celebrar tu cumpleaños *(15°)*.
5. Vives en un apartamento en el *(1°)* piso.
6. Caminas a la escuela por la Calle *(8°)*.
7. El español es tu *(3°)* clase del día.
8. Estudias el *(2°)* semestre de español.
9. Estamos en la *(10°)* lección.
10. Debes hacer el *(4°)* ejercicio.

◆ 4 ◆ Fractions

½ un medio, medio (-a), una mitad de	*(a/one) half, half of*
⅓ un tercio, una tercera parte de	*(a/one) third, the third part of*
¼ un cuarto, una cuarta parte de	*(a/one) fourth, a quarter of*
⅔ dos tercios, las dos terceras partes de	*two-thirds, two-thirds of*
¾ tres cuartos, las tres cuartas partes de	*three-fourths, three quarters of*
⅘ cuatro quintos, las cuatro quintas partes de	*four-fifths of*
¹/₁₀ un décimo, la décima parte de	*(a/one) tenth, a tenth of*

NOTE:

1. Except for *medio* and *tercio*, noun fractions are formed with ordinal numbers up through *décimo* (tenth). Thereafter, the ending *-avo* is usually added to the cardinal number to express fractions smaller than a tenth.

    ¹/₁₂ un doceavo, una doceava parte de   *(a/one) twelfth of*

2. Fractions are masculine nouns.

3⅓ tres y un tercio   *three and one-third*

When the fraction precedes the thing divided, it may be used with the feminine noun *parte*, unless a unit of measure is expressed:

una tercera **parte** (un tercio) del libro   *a third of the book*

BUT

un tercio de libra   *a third of a pound*

3. The adjective *medio (-a)* means "half," while the noun *la mitad (de)* means "half (of)."

media docena de huevos   *half a dozen eggs*

la mitad de la clase   *half of the class*

(**EXERCISE O**)

Copy the following shopping list, writing out fractions in full.

Lista de compras
½ docena de huevos
½ galón de leche
¼ libra de jamón
¾ libra de queso
½ pan
1½ libra de galletas
½ melón
½ sandía

◆ 5 ◆ Multiples

Terms that indicate that one quantity is a multiple of another are used in the same manner as their English equivalents.

una vez	*once*	simple	*single, simple*
dos veces	*twice*	doble	*double*
tres veces	*three times*	triple	*triple*

Me visitó **una vez**.	*She visited me once.*
Lo leí **dos veces**.	*I read it twice.*
Escribí el **doble** de lo que escribiste tú.	*I wrote twice as much as you.*

NOTE:

1. Adverbial phrases expressing the number of times that an event occurs are formed by a cardinal number and the feminine noun *vez* (a time).

Leí el libro **tres veces**.   *I read the book three times.*

2. Multiples like *doble, triple* may be either adjectives or nouns.

Es una máquina de **doble** motor.   *It's a double-motor machine.*

Este carro cuesta hoy el **doble**.   *This car costs twice as much today.*

EXERCISE P

You overhear your younger sister tell a friend how many times she has done some activities. Tell what she says using the cues in parentheses.

EXAMPLE: ir al parque zoológico *(10)*
       Fui al parque zoológico **diez veces**.

1. volar en avión *(5)*

2. esquiar *(20)*

3. ver la película «Fantasma» *(2)*

4. jugar al fútbol *(50)*

5. comer al aire libre *(8)*

6. ir a la playa *(100)*

7. preparar la cena *(1)*

MASTERY EXERCISES

EXERCISE Q

Your parents have remodeled the house to give you a larger room. Write sentences telling how much different things cost.

1. pintura $790

2. ventanas $1,200

3. muebles $920

4. alfombra $444

5. televisor $389

6. cortinas $56

7. total $3,799

EXERCISE R

You are visiting a cousin in Spain. She mentions several tourist attractions and indicates how many times she has visited each one of them. Use the cues in parentheses to express what she says.

EXAMPLE: el Escorial (3)
> **Visité el Escorial tres veces.**

1. el Valle de los Caídos (5)

2. el Museo del Prado (12)

3. la Plaza Mayor (20)

4. el Palacio Real (1)

5. la ciudad de Toledo (7)

6. el Parque del Buen Retiro (25)

EXERCISE S

Before going back to school in the fall, you write to a friend to describe the summer job you had in a retail store. You may wish to include the following: number of hours per week you worked, number of weeks you worked, total number of hours you worked, your weekly salary, how much time you had for lunch, number of employees, average number of customers each day, company earnings, how most purchases are made, when the business opened for the first time.

Times and Dates

♦ 1 ♦ Time Expressions

a. *¿Qué hora es?* is equivalent to "What time is it?"

b. In expressing time, "It is" is expressed by *Es la* (for one o'clock), and *Son las* for other hours (two o'clock, three o'clock, and so on).

Es la una.	*It's one o'clock.*
Son las dos (tres).	*It's two (three) o'clock.*

c. Time after or past the hour (up to half past) is expressed by the hour + *y*, followed by the number of minutes. "Half past" is expressed by *y media*; "a quarter past" is expressed by *y cuarto*.

Es la una **y** diez.	*It's ten (minutes) after one. It's 1:10.*
Son las seis **y media**.	*It's half past six. It's 6:30.*
Son las diez **y cuarto**.	*It's a quarter after ten. It's 10:15*

d. After half past, the time is expressed in terms of the following hour *menos* (minus) the minutes.

Son las dos **menos** veinte.	*It's twenty minutes to two. It's 1:40.*
Son las nueve **menos** cuarto.	*It's a quarter to nine. It's 8:45*

e. The expression *de la mañana* corresponds to English A.M. (in the morning). *De la tarde* (in the afternoon) and *de la noche* (in the evening) correspond to English P.M. *En punto* means "sharp" or "on the dot."

Son las ocho **de la mañana**.	*It's 8:00 A.M.*
Es la una **de la tarde**.	*It's 1:00 P.M.*
Son las ocho **de la noche en punto**.	*It's 8:00 P.M. sharp.*

NOTE:

1. Instead of *media* and *cuarto*, the number of minutes may be used *(treinta, quince)*.

Son las cinco **y treinta**.	*It's five-thirty. It's half past five.*
Es la una y **quince**.	*It's one-fifteen. It's a quarter past one.*

2. It's not uncommon to hear times like 12:45 and 12:50 expressed with *y*.

Son las doce **y cuarenta y cinco**.   *It's twelve-forty-five.*

Son las doce **y cincuenta**.   *It's twelve-fifty.*

f. Common time expressions

¿Qué hora es?   *What time is it?*

¿A qué hora?   *At what time?*

a las dos (tres)   *at two (three) o'clock*

de la mañana   *in the morning, A.M.*

de la tarde   *in the afternoon, P.M.*

de la noche   *at night, P.M.*

Es mediodía   *It's noon.*

a mediodía   *at noon*

Es medianoche   *It's midnight*

a medianoche   *at midnight*

Es tarde.   *It's late.*

Es temprano.   *It's early.*

a tiempo   *on time*

en punto   *exactly, sharp*

EXERCISE A

You're teaching your younger sister to tell time in Spanish. Express the hours indicated on the clocks.

EXAMPLE: Son las **diez menos cuarto**.

1.

2.

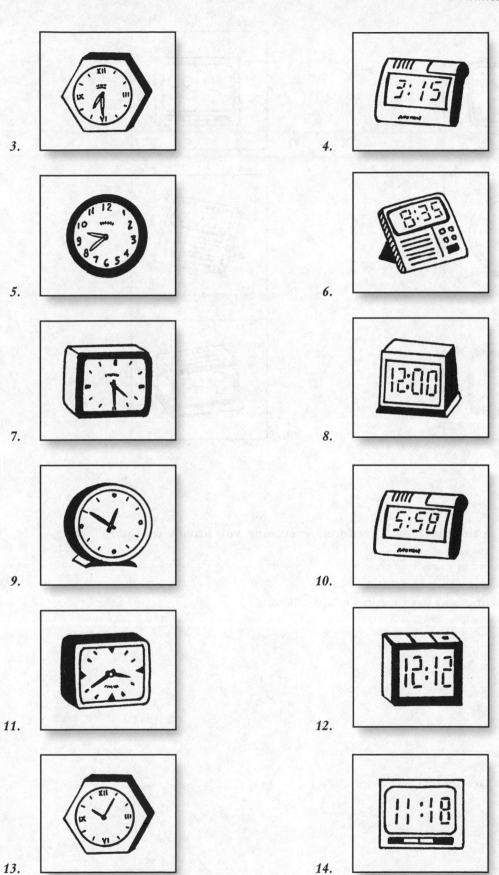

3.

4.

5.

6.

7.

8.

9.

10.

11.

12.

13.

14.

15.   16.

17.   18.

19.   20.

EXERCISE B

Tell at what time in the morning, afternoon, or evening you usually do the following activities.

EXAMPLE: desayunarse
        Me desayuno a las seis y media **de la mañana**.

1. ir a la escuela

2. almorzar

3. preparar la tarea

4. jugar con los amigos

5. salir de la escuela

6. cenar

7. ver su programa favorito de televisión

8. acostarse

9. practicar un deporte

10. bañarse

EXERCISE C

You don't know where the day has gone. Using the notes below, tell at what time you completed each activity.

EXAMPLE: Tú ayudas a tu papá a lavar el carro. Son las ocho y media cuando empiezan. Tardan una hora y media en lavar el carro. ¿Qué hora es?

Son las diez.

1. Tú acompañas a tu mamá al supermercado. Salen de la casa a las diez y cuarto. Regresan a casa ochenta minutos después. ¿Qué hora es?

2. Tu amiga te llama por teléfono a las doce menos cinco. Hablan por quince minutos. ¿A qué hora terminan de hablar?

3. A la una tú arreglas tu cuarto. Necesitas setenta y cinco minutos. ¿Qué hora es?

4. Tienes que sacar un libro de la biblioteca. Sales de tu casa a las tres menos cuarto y vuelves a la casa en dos horas y media. ¿A qué hora vuelves a casa?

5. Después de cenar, estudias para un examen por tres horas y quince minutos. Empiezas a estudiar a las siete y diez. ¿Qué hora es cuando terminas de estudiar?

♦ 2 ♦ Dates

a. Days of the week (*Los días de la semana*)

lunes *Monday*

martes *Tuesday*

miércoles *Wednesday*

jueves *Thursday*

viernes *Friday*

sábado *Saturday*

domingo *Sunday*

NOTE:

1. "On" before a day of the week is expressed by *el* for the singular and *los* for the plural.

el lunes *on Monday*   los lunes *on Mondays*

el viernes *on Friday*   los viernes *on Fridays*

el sábado *on Saturday*   los sábados *on Saturdays*

el domingo *on Sunday*   los domingos *on Sundays*

2. Days of the week whose names end in -s do not change their form in the plural.

3. The days of the week are not capitalized in Spanish.

b. Months *(Los meses)*

enero	*January*	julio	*July*
febrero	*February*	agosto	*August*
marzo	*March*	septiembre	*September*
abril	*April*	octubre	*October*
mayo	*May*	noviembre	*November*
junio	*June*	diciembre	*December*

NOTE:

Like the days of the week, the months are written with lowercase (small) letters in Spanish.

c. Dates

¿Cuál es la fecha de hoy? ⎫
¿A cuántos estamos hoy? ⎬ *What is today's date?*

Es el primero de enero. ⎫
Estamos a primero de enero. ⎬ *It's January 1.*

Es el dos de febrero	*It's February 2.*
Es el tres (cuatro) de mayo.	*It's May 3 (4)*
mil ochocientos doce	*1812*
el quince de abril de	*April 15, 2008*
dos mil ocho	

NOTE:

1. Cardinal numbers are used for all dates except *primero* (first).

el **primero** de abril	*April 1*
el tres (cuatro, cinco) de abril	*April 3 (4,5)*

2. The year is expressed in Spanish by thousands and hundreds, not by hundreds alone as in English.

3. The date and month are connected by the preposition *de*. The month and the year are also connected by *de*.

el diez **de** junio **de**	*(on) June 10, 1840*
mil ochocientos cuarenta	

With dates, *el* corresponds to "on."

EXERCISE D

You're telling an exchange student at your school about important dates in the United States. Give the Spanish equivalent for the dates indicated.

1. February 22
2. December 25
3. February 14
4. January 1
5. October 12
6. July 4
7. November 11
8. April 1
9. October 31
10. February 12

EXERCISE E

You're reading a list of Mexican national holidays. Express these dates in Spanish.

1. May 5
2. September 16
3. November 20
4. May 1
5. February 5
6. March 21
7. January 1
8. December 25

EXERCISE F

Tell the date of birth (including the year) of the following members of your family.

EXAMPLE: tu tía favorita *(mi tía favorita)*
Mi tía favorita **nació** el **dos de agosto** de **mil novecientos sesenta y uno**.

1. tu madre *(mi madre)*

2. tu padre *(mi padre)*

3. tu abuelo materno *(mi abuelo materno)*

4. tu abuela paterna *(mi abuela paterna)*

5. tu hermano(-a) *(mi hermano(-a))*

6. tu primo(-a) favorito(-a) *(mi primo(-a) favorito(-a))*

7. tú *(Yo)*

EXERCISE G

Express the following dates in Spanish.

1. March 15, 1271
2. February 2, 1588
3. April 17, 1942
4. May 23, 1848
5. July 4, 1776
6. January 30, 1660
7. July 18, 1395
8. December 13, 1969
9. June 22, 2002
10. March 25, 1124

MASTERY EXERCISES

EXERCISE H

A friend is helping you study for a Spanish test. Answer the questions your friend asks.

1. Si hoy es lunes, ¿qué día es mañana?

2. ¿Cuál es el segundo mes del año?

3. ¿En qué mes celebramos la Navidad?

4. ¿Cuál es el noveno mes del año?

5. ¿Si hoy es jueves, ¿qué día fue ayer?

6. ¿Cuáles son los meses que tienen treinta días?

7. ¿Qué mes tiene veintiocho o veintinueve días?

8. ¿Qué meses tienen treinta y un días?

9. ¿En qué días no hay clases?

10. ¿En qué días vas a la escuela?

11. ¿Cuál es la fecha de hoy?

12. ¿En qué mes celebramos la fiesta nacional de los Estados Unidos?

13. ¿Cuál es el séptimo mes del año?

14. ¿En qué mes celebramos el Año Nuevo?

15. ¿En qué fecha celebras tu cumpleaños?

EXERCISE I

In one of your classes you have been discussing the concept of time management. Prepare a journal entry in which you log and describe all of the activities that you did today. Be sure to include the time you started and ended each activity. Also include how long you spent on each activity.

CHAPTER 24

Interrogatives

a. Common interrogative expressions

¿qué? *what?*

¿quién (-es)? *who?*

¿a quién (-es)? *whom? to whom?*

¿de quién (-es)? *whose? of whom?*

¿con quién (-es)? *with whom?*

¿cuál (-es)? *which? which one(s)?*

¿cuándo? *when?*

¿cuánto (-a)? *how much?*

¿cuántos (-as)? *how many?*

¿cómo? *how?*

¿por qué? *why?*

¿dónde? *where?*

¿de dónde? *(from) where?*

¿adónde? *(to) where?*

NOTE:

1. All interrogative words have a written accent.

2. In Spanish, questions have an inverted question mark (¿) at the beginning and a standard one (?) at the end.

3. When interrogatives (words such as; *¿qué?, ¿cuándo?, ¿dónde?*) are used in a question, the subject-verb order is reversed from the order in statements.

¿Qué **hacen ellos**?	*What are they doing?*
Ellos bailan.	*They are dancing.*
¿Dónde **está María**?	*Where is Mary?*
Ella está aquí.	*She is here.*

EXERCISE A

You're talking to a new student in your class for the first time. Write the questions that he has answered.

1. Me llamo Enrique Casas.

2. Yo soy de Colombia.

3. Vivo en la calle Oak.

4. Vivo con mis padres y mis dos hermanos.

5. Llegué a los Estados Unidos el mes pasado.

6. Tengo quince años.

7. Me gustan el tenis y el fútbol.

8. Tengo seis clases.

9. Son el inglés, la historia, la biología, las matemáticas, el español y la educación física.

10. El señor Época es mi profesor de historia.

11. Me gusta más la clase de inglés.

12. Después de las clases voy al parque.

13. Voy al parque porque me gusta remar en el lago.

> **b.** Both *¿qué?* and *¿cuál?* are equivalent to English "what?" and "which?," but the two words are not usually interchangeable in Spanish.
>
> **(1)** *¿Qué?* seeks a description, definition, or explanation.
>
> **¿Qué** es eso?   *What is that?*
>
> **(2)** *¿Cuál?* implies a choice or selection.
>
> **¿Cuál** perfume prefiere Ud.?   *Which perfume do you prefer?*
>
> NOTE:
>
> It's common practice in modern Spanish to substitute *¿qué?* for *¿cuál?*
>
> **¿Qué** camisa prefiere José? ⎫
>   ⎬ *Which shirt does José prefer?*
> **¿Cuál** camisa prefiere José? ⎭

EXERCISE B

Underline the interrogative word that is needed in each question.

1. ¿(Cuál /Qué) es esto?

2. ¿(Cuál / Qué) comes por la mañana?

3. ¿(Cuál /Qué) día es hoy?

4. ¿(Cuál / Cuáles) son los meses del año?

5. ¿(Cuál / Qué) es tu número de teléfono?

6. ¿(Cuál / Cuáles) postres te gustan más?

7. ¿(Cuál / Qué) vas a hacer con el dinero?

8. ¿(Cuál / Qué) haces cuando llueve?

9. ¿(Cuál / Qué) comes en un restaurante mexicano?

10. ¿(Cuál / Qué) libros leíste el año pasado?

EXERCISE C

While Linda is trying to study, her little sister is looking through a book that has many words she doesn't understand. According to the answers given, write the questions Linda's sister asks.

EXAMPLE: Un clavel es una flor.
   ¿Qué es **un clavel**?

1. Un pasaporte es un documento.

2. Una vaca es un animal.

3. Una manzana es una fruta.

4. El oro es un metal.

5. Un diccionario es un libro.

c. *¿Quién (-es)?, ¿a quién (-es)?,* and *¿de quién (-es)?*

(1). *¿Quién (-es)?* (who?) is used as the subject of the sentence.

¿Quién es este alumno?	*Who is this student?*
¿Quiénes son estos alumnos?	*Who are these students?*

(2). *¿A quién (-es)?* (whom?, to whom?) is used as the object of the verb (either direct or indirect object).

¿A quién ve Ud.?	*Whom do you see?*
¿A quiénes habla Ud.?	*To whom are you speaking?*

(3). *¿De quién (-es)* (whose?) is used to express possession.

¿De quién es el libro?	*Whose book is it? (Of whom is the book?)*
¿De quién (-es) son los libros?	*Whose books are they? (Of whom are the books?)*

EXERCISE D

Pablo never listens carefully when his friends are talking and always has to ask whom they're speaking about. Write the questions Pablo asks to find out who does the following.

EXAMPLE: Daniel juega al fútbol.
    ¿Quién juega al fútbol?

1. Mis hermanas van a una fiesta.

2. Carlos trabaja en el cine.

3. Nosotros vamos al cine esta noche.

4. Rosa no habla con su hermano.

5. Alberto quiere vender su bicicleta.

6. Yo tengo que estudiar para un examen.

7. Mis tíos llegan mañana.

EXERCISE E

You're with a friend at a party, but you don't know many of the people there. Write what you ask your friend about the other people at the party. They're indicated in parentheses.

EXAMPLE: Marta / hablar *(Gerardo y Hugo)*
    ¿A quiénes habla Marta?

1. Gloria / mirar *(su novio)*

2. Vincent y Sara / ver *(los señores Junco)*

3. Carmen / hablar *(Jorge y Fergus)*

4. tú / saludar *(Pilar)*

5. la señora Junco / servir café *(Jamal y Tony)*

6. Esteban / llamar *(sus padres)*

EXERCISE F

After the party, Mrs. Junco finds that several guests left things at the house. Write what Mrs. Junco asks her daughter, Raquel.

EXAMPLE: **¿De quién** es la bolsa?

1.

2.

3.

4.

5.

d. *¿Dónde?, ¿adónde?,* and *¿de dónde?*

    (1) *¿Dónde?* (where?) expresses location.

        ¿Dónde está Ana?   *Where's Ana?*

    (2) *¿Adónde?* (to where?) expresses motion to a place.

        ¿Adónde va Ud.?   *Where are you going?*

    (3) *¿De dónde?* (from where?) expresses origin.

        ¿De dónde es Ud.?   *Where are you from?*

EXERCISE G

When Julio's grandmother comes to visit, she wants to know where everyone is. Based on Julio's answers, tell what she asks him.

EXAMPLE: Mi papá está en el jardín.

          ¿Dónde está tu papá?

1. Mi mamá está en la cocina.

2. Mis hermanas están en el centro.

3. Mis amigos están en el parque.

4. Alfredo está en su dormitorio.

5. El perro está en el sótano.

EXERCISE H

As you go home on the last day of school, a friend asks you about other people's summer plans. Write down his questions.

EXAMPLE: Ricardo

¿**Adónde va** Ricardo durante las vacaciones?

1. Sue y Helen   *4.* los hermanos Pirelli

2. tú   *5.* Álvaro y su familia

3. la señora Núñez

EXERCISE I

You invite your cousin to an international fair at your school, where dishes from different countries are being served. Tell what she asks you about each dish.

EXAMPLE: los tacos

¿**De dónde son** los tacos?

1. la paella   *4.* el arroz con pollo

2. el asopao   *5.* la pizza

3. los frijoles negros   *6.* las empanadas

MASTERY EXERCISES

EXERCISE J

A friend is helping you study for a Spanish test. She gives you cards that contain statements. You are to form questions using an interrogative expression in place of the word(s) in boldface.

EXAMPLE: José vive en **Colorado**.

¿**Dónde** vive José?

1. **Pedro** es muy aplicado.

    ¿_____ es muy aplicado?

2. El cuaderno es **de Ana**.

    ¿_____ es el cuaderno?

3. Mis bebidas favoritas son **los jugos y las gaseosas**.

    ¿_____ tus bebidas favoritas?

4. Guatemala está **en la América Central**.

¿_____ está Guatemala?

5. Hoy es **el catorce de noviembre**.

¿_____ es la fecha de hoy?

6. El director va **a Italia**.

¿_____ va el director?

7. Un resfriado es **una enfermedad**.

¿_____ es un resfriado?

8. Pienso visitar **Inglaterra**.

¿_____ país piensas visitar?

9. La señora admira **el vestido de seda**.

¿_____ vestido admira la señora?

10. Hay **cincuenta y dos** semanas en un año.

¿_____ semanas hay en un año?

11. Juana tiene **dos** pares de zapatos.

¿_____ pares de zapatos tiene Juana?

12. Da un paseo **con su hija**.

¿_____ da un paseo?

13. **La bicicleta** vale doscientos dólares.

¿_____ vale doscientos dólares?

14. **Los alumnos** traducen mal.

¿_____ traducen mal?

15. Javier besó **a su abuela**.

¿_____ besó Javier?

16. Almuerzan **porque tienen hambre**.

¿_____ almuerzan?

17. Pablo invitó **a Luisa y Alfredo**.

¿_____ invitó Pablo?

18. Francisco tiene **dolor de muelas**.

¿——————————— tiene Francisco?

19. Mi abuelo cenó **a las seis y cuarto**.

¿——————————— cenó tu abuelo?

20. **Los alumnos** abrieron las ventanas.

¿——————————— abrieron las ventanas?

EXERCISE K

An exchange student from Argentina will be staying with your family. Write the questions that you'll ask her when you meet for the first time. From the list below, be sure to use a different interrogative expression in each question.

¿adónde?	¿cuál(es)?	¿cuánto?	¿dónde?	¿qué?
¿cómo?	¿cuándo?	¿de dónde?	¿por qué?	¿quién(es)?

EXERCISE L

You find a message on your answering machine but you cannot understand certain words in the message. Write the questions that you want to ask as you hear the following message.

1. Habla★★★★★★.

2. Son las ★★★★★★ de la tarde.

3. Estoy en el Hotel ★★★★★★.

4. Viajo con dos ★★★★★★.

5. Son muy ★★★★★★.

6. Ellas se llaman ★★★★★★ y ★★★★★★.

7. Vamos a pasar ★★★★★★ días en esta ciudad.

8. Espero ★★★★★★.

9. Llámame al número ★★★★★★.

10. Esta noche vamos al ★★★★★★.

11. Mis ★★★★★★ mandan muchos saludos.

EXERCISE M

You and a classmate are going to interview a group of Spanish-speaking students who are visiting your school for a month. You will then publish their answers in the school newspaper. Working with a classmate, prepare the questions that you will ask them in the interview. You may wish to include questions related to their indentity, nationality, age, purpose of the visit, length of the visit, their education system, special interests, places they have visited, impressions of their visit, etc.

Exclamations

Exclamatory words, like interrogative words, have written accents. The most common exclamatory words are:

¡Qué...!	*What ...! What a ...! How ...!*
¡Cuánto (-a) ...!	*How much ...!*
¡Cuántos (-as) ...!	*How many ...!*

¡**Qué** libro!	*What a book!*
¡**Qué** grande es!	*How large it is!*
¡**Cuántos** perros tienen!	*How many dogs they have!*
¡**Qué rápido** corre el coche!	*How fast the car runs!*

NOTE:

1. Exclamatory sentences have an inverted exclamation mark (¡) at the beginning and a standard one (!) at the end.

2. If there is an adjective next to a noun, the exclamation is made more intense by placing *tan* or *más* before the adjective.

¡Qué niño *tan (más)* inteligente!   *What an intelligent child!*

EXERCISE A

Two friends are raving about their vacation in Puerto Rico. Write what they say.

EXAMPLE: isla/bonita
¡**Qué** isla **tan (más)** bonita!

1. vacaciones/fabulosas
2. sol /fuerte
3. piscina /grande
4. clima/agradable
5. deliciosa /ser / la comida
6. playas/hay
7. simpáticos /ser/los puertorriqueños
8. bien /pasar /nosotros /las vacaciones

EXERCISE B

You take your younger brother to the zoo. Write what he exclaims upon seeing the following.

EXAMPLE: tren / moderno
¡Qué tren **más** moderno

1. cola / larga

2. tigre / feroz

3. globos / bonitos

4. pájaros / tranquilos

5. oso / grande

6. monos / cómicos

7. pavo real / elegante

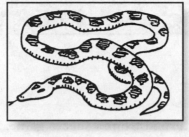

8. serpiente / larga

9. patos / graciosos

10. zoológico / interesante

EXERCISE C

You and some friends are returning home from a gathering where you heard about the trip another friend made last summer. Select the correct exclamatory word.

1. ¡(Qué /Cuánto) aburrido! Pasó el verano con su familia.

2. ¡(Qué /Cuánto) viaje más emocionante!

3. ¡(Cuántos /Cuántas) fotos sacó!

4. ¡(Qué /Cuánto) lugares más interesantes visitó!

5. ¡(Cuántos /Cuántas) cosas bonitas compró!

6. ¡(Qué /Cuánto) dinero costó!

7. ¡(Qué /Cuánto) cuentos más divertidos tiene del viaje!

8. ¡(Qué /Cuánto) simpática es su familia!

MASTERY EXERCISES

EXERCISE D

You've just returned from a soccer game. Your friend watched it on television and agrees with your comments. Tell what your friend exclaims when he hears your comments.

EXAMPLE: Era un partido aburrido.
             ¡**Qué** partido **más (tan)** aburrido!

1. Los futbolistas jugaron mal.

2. Necesitan más práctica.

3. El estadio es muy moderno.

4. Mucha gente salió temprano.

5. Perdieron muchos fanáticos.

6. Parecía un partido de aficionados.

EXERCISE E

Tell what comment you would make about the following things.

1. un día caluroso

2. una comida sabrosa

3. muchos amigos buenos

4. una película horrible

5. una fiesta divertida

6. una noticia increíble

CHAPTER 26

Possession

♦ 1 ♦ Expressing Possession

a. Possession is normally expressed in Spanish by *de* + the possessor.

el libro **de Juan**	*John's book*
la casa **de los señores Camacho**	*the Camachos' house*
los regalos **de los niños**	*the children's gifts*
el suéter **de mi hermana**	*my sister's sweater*

b. When the preposition *de* is followed by the definite article *el*, the contraction *del* is formed.

el juguete **del** niño	*the boy's toy*

c. When followed by a form of *ser*, *¿De quién (-es). . . ?* is equivalent to the English interrogative "Whose?".

¿De quién es la pelota?	*Whose ball is it?*
¿De quién son los guantes?	*Whose gloves are they?*
¿De quién es el coche nuevo?	*Whose new car is it?*
¿De quiénes son las revistas?	*Whose magazines are they?*

EXERCISE A

While visiting your house, Antonio wants to know whom the various things he sees there belong to. Using the cues provided, write Antonio's questions.

EXAMPLE: el televisor

   ¿De quién es el televisor?

1. los libros

2. la muñeca

3. los patines

4. los relojes

5. las llaves

6. las camisetas

7. las revistas

8. la calculadora

9. los anteojos

10. el estéreo

EXERCISE B

Using the cues provided, answer the questions Antonio asked you in Exercise A.

EXAMPLE: el televisor / mi papá
El televisor **es de** mi papá.

1. los libros / María

2. la muñeca / mi hermana

3. los patines / mi primo

4. los relojes / mis padres

5. las llaves / mi abuela

6. las camisetas / mis hermanos

7. las revistas / el vecino

8. la calculadora / mi madre

9. los anteojos / mi abuelo

10. el estéreo / mi mamá

EXERCISE C

While sitting in the dentist's waiting room, Gloria comments on the people she sees there. Tell what she says.

EXAMPLE: las uñas / la señora / largo
Las uñas **de** la señora **son largas**.

1. el sombrero / el niño / grande

2. los zapatos / la chica / feo

3. la pulsera / la enfermera / bonito

4. la máscara / el dentista / cómico

5. el suéter / el señor / ridículo

♦ 2 ♦ Possessive Adjectives

Singular	Plural	Meaning
mi amigo (-a)	**mis amigos (-as)**	*my*
tu amigo (-a)	**tus amigos (-as)**	*your (fam. sing.)*
su amigo (-a)	**sus amigos (-as)**	*his, her, its, their; your (formal)*
nuestro amigo	**nuestros amigos**	*our*
nuestra amiga	**nuestras amigas**	
vuestro amigo	**vuestros amigos**	*your (fam. pl.)*
vuestra amiga	**vuestras amigas**	

NOTE:

1. Possessive adjectives agree in gender (masculine or feminine) and number (singular or plural) with the person or thing possessed, not with the possessor.

nuestra madre	*our mother*
nuestras madres	*our mothers*
su libro	*his, her, its, their, your (formal), your (pl.) book*
sus libros	*his, her, its, their, your (formal), your (pl.) books*

2. *Nuestro* and *vuestro* have four forms. The other possessive adjectives have two forms.

EXERCISE D

Complete the description that Pedro wrote about a member of his family by inserting the appropriate possessive adjective in the spaces.

_____ familia y yo vivimos en la ciudad. _____ casa no es muy
          1.   2.

grande. Yo comparto _____ dormitorio con uno de _____
                              3.   4.

hermanos. _____ nombre es Enrique. _____ dormitorio es
                    5.   6.

amplio pero tengo que guardar todas _____ cosas en otro cuarto. Enrique tiene
                                              7.

muchos juguetes pero él tiene la costumbre de dejar _____ cosas en los otros cuartos
                                                              8.

de la casa. Enrique nunca usa _____ propia ropa. Le gusta usar _____ ropa.
                                        9.   10.

Usa _____ camisas y _____ suéteres. Aunque Enrique es _____
          11.   12.   13.

hermano menor, _____ talla es la misma. También le gusta molestar a _____
                        14.   15.

hermana. Siempre usa _____ cámara para sacar fotos. Entonces ella esconde
                              16.

_____ fotos. _____ papás van a darle a Enrique _____ propia
          17.   18.   19.

cámara para _____ cumpleaños.
                    20.

(EXERCISE E)

Roberta and some friends are returning from a camping trip. As they unpack the car, Roberta indicates whom the different things belong to. Use the appropriate possessive adjective to tell what she says.

EXAMPLE: una linterna / de Roberta
          Es mi linterna.

1. una cámara /de Alfredo

2. una grabadora /de nosotros

3. unas revistas / de Gregorio

4. una mochila /de Alfredo y Javier

5. los anteojos /de Roberto

6. unas monedas /de Pepe

(EXERCISE F)

Teresa is guessing who's who in the Jiménez family, but she doesn't know how to read a family tree. Help Teresa figure out the correct family relationships among the following people.

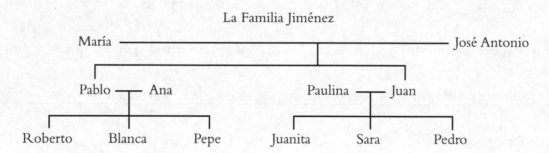

La Familia Jiménez

EXAMPLES: María es la madre de Pepe.
           No, María no es la madre de Pepe. **Ella es su abuela.**

OR: **No, María no es** la madre de Pepe. **Ella es la madre de Juan y de Pablo.**

1. Pablo es el padre de María.

2. Blanca es la hermana de Ana.

3. Juan y Paulina son los padres de María y José Antonio.

4. María y José Antonio son los primos de Juanita, Sara y Pedro.

5. Pedro es el hermano de Roberto, Blanca y Pepe.

6. Juanita y Sara son las primas de Pedro.

MASTERY EXERCISES

EXERCISE G

Answer these questions that your parent asks you about some new friends of yours. Use the appropriate possessive adjective in your responses.

1. ¿Cómo se llaman tus amigos nuevos? *(Jorge y Paco)*

2. ¿Cuáles son sus apellidos? *(Nogales, Fuentes)*

3. ¿Dónde está su casa? *(la calle Olmo)*

4. ¿Qué es su padre? *(ingeniero)*

5. ¿Viven cerca de tu tío Daniel? *(sí)*

6. ¿Cuántas personas hay en su familia? *(5)*

7. ¿Son miembros de tu equipo de baloncesto? *(sí)*

8. ¿Salen bien en sus exámenes? *(sí)*

9. ¿Conocen a tus otros amigos? *(sí)*

10. ¿Cuándo vas a su casa? *(mañana)*

EXERCISE H

Your host family in Guatemala wants to know about your family. In Spanish, write a note to your host family in which you describe your family. You may wish to include the following: the size of your family, who the family members are, descriptions of your siblings, their hobbies or interests, the house you live in, etc.

Demonstrative Adjectives

Demonstrative adjectives, like other adjectives, agree with their nouns in gender (masculine or feminine) and number (singular or plural).

	Masculine	Feminine	Meaning
Singular	este libro	esta casa	*this*
Plural	estos libros	estas casas	*these*

	Masculine	Feminine	Meaning
Singular	ese libro	esa casa	*that (near you)*
Plural	esos libros	esas casas	*those (near you)*

	Masculine	Feminine	Meaning
Singular	aquel libro	aquella casa	*that (at a distance)*
Plural	aquellos libros	aquellas casas	*those (at a distance)*

NOTE:

1. *Este (esta, estos, estas)* refers to what is near. *Ese (esa, esos, esas)* refers to what isn't so near. *Aquel (aquella, aquellos, aquellas)*, "that" (those), refers to what is remote from both the speaker and the person addressed.

Esta blusa es negra.	*This blouse is black.*
Mary, dame **esa** blusa que tienes en la mano.	*Mary, give me that blouse that you have in your hand.*
Mary, dame **aquella** blusa.	*Mary, give me that blouse over there.*

2. The adverbs *aquí* (here), *ahí* (there), and *allí* ([over] there) correspond to the demonstrative adjectives *este*, *ese*, and *aquel*.

Pon
{
este libro **aquí**.
ese cuaderno **ahí**.
aquel lápiz **allí**.
}

Put
{
this book here.
that notebook there.
that pencil over there.
}

EXERCISE A

A week before Mother's Day, Federico accompanies his mother to a department store. He tries to find out what she likes. Tell what he asks her.

EXAMPLE: prendedor
¿Te gusta **este** prendedor?

1. aretes **3.** anillos **5.** cadenas **7.** reloj

2. pulsera **4.** billetera **6.** perfume **8.** bolsa

EXERCISE B

Pilar and a friend are visiting a botanical garden. Tell what they say about the plants and flowers they see.

EXAMPLE: árboles /altos
Esos árboles **son** altos.

1. rosas /delicadas **3.** gladiolas /bonitas **5.** tulipanes /rojos **7.** pino / viejo

2. planta /pequeña **4.** orquídeas /exóticas **6.** cacto /feo **8.** dalia / elegante

EXERCISE C

You and a friend are visiting the observation deck at the tallest building in the city. As you look through the telescope, describe what you see.

EXAMPLE: iglesia /antigua
Aquella iglesia es antigua.

1. puente / largo **6.** estatua / famosa

2. barcos /caros **7.** parques / bonitos

3. estadio / grande **8.** casas / pequeñas

4. calle /corta **9.** universidad / privada

5. barrio / interesante

EXERCISE D

Alice is in a toy store looking for a gift for her brother and sister. She wants to know the price of the things she sees. Tell what she asks.

EXAMPLES: guante de béisbol /aquí
   ¿Cuánto cuesta este guante de béisbol?

   juego electrónico/ahí
   ¿Cuánto cuesta ese juego electrónico?

   muñecas/allí
   ¿Cuánto cuestan aquellas muñecas?

1. bicicletas / allí

2. patines/ ahí

3. osito de peluche / aquí

4. pelota / allí

5. discos compactos/ ahí

6. grabadora / aquí

7. raqueta de tenis / ahí

8. radio portátil / ahí

9. casa de muñecas / aquí

10. juego de damas / allí

EXERCISE E

Pepe is helping his mother do the shopping. Answer the questions he asks his mother, using the appropriate demonstrative adjective.

EXAMPLE: ¿Prefieres la sandía de ahí?
   Prefiero esa sandía.

1. ¿Te gustan los plátanos de allí?

2. Prefieres los tomates de aquí?

3. ¿Prefieres el melón de allí?

4. ¿Te gustan las manzanas de ahí?

5. ¿Te gusta la piña de aquí?

6. ¿Prefieres las peras de ahí?

7. ¿Quieres las uvas de aquí?

8. ¿Te gusta la fruta de allí?

EXERCISE F

Mr. Molina takes his family on a tour of the city where he went to college. Complete his statements with the appropriate demonstrative adjective.

Yo vivía aquí, en _____ pensión aquí. De _____ ventana en el tercer piso veía
          1.   2.

_____ monumentos que visitamos ayer. En _____ calle ahí había muchos
     3.   4.

restaurantes buenos y baratos. Tomaba el desayuno en _____ café; almorzaba en
                                                               5.

_____ restaurante de aquí y cenaba en _____ restaurante que está en la esquina.
     6.   *7.*

Compraba el periódico en _____ tienda que está al lado de la pensión. Allí había un cine, no
                                     8.

existía _____ biblioteca. _____ señor que anda ahí vendía los boletos. Vi muchas
         9.   *10.*

películas buenas en _____ cine. Jugaba al fútbol en _____ parque de allí. En el verano
                    11.   *12.*

iba a nadar en _____ piscina que está dentro del parque. Ahí conocí a _____
               13.   *14.*

señores que Uds. conocieron ayer. ¡Cómo me divertí en _____ ciudad!
                                               15.

◀⟨ MASTERY EXERCISES ⟩▶

EXERCISE G

You're in the cafeteria with a friend who's visiting your school. As you point to the different kinds of food, you comment on them. Use a demonstrative adjective to describe five of the items you see.

carne   galletas   papas fritas   postres

ensaladas   helado   pastel   sopa

EXAMPLE: **Este plátano** es delicioso.
                 Esas hamburguesas tienen queso.
                 Aquel pan es dulce.

EXERCISE H

You visit your sister at her college dormitory. In Spanish, write an entry in your journal in which you describe your visit. Use as many demonstrative adjectives as possible. You may wish to include the following: the size of the dormitory room, the decorations, e.g., posters, stuffed animals, etc., the computer, some items you recognize as yours, e.g., CDs, magazines, etc., the other students.

Word Study

CHAPTER

28

Cognates

Many Spanish and English words are related in form (spelling) and meaning because they derive from the same Latin or Greek root. Such pairs of words are called cognates, from *cognatus*, the Latin word for *relative*.

◆ 1 ◆ Exact Cognates

Spanish words spelled exactly as in English are called exact cognates.

actor	doctor	piano
central	hotel	radio (*m. & f.*)
color	idea	terrible
chocolate	motor	horrible

NOTE:

Although the spellings are identical in both languages, the pronunciations are different.

◆ 2 ◆ Direct Cognates

Many other cognates can be recognized if we bear in mind certain rules of Spanish spelling and pronunciation.

a. Many Spanish words that end in *-ción* have a corresponding English word that ends in *-tion*.

la pronunciación   *pronunciation*
la combinación   *combination*

EXERCISE A

Write the English words that correspond to the following Spanish words.

1. admiración

2. aviación

3. celebración

4. civilización

5. dirección

6. invitación

7. nación

8. producción

9. repetición

10. sección

b. The Spanish ending *–dad* corresponds to the English ending *–ty*

la sociedad   *society*

la electricidad   *electricity*

EXERCISE B

Write the English words that correspond to the following Spanish words.

1. autoridad   *5.* generosidad   *8.* realidad

2. capacidad   *6.* necesidad   *9.* universidad

3. curiosidad   *7.* posibilidad   *10.* variedad

4. eternidad

c. Many Spanish words that end in *-ia*, *-ía*, or *-io* end in *y* in English.

familia   *family*

fotografía   *photography*

vocabulario   *vocabulary*

EXERCISE C

Write the English words (or names) that correspond to the following Spanish words (or names).

1. Antonio   *5.* geografía   *8.* memoria

2. democracia   *6.* historia   *9.* necesario

3. dormitorio   *7.* María   *10.* remedio

4. farmacia

d. The Spanish ending *-oso* corresponds to the English ending *-ous*.

misterioso   *mysterious*

rigoroso   *rigorous*

EXERCISE D

Write the English words that correspond to the following Spanish words.

1. curioso   *5.* glorioso   *8.* numeroso

2. famoso   *6.* montañoso   *9.* precioso

3. furioso   *7.* nervioso   *10.* religioso

4. generoso

e. The Spanish adverbial ending *-mente* corresponds to the English adverbial ending - *ly*.

finalmente   *finally*

EXERCISE E

Write the English adverbs that correspond to the following Spanish adverbs.

1. correctamente

2. diligentemente

3. exactamente

4. frecuentemente

5. inmediatamente

6. naturalmente

7. perfectamente

8. rápidamente

9. recientemente

10. sinceramente

> **f.** In Spanish, there are almost no words beginning with *s* + consonant. Many English words beginning with *s* + consonant have corresponding Spanish words beginning with *-es*.
>
> espacio   *space*

EXERCISE F

Write the English words that correspond to the following Spanish words.

1. escena

2. escriba

3. España

4. especial

5. espectáculo

6. espíritu

7. espléndido

8. estudiante

9. estación

10. estúpido

♦ 3 ♦ Indirect Cognates (Part I)

Many Spanish words are indirectly related in form and meaning to English words. That is, there is a recognizable similarity in the forms of the two words, and an indirect connection in meaning. For example: *libro* means "book," and is related in form and meaning to the English word *library*.

SPANISH WORD	ENGLISH MEANING	ENGLISH COGNATE
agua	*water*	*aquarium*
alto	*high*	*altitude*
aprender	*to learn*	*apprentice*
árbol	*tree*	*arbor*
ascensor	*elevator*	*to ascend, rise*

SPANISH WORD	ENGLISH MEANING	ENGLISH COGNATE
avión	*airplane*	*aviation*
azul	*blue*	*azure*
bailar	*to dance*	*ballet*
beber	*to drink*	*beverage*
biblioteca	*library*	*bibliography (list of books)*
brazo	*arm*	*bracelet; embrace*
caliente	*hot*	*caloric*
calor	*heat*	*calorie*
cantar	*to sing*	*chant*
carne	*meat*	*carnivore (meat eater)*
carnicería	*butcher shop*	*carnivorous*
carnicero	*butcher*	*carnage (slaughter)*
cien, ciento	*hundred*	*century*
cine	*movies*	*cinema*
comprender	*to understand*	*comprehend*
contra	*against*	*contrary*
correr	*to run*	*current, courier (messenger, runner)*
creer	*to believe*	*credible, creed (belief)*
¿cuánto?	*how much?*	*quantity*
deber	*to owe*	*debt, debtor (ower)*
décimo	*tenth*	*decimal*
día	*day*	*diary*
diente	*tooth*	*dental, dentist*
dormir	*to sleep*	*dormant*
dormitorio	*bedroom*	*dormitory*
duro	*hard*	*endure*

EXERCISE G

For each of the English words given, write the related Spanish word and its meaning in English.

EXAMPLE: chant **cantar** (to sing)

1. ballet
2. dental
3. beverage
4. century
5. debt
6. apprentice
7. durable
8. aviation
9. quantity
10. comprehend
11. cinema
12. altitude
13. creed
14. dormitory
15. contrary

(EXERCISE H)

Match the Spanish words in column A with their English indirect cognates in column B.

_A_	_B_
1. día	**a.** carnivorous
2. agua	**b.** decimal
3. biblioteca	**c.** bibliography
4. décimo	**d.** diary
5. brazo	**e.** ascend
6. árbol	**f.** bracelet
7. carne	**g.** aquarium
8. azul	**h.** azure
9. ascensor	**i.** arbor
10. calor	**j.** caloric

(EXERCISE I)

Select the English word that expresses the meaning of the Spanish words given.

1. deber	to drink, to owe, to tell
2. cantar	to count, to sing, to buy
3. duro	tooth, dear, hard
4. comprender	to buy, to understand, to learn
5. ciento	scientist, hundred, central
6. bailar	to dance, to play ball, to believe
7. aprender	to open, to learn, to understand
8. cine	sign, century, movies
9. correr	to believe, to run, to want
10. alto	high, elevator, alter

(EXERCISE J)

Select the Spanish word that expresses the meaning of the English word given.

1. arm	brazo, amar, armario
2. against	contar, contestar, contra
3. library	libro, libre, biblioteca

4. heat   color, calor, carne

5. airplane   playa, aire, avión

6. how much?   ¿cuánto?, ¿cuándo?, ¿cuál?

7. tree   tres, árbol, alto

8. to drink   creer, bailar, beber

9. to sleep   dormir, decir, morir

10. tooth   día, duro, diente

♦ 4 ♦ Indirect Cognates (Part II)

SPANISH WORD	ENGLISH MEANING	ENGLISH COGNATE
edificio	*building*	*edifice (large building)*
enfermedad	*illness*	*infirmity*
enfermo	*sick, ill*	*infirmary*
escribir	*to write*	*scribble, scribe*
fábrica	*factory*	*fabricate (manufacture)*
fácil	*easy*	*facilitate (make easy)*
fácilmente	*easily*	*facile*
feliz	*happy*	*felicity (happiness)*
felizmente	*happily*	*felicitous*
flor	*flower*	*florist*
guante	*glove*	*gauntlet*
habitación	*room*	*habitation*
habitante	*inhabitant*	*inhabit*
hierba	*grass*	*herb*
lavar	*to wash*	*lavatory*
leer	*to read*	*legible*
lengua	*language*	*linguist (language specialist)*
libre	*free*	*liberty*
libremente	*freely*	*liberally*
libro	*book*	*library*
luna	*moon*	*lunar*
malo	*bad*	*malefactor (evildoer)*

SPANISH WORD	ENGLISH MEANING	ENGLISH COGNATE
mano	*hand*	*manually (by hand)*
mayor	*older, greater*	*major, majority*
médico	*doctor*	*medical*
menor	*lesser, younger*	*minor, minority*
menos	*less*	*minus*
mirar	*to look at*	*mirror*
morir	*to die*	*mortal, mortuary*
nuevo	*new*	*novelty*

EXERCISE K

For each English word, write the Spanish cognate and its meaning.

EXAMPLE: linguist **lengua** (language)

1. lunar
2. florist
3. malefactor
4. manual
5. facilitate
6. edifice
7. felicity
8. library
9. herb
10. scribble
11. majority
12. minor
13. mirror
14. medical
15. lavatory

EXERCISE L

Match the Spanish words in column A with their English cognates in column B.

A	*B*
1. habitación	*a.* liberty
2. menos	*b.* linguist
3. fábrica	*c.* mortal
4. guante	*d.* infirmary
5. leer	*e.* novelty
6. enfermo	*f.* gauntlet
7. libre	*g.* minus
8. nuevo	*h.* inhabit
9. morir	*i.* legible
10. lengua	*j.* fabricate

EXERCISE M

Select the English word that expresses the meaning of the Spanish words given.

1. menos   less, younger, lesser

2. morir   to look at, to die, to show

3. flor   flower, florist, flour

4. malo   mallet, male, bad

5. lavar   to wash, to arrive, to carry

6. habitación   habit, room, to inhabit

7. fácil   easy, factory, flower

8. edificio   office, building, exercise

9. mayor   greater, better, mayor

10. mano   man, manage, hand

EXERCISE N

Select the Spanish word that expresses the meaning of the English words given.

1. younger   mano, menor, menos

2. free   libro, libre, fresco

3. factory   fábrica, flor, fecha

4. happy   feliz, tristemente, bonito

5. grass   hoja, hierba, árbol

6. moon   lunes, moneda, luna

7. new   nuevo, nieve, nueve

8. to look at   ver, mirar, buscar

9. glove   mano, corbata, guante

10. doctor   médico, medio, enfermedad

♦ 5 ♦ Indirect Cognates (Part III)

SPANISH WORD	ENGLISH MEANING	ENGLISH COGNATE
patria	(native) country	patriotic
pedir	to request	petition
pensar	to think	pensive (thoughtful)
periódico	newspaper	periodical

SPANISH WORD	ENGLISH MEANING	ENGLISH COGNATE
pluma	*pen, feather*	*plume*
pobre	*poor*	*poverty*
precio	*price*	*precious*
primero	*first*	*primary*
pronto	*soon*	*prompt*
revista	*magazine*	*review*
sala	*hall, parlor*	*salon*
sentir	*to feel*	*sentiment*
sol	*sun*	*solar*
sonar	*to sound*	*sonorous (full sounding)*
tarde	*late*	*tardy*
tiempo	*time*	*tempo, temporary*
tierra	*earth, land*	*territory*
todo	*all*	*total*
valer	*to be worth*	*value*
vecino	*neighbor*	*vicinity (neighborhood)*
vender	*to sell*	*vendor*
ventana	*window*	*ventilate*
verdad	*truth*	*verify*
verde	*green*	*verdant (green)*
vida	*life*	*vital, vitality*
vivir	*to live*	*revive, vivid*

EXERCISE O

For each English word, give the Spanish indirect cognate and its meaning.

EXAMPLE: vicinity **vecino** (neighbor)

1. periodical

2. territory

3. poverty

4. salon

5. primary

6. solar

7. total

8. vivid

9. prompt

10. tempo

11. patriot

12. ventilate

13. plume

14. verdant

15. pensive

EXERCISE P

Match the Spanish words in column A with their English cognates in column B.

	A		B
1.	valer	a.	review
2.	vida	b.	sonorous
3.	precio	c.	precious
4.	revista	d.	value
5.	verdad	e.	verify
6.	pedir	f.	sentiment
7.	sonar	g.	vital
8.	tarde	h.	tardy
9.	sentir	i.	vendor
10.	vender	j.	petition

EXERCISE Q

Select the English word that expresses the meaning of the Spanish words given.

1.	periódico	newspaper, period, periodical
2.	sala	sale, hall, saloon
3.	verde	vertical, divert, green
4.	valer	bravery, to be worth, to fly
5.	pluma	pen, pencil, plum
6.	todo	bull, land, all
7.	vecino	time, summer, neighbor
8.	patria	country, father, courtyard
9.	ventana	window, vent, ventilate
10.	tierra	time, earth, terror

EXERCISE R

Select the Spanish word that expresses the meaning of the English words given.

1.	sun	sol, hijo, soldado
2.	price	costar, precio, valer
3.	to request	pedir, perder, poder
4.	truth	verdad, verde, viento

5. first   pronto, primero, primo

6. to sell   venir, ver, vender

7. to regret   sentir, sentar, triste

8. poor   pueblo, pobre, pronto

9. late   tiempo, ayer, tarde

10. life   vida, vivir, libre

♦ 6 ♦ Words Frequently Confused

In Spanish, there are many pairs of words that are written alike or sound alike, but have different meanings.

a. An accent mark is used to distinguish the following pairs of words:

como	*as, like*	que	*which, that, who*
¿cómo?	*how?*	¿qué?	*what?*
de	*of, from*	se	*himself, herself, yourself, themselves*
dé	*(Ud.) give (command)*	sé	*I know*
el	*the*	si	*if*
él	*he, him*	sí	*yes*
mas	*but*	te	*you, yourself*
más	*more*	té	*tea*
mi	*my*	tu	*your*
mí	*me*	tú	*you*

b. Some words are spelled identically even though they have very different meanings. Their meaning must be determined from the context.

cara	*face*	nada	*nothing, not …anything*
cara (caro)	*expensive*	nada	*you, he, she swims*
como	*as, like*	(la) parte	*part*
como	*I eat*	parte	*you, he, she departs*
entre	*between, among*	sobre	*on, over*
entre	*enter (command)*	(el) sobre	*envelope*
este	*this*	tarde	*late*
este	*east*	(la) tarde	*afternoon*
mañana	*tomorrow*	(el) traje	*suit*
mañana	*morning*	traje	*I brought*
media	*stocking*	vino	*wine*
media (medio)	*half*	vino	*you, he, she came*

c. The following groups of words may cause confusion because of their similar spelling and pronunciation.

cantar	*to sing*	llegar	*to arrive*
contar	*to count*	llevar	*to carry, to wear*
¿cuánto?	*how much?*	llorar	*to cry*
¿cuándo?	*when?*	llover	*to rain*
cuento	*story*	música	*music*
cuenta	*account; you, he, she counts*	música (músico)	*musician*
cuarto	*room, fourth*	nueve	*nine*
cuatro	*four*	nuevo	*new*
dólar	*dollar*	pero	*but*
dolor	*ache, pain*	perro	*dog*
falda	*skirt*	plata	*silver*
falta	*mistake, error*	plato	*dish, plate*
hermano	*brother*	primo	*cousin*
hermoso	*beautiful*	primero	*first*
hambre	*hunger*	queso	*cheese*
hombre	*man*	quiso	*you, he, she wanted*
hay	*there is, there are*	quince	*fifteen*
hoy	*today*	quinto	*fifth*
inglesa (inglés)	*English*	sentarse	*to sit down*
iglesia	*church*	sentirse	*to feel*
libre	*free*	veinte	*twenty*
libro	*book*	viento	*wind*
luna	*moon*	viaje	*trip*
lunes	*Monday*	viejo	*old, old man*

EXERCISE S

Select the word in parentheses that correctly completes each sentence.

1. ¿Expresas bien (tu / tú) idea?

2. ¿Expresas (tu / tú) bien la idea?

3. (Si / Sí), señor, soy norteamericana.

4. Su (pero / perro) es muy (hermano / hermoso).

5. ¿Cómo (se / sé) llama Ud.?

6. Colón es el (hambre / hombre) (que / qué) descubrió el Nuevo Mundo.

7. Su (primo / primero) habla demasiado.

8. ¿(Como / Cómo) están Uds.?

9. ¿Quién inventó (el / él) teléfono?

10. (De / Dé) Ud. el examen al maestro.

11. No vi (la luna / el lunes) anoche.

12. No (te / té) reconozco con la máscara.

13. El vapor (llega / lleva) el martes próximo.

14. Vamos al restaurante. Tengo (hambre / hombre).

15. Esa invitación es para (mi / mí).

EXERCISE T

Select the Spanish word that expresses the meaning of the English words given.

1.	fifth	quince, quinientos, quinto
2.	skirt	fábrica, falda, falta
3.	brother	hermano, hermoso, hierro
4.	ache	cabeza, dólar, dolor
5.	stocking	media, medio, mientras
6.	today	hay, hoja, hoy
7.	trip	viaje, viejo, vieja
8.	how much?	¿cómo?, ¿cuándo?, ¿cuánto?
9.	music	museo, música, músico
10.	silver	plata, plato, plaza
11.	cheese	queso, quise, quiso
12.	to rain	llenar, llorar, llover
13.	new	nieve, nueve, nuevo
14.	twenty	veinte, ventana, viento
15.	four	cuadro, cuarto, cuatro

MASTERY EXERCISES

Complete the crossword puzzle by filling in the Spanish cognates of the words given.

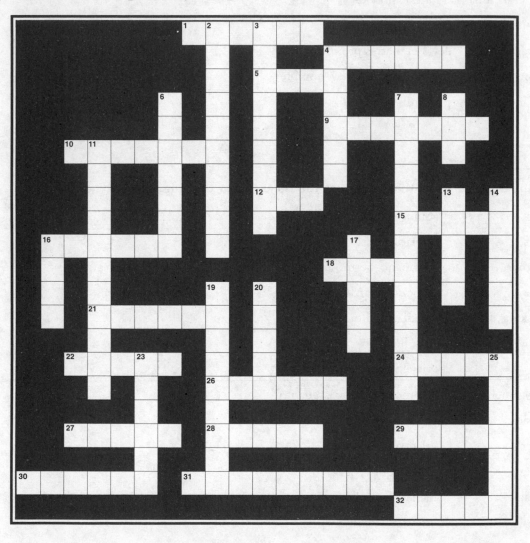

ACROSS

1. herb
4. prompt
5. lunar
9. remedy
10. memory
12. solar
15. carnivorous
16. decimal
18. salon
21. contrary
22. plume
24. tardy
26. tempo
27. mortal
28. novelty
29. poverty
30. quantity
31. geography
32. library

DOWN

2. invitation
3. religious
4. patriotic
6. furious
7. perfectly
8. diary
11. spectacle
13. bracelet
14. verify
16. endure
17. facilitate
19. inhabit
20. liberty
23. medical
25. infirmary

EXERCISE V

Write two meanings for each of the following words.

1. nada   *5.* parte   *8.* vino

2. tarde   *6.* sobre   *9.* media

3. mañana   *7.* como   *10.* este

4. cara

Synonyms and Antonyms

◆ 1 ◆ Synonyms

Synonyms are two or more words or expressions with the same meaning.

SYNONYMS	ENGLISH MEANINGS
a menudo, frecuentemente, muchas veces	*often, frequently*
a veces, algunas veces	*at times, sometimes*
al fin, finalmente	*finally, at last*
la alcoba, el dormitorio	*bedroom*
alegre, contento, feliz	*merry, happy*
algunos, unos, varios	*some, several*
la alumna, la estudiante	*pupil, student (f.)*
el alumno, el estudiante	*pupil, student (m.)*
la amiga, la compañera	*friend, companion (f.)*
el amigo, el compañero	*friend, companion (m.)*
andar, caminar, ir a pie	*to walk*
aplicado, diligente	*diligent, studious*
el automóvil, el carro, el coche	*automobile, car*
bonito, lindo	*pretty*
la camarera, la mesera, la moza	*waitress*
el camarero, el mesero, el mozo	*waiter*
el catarro, el resfriado	*cold (illness)*
comenzar, empezar	*to begin*
completar, terminar	*to complete, to finish*
comprender, entender	*to understand*
contestar, responder	*to answer*
el cuarto, la habitación	*room*

el cuento, la historia	*story*
la chica, la niña	*child (f.)*
el chico, el niño	*child (m.)*
delante de, en frente de	*in front of, opposite*
de nuevo, otra vez	*again*
desear, querer	*to wish; to want*
el doctor, el médico	*doctor (m.)*
la doctora, la médico	*doctor (f.)*
encontrar, hallar	*to find*
entonces, luego	*then*
el error, la falta	*error, mistake*
la esposa, la mujer	*wife*
el esposo, el marido	*husband*
el examen, la prueba	*test, examination*
la maestra, la profesora	*teacher (f.)*
el maestro, el profesor	*teacher (m.)*
la montaña, el monte	*mountain*
la nación, el país	*nation, country*
partir, salir	*to leave, to depart*
poseer, tener	*to own, to have*
regresar, volver	*to return*

EXERCISE A

Select the synonym of the words given.

1. amigo   dueño, compañero, hombre

2. delante de   alguna vez, sobre, enfrente de

3. cuarto   habitación, casa, jardín

4. unos   muchos, varios, pocos

5. estudiante   maestro, amigo, alumno

6. bonito   lindo, simpático, joven

7. examen   nota, prueba, trabajo

8. país   ciudad, nación, estado

9. niño   chico, esposo, hermano

10. desear   respetar, gastar, querer

11. poseer   conservar, tener, recordar

12. entonces   pronto, primero, luego

13. alegre   generoso, contento, triste

14. historia   cuento, noticia, propina

15. no hay de qué   por favor, gracias, de nada

EXERCISE B

Match the words in column A with their synonyms in column B.

A		*B*	
1. andar		**a.** terminar
2. empezar		**b.** maestro
3. salir		**c.** aplicado
4. encontrar		**d.** ir a pie
5. diligente		**e.** falta
6. profesor		**f.** alcoba
7. error		**g.** automóvil
8. completar		**h.** comenzar
9. coche		**i.** partir
10. dormitorio		**j.** hallar

EXERCISE C

Retell Hector's story by replacing the words in parentheses with their synonyms.

No voy al doctor *(a menudo)* _____ . Nunca *(quiero)* _____ ir al
                                    1.   2.

doctor. Pero la semana pasada tenía *(un catarro)* _____ muy fuerte. Llamé al doctor
                                                              3.

para hacer una cita. Mi mamá tenía *(el automóvil)* _____ y tuve que *(caminar)*
                                                                4.

_____ a su oficina. Había *(varias)* _____ personas en su consultorio.
         5.   6.

El doctor *(empezó)* _____ a examinarme la boca. Me dio una receta. Le di las gracias y
                          7.

él respondió: *(No hay de qué)* _____ . *(Volví)* _____ a casa a las cinco.
                                          8.   9.

Ahora estoy *(contento)* _____ porque no tengo catarro.
                                10.

EXERCISE D

Complete the crossword puzzle with the synonym of the words given.

ACROSS

1. estudiante

3. error

5. dormitorio

7. montaña

9. andar

10. responder

12. finalmente

13. desear

15. niño

17. maestro

20. país

21. frecuentemente

22. no hay de qué

DOWN

2. algunos

4. completar

5. contento

6. compañero

8. mozo

9. automóvil

10. historia

11. comprender

14. mujer

16. poseer

17. examen

18. de nuevo

19. regresar

♦ 2 ♦ Antonyms (Part I)

An antonym is a word or expression opposite in meaning to another word.

WORD / EXPRESSION	ANTONYM
a menudo, frecuentemente *frequently*	pocas veces *rarely*
abajo *down, downstairs*	arriba *up, upstairs*
abrir *to open*	cerrar *to close*
abuelo *grandfather*	nieto *grandson*
ahora *now*	después *later*
alegre, feliz *happy*	triste *sad*
algo *something*	nada *nothing*
alguien *someone*	nadie *no one*
alguno *some*	ninguno *none*
allí *there*	aquí *here*
alto *high*	bajo *low*
amigo *friend*	enemigo *enemy*
ancho *wide*	estrecho *narrow*
antes de *before*	después de *after*
aplicado, diligente *diligent*	perezoso *lazy*
ayer *yesterday*	mañana *tomorrow*
barato *cheap*	caro *expensive, dear*
bien *well*	mal *badly*
blanco *white*	negro *black*
bueno *good*	malo *bad*
caliente *hot, warm*	frío *cold*
cerca de *near*	lejos de *far from*
comprar *to buy*	vender *to sell*
con *with*	sin *without*
corto *short*	largo *long*
dar *to give*	tomar *to take*
debajo de *under, beneath*	sobre *upon, over*

delante de   *in front of*   detrás de   *in back of*

derecho   *right*   izquierdo   *left*

despacio   *slowly*   rápidamente   *quickly*

día   *day*   noche   *night*

EXERCISE E

Select the antonym of the word or expression given.

1. ancho   derecho, bastante, estrecho
2. enemigo   amigo, primo, dueño
3. arriba   hacia, abajo, detrás de
4. mal   demasiado, mucho, bien
5. blanco   plata, negro, alto
6. vender   comprar, valer, prestar
7. despacio   poco a poco, espacio, rápidamente
8. nada   alguno, algo, corto
9. bajo   alto, vacío, grande
10. abrir   cenar, celebrar, cerrar
11. frío   nieve, caliente, sur
12. caro   rico, barato, mucho
13. alguien   unos, muchos, nadie
14. más tarde   ahora, pocas veces, al fin
15. feliz   contento, gordo, triste

EXERCISE F

Match the word in column A with its antonym in column B.

A	*B*
1. frecuentemente	*a.* nieto
2. diligente	*b.* dar
3. tomar	*c.* corto
4. derecho	*d.* perezoso
5. alguno	*e.* mañana
6. largo	*f.* debajo de
7. sobre	*g.* pocas veces
8. abuelo	*h.* ninguno
9. ayer	*i.* día
10. noche	*j.* izquierdo

EXERCISE G

Sam and his brother have returned from visiting a friend's new home. His brother always contradicts what Sam says. Tell what his brother says by using an appropriate antonym in each sentence.

EXAMPLE: Ricky es nuestro amigo.
          Ricky es nuestro **enemigo**.

1. Hay una piscina detrás de la casa.

2. El agua de la piscina está fría.

3. Su hermana está muy contenta.

4. Antes de salir de la casa tomamos un café.

5. Arturo es una persona diligente.

6. Le gusta salir con sus amigos.

7. Viven cerca de la universidad.

8. Nadie estaba en la piscina.

9. Viven en la parte alta de la ciudad.

10. La casa es de color blanco.

EXERCISE H

Answer your parents' questions using the antonym in parentheses.

1. ¿Deseas comer ahora? *(después)*

2. ¿Compras las plumas baratas? *(caras)*

3. ¿Te gusta comer pescado a menudo? *(pocas veces)*

4. ¿Estudias antes de cenar? *(después de)*

5. ¿Vas a vender limonada? *(comprar)*

♦ 3 ♦ Antonyms (Part II)

WORD / EXPRESSION	ANTONYM
empezar *to begin*	terminar *to end, to finish*
entrar *to enter*	salir (de) *to leave*
este *east*	oeste *west*
fácil *easy*	difícil *difficult, hard*
feo *ugly*	hermoso *beautiful*

feo *ugly*	bonito, lindo *pretty*
fuerte *strong*	débil *weak*
gordo *chubby, fat*	flaco *thin*
grande *large, big*	pequeño *small, little*
hombre *man*	mujer *woman*
invierno *winter*	verano *summer*
levantarse *to stand up*	sentarse *to sit down*
lleno *full*	vacío *empty*
más *more*	menos *less*
mayor *greater, older*	menor *lesser, younger*
mediodía *noon*	medianoche *midnight*
moreno *brunette*	rubio *blond*
mucho *much*	poco *little*
no *no*	sí *yes*
norte *north*	sur *south*
nunca *never*	siempre *always*
olvidar *to forget*	recordar *to remember*
perder *to lose*	encontrar, hallar *to find*
perder *to lose*	ganar *to win*
pobre *poor*	rico *rich*
ponerse *to put on*	quitarse *to take off*
pregunta *question*	respuesta *answer*
preguntar *to ask*	contestar, responder *to answer*
presente *present*	ausente *absent*
presente *present*	pasado *past*
ruido *noise*	silencio *silence*
subir *to go up*	bajar *to go down*
tarde *late*	temprano *early*
viejo *old*	joven *young*
viejo *old*	nuevo *new*
vivir *to live*	morir *to die*

EXERCISE I

Select the antonym of the words given.

1. empezar   lograr, comenzar, terminar

2. mediodía   media, medianoche, remedio

3. mayor   numeroso, menor, medio

4. viejo   nuevo, noveno, nueve

5. encontrar   perder, inventar, desaparecer

6. olvidar   recordar, reconocer, referir

7. moreno   pardo, rubio, rosado

8. norte   sur, este, oeste

9. fuerte   duro, nervioso, débil

10. pregunta   contestar, responder, respuesta

11. más   menor, poco, menos

12. vivir   existir, morir, romper

13. subir   sentir, bajar, poseer

14. nunca   siempre, nadie, algo

15. entrar   sacar, llenar, salir

EXERCISE J

Match the words in column A with their antonyms in column B.

_A_	_B_
1. este	a. silencio
2. levantarse	b. mujer
3. no	c. poco
4. ponerse	d. vacío
5. mucho	e. viejo
6. hombre	f. contestar
7. joven	g. oeste
8. preguntar	h. sí
9. ruido	i. quitarse
10. lleno	j. sentarse

EXERCISE K

Laura's grandfather always mixes up his stories. Correct the following one by replacing the words in parentheses with their antonyms.

Ayer vimos una escena *(fea)* _____ . *(Enfrente de)* _____ las dos casas hay un

1.   2.

espacio *(pequeño)* _____ . La niña que vive *(aquí)* _____ estaba muy *(contenta)*

3.   4.

_____ . Ella *(compraba)* _____ limonada porque hacía *(frío)* _____ .

5.   6.   7.

Una mujer muy *(alta)* _____ y *(flaca)* _____ llegó. Quería *(vender)*

8.   9.

_____ una limonada porque era *(cara)* _____ . Tenía *(poco)* _____

10.   11.   12.

dinero y bebió toda la limonada. Ahora todas las botellas están *(llenas)* _____ y

13.

todo el mundo está *(triste)* _____ .

14.

EXERCISE L

Adrián's brother never listens to what he says and usually answers his questions foolishly. Answer Adrian's questions negatively, using an antonym for the words in boldface.

EXAMPLE: ¿Es **difícil** la geografía?

        No, la geografía es **fácil**.

1. ¿Es **bonita** tu amiga?

2. ¿Hay mucha nieve en el **invierno**?

3. ¿Hace calor en el **sur**?

4. ¿Hace sol al **mediodía**?

5. ¿Tienen muchos juguetes los niños **ricos**?

6. ¿Son **grandes** los elefantes?

7. ¿Sacas tú **buenas** notas en las clases?

8. ¿Te gusta el **silencio**?

9. ¿Llegas **temprano** a la escuela?

10. ¿Siempre **encuentras** las llaves?

EXERCISE M

Complete the crossword puzzle with the antonym of the words given.

ACROSS

2. comprar
3. nada
4. delante de
5. a menudo
9. alguno
10. caliente
11. ayer
13. alto
14. allí
16. alegre
18. con
19. abuelo
21. enemigo
22. diligente
23. corto
24. sobre

DOWN

1. lejos de
3. abajo
6. después
7. abrir
8. caro
9. alguien
12. día
15. derecho
17. ancho
20. blanco

EXERCISE N

Match the words in column A with their synonyms in column B and their antonyms in column C.

A	B (synonym)	C (antonym)
1. alegre	**a.** comenzar	**A.** preguntar
2. delante de	**b.** unos	**B.** terminar
3. bonito	**c.** diligente	**C.** triste
4. amigo	**d.** lindo	**D.** feo
5. empezar	**e.** hallar	**E.** ningunos
6. a menudo	**f.** feliz	**F.** detrás de
7. responder	**g.** contestar	**G.** enemigo
8. algunos	**h.** enfrente de	**H.** perezoso
9. aplicado	**i.** frecuentemente	**I.** perder
10. encontrar	**j.** compañero	**J.** pocas veces

EXERCISE O

Describe the pictures using the following words.

ancho	invierno	mediodía	quitarse
bajar	lleno	menor	rubio
débil	más	menos	subir
estrecho	mayor	moreno	vacío
fuerte	medianoche	ponerse	verano

1.

2.

3.

4.

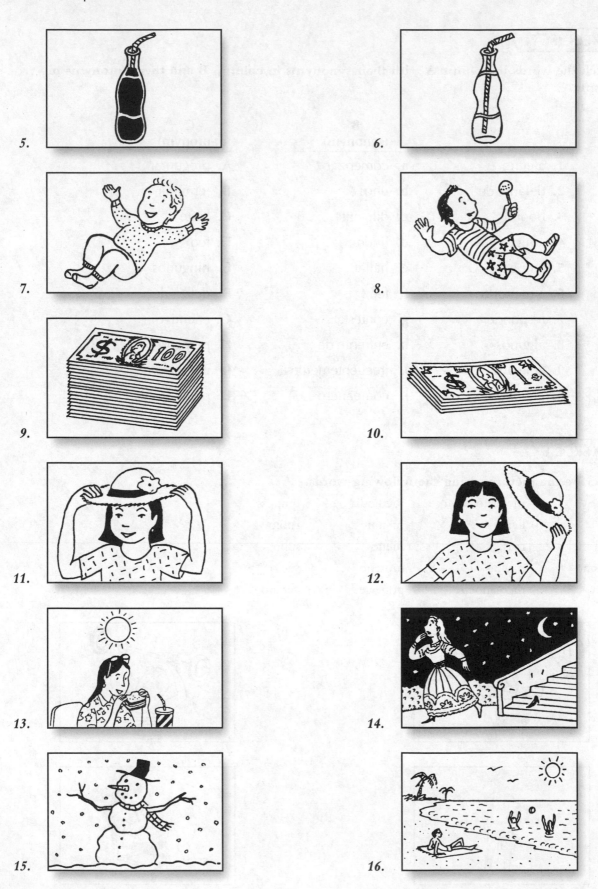

17.

18.

19.

20.

CHAPTER 30

Topical (Thematic) Vocabulary

◆ 1 ◆ Personal Identification

a. Características físicas

alto, -a *tall*	joven *young*
bajo, -a *short*	lindo, -a *pretty*
bonito, -a *pretty*	moreno, -a *dark-haired, dark-skinned*
delgado, -a *thin*	pelirrojo, -a *redheaded*
feo, -a *ugly*	rubio, -a *fair, blond*
gordo, -a *fat*	trigueño, -a *dark-skinned*
guapo -a *handsome*	viejo, -a *old*

b. Características de la personalidad

aburrido, -a *boring*	independiente *independent*
agradable *pleasant, nice, likable*	inteligente *intelligent*
amable *courteous, kind*	interesante *interesting*
antipático, -a *unpleasant, not nice*	irresponsable *irresponsible*
bueno, -a *good*	malo, -a *bad*
cariñoso, -a *affectionate*	paciente *patient*
desagradable *unpleasant*	popular *popular*
divertido, -a *fun, amusing*	responsable *responsible*
egoísta *selfish*	simpático, -a *friendly, nice, likable*
generoso, -a *generous*	tacaño, -a *stingy*
impaciente *impatient*	tonto, -a *dumb; stupid*

c. Otras palabras

el apellido *last name*	el lugar de nacimiento *place of birth*
el cumpleaños *birthday*	la nacionalidad *nationality*
la dirección *address*	el nombre *name*
la edad *age*	el número de teléfono *telephone number*
la fecha de nacimiento *date of birth*	

EXERCISE A

Select the word in each group that is in a different category from the other three.

1. gordo, desagradable, lindo, alto

2. generoso, divertido, cariñoso, bajo

3. paciente, bueno, pelirrojo, independiente

4. tacaño, moreno, rubio, pelirrojo

5. edad, simpático, cumpleaños, fecha de nacimiento

6. egoísta, joven, bueno, popular

7. apellido, tacaño, lugar de nacimiento, dirección

8. aburrido, desagradable, guapo, irresponsable

9. delgado, tonto, viejo, moreno

10. impaciente, responsable, malo, rubio

EXERCISE B

How would you describe yourself? Make a list of five adjectives that describe your appearance; and then, make a list of five adjectives that describe your personality.

EXERCISE C

Your new key pal would like to know more about you. She asks you to write a description of yourself in a minimum of five sentences.

EXERCISE D

You have to exchange a gift you bought but you can't find the salesperson who helped you. In a minimum of five sentences, describe him (her) to the store manager.

EXERCISE E

Mrs. García is talking about Luis and Ricky, her twin grandsons. Their personalities are complete opposites. List at least five adjectives that she would use to describe each boy.

EXERCISE F

Complete the crossword puzzle with the appropriate Spanish words for the clues given in English.

ACROSS

1. patient
5. selfish
7. interesting
10. name
11. fat
16. intelligent
17. dumb
18. young
19. handsome
20. age
22. friendly
25. bad
26. blonde
27. pretty
28. last name
29. dark hair

DOWN

1. redheaded
2. good
3. ugly
4. generous
6. courteous, kind
8. tall
9. stingy
12. amusing
13. thin
14. old
15. independent
21. address
23. boring
24. affectionate

◆ 2 ◆ House and Home

a. La casa

la alcoba *bedroom*	el estudio *study, den*
el apartamento *apartment*	el garaje *garage*
el ascensor *elevator*	la habitación *room*
el balcón *balcony*	el jardín *garden*
el (cuarto de) baño *bathroom*	el pasillo *corridor, hall*
la casa *house, home*	el patio *courtyard*
la casa particular *private house*	la piscina *swimming pool*
la cocina *kitchen*	el piso *floor, story, apartment*
el comedor *dining room*	la sala *parlor, living room*
el cuarto *room*	la sala de estar *family room*
el desván *attic*	el sótano *cellar, basement*
el dormitorio *bedroom*	el suelo *floor, ground*
la escalera *stairs, staircase*	la terraza *terrace*

b. Los muebles

la alfombra *rug, carpet*	la lámpara *lamp*
el armario *closet*	la mesa *table*
la cama *bed*	los muebles *furniture*
la cómoda *bureau, dresser*	la silla *chair*
la cortina *curtain*	el sillón *armchair*
el escritorio *desk*	el sofá *sofa*

EXERCISE G

In each group, select the word that is not thematically in the same category as the other three.

1. comedor, alcoba, sótano, libro
2. dormitorio, habitación, coche, sala
3. sótano, cama, armario, silla
4. mesa, patio, sofá, cómoda
5. escalera, ascensor, alfombra, piso

6. pasillo, estudio, desván, lámpara
7. terraza, sala, cortina, patio
8. armario, mesa, cómoda, garaje
9. alfombra, apartamento, casa particular, piso
10. garaje, estudio, cama, patio

EXERCISE H

Match the activities in column A with the appropriate room in column B.

	A		*B*
1.	dormir	*a.*	baño
2.	preparar la comida	*b.*	garaje
3.	plantar flores	*c.*	alcoba
4.	lavarse la cara	*d.*	sala
5.	nadar	*e.*	pasillo
6.	estacionar el carro	*f.*	cocina
7.	estudiar y hacer la tarea	*g.*	piscina
8.	subir de un piso a otro	*h.*	jardín
9.	ir de un cuarto a otro	*i.*	estudio
10.	ver la televisión	*j.*	escalera

EXERCISE I

You're planning your dream house. Using the plan below, label the different rooms shown in the floor plan.

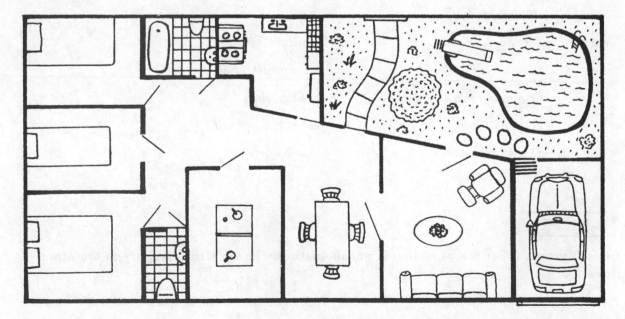

EXERCISE J

Your family is moving to a larger house and you will no longer have to share your room with a sibling. Prepare a list of 5 pieces of furniture and 5 accessories you would like to have in your room.

EXERCISE K

A friend is telling you about her house. If the statement is true, write *Sí*; if it's false, correct it by replacing the word(s) in boldface.

1. Puse una alfombra en **la mesa**.
2. Solamente **una familia** vive en una casa particular.
3. **El suelo** es el cuarto más grande del apartamento.
4. La lámpara y la mesa son **muebles**.
5. Mi madre prepara las comidas en **la escalera**.
6. Mi papá estaciona el carro en **la sala**.
7. Ponemos las cortinas en **las camas**.
8. Mi abuelo se sienta en **la cómoda** para leer el periódico.
9. Guardo la ropa en **el balcón**.
10. Uso **el desván** para ir de un piso a otro.

◆ 3 ◆ Family Life

la abuela	*grandmother*	la niña	*girl*
el abuelo	*grandfather*	el niño	*boy*
los abuelos	*grandparents*	la nuera	*daughter-in-law*
el cuñado	*brother-in-law*	el padrastro	*stepfather*
la cuñada	*sister-in-law*	el padre	*father*
la esposa	*wife*	los padres	*parents*
el esposo	*husband*	el padrino	*godfather*
la familia	*family*	los papás	*parents*
la hermana	*sister*	el pariente	*relative*
el hermano	*brother*	la prima	*cousin*
los hermanos	*brothers, brothers and sisters*	el primo	*cousin*
la hija	*daughter*	la sobrina	*niece*
el hijo	*son*	el sobrino	*nephew*
los hijos	*children, sons and daughters*	el suegro	*father-in-law*
la madrastra	*stepmother*	la suegra	*mother-in-law*
la madre	*mother*	la tía	*aunt*
la madrina	*godmother*	el tío	*uncle*
la mamá	*mom, mother*	los tíos	*uncles, aunts and uncles*
la nieta	*granddaughter*	el yerno	*son-in-law*
el nieto	*grandson*		

EXERCISE L

If the statement is true, write *Sí*; if it's false, correct it by replacing the words in boldface.

1. El hijo de mi tío es **mi hermano**.

2. La madre de mi madre es **mi abuela**.

3. La hermana de mi papá es **mi prima**.

4. El yerno de mi abuelo es **mi sobrino**.

5. Yo soy **el hijo** de mi abuelo.

6. Mis abuelos son los suegros de **mis hermanos**.

7. **Mi sobrino** es el hijo de mis padres.

8. Mi madre **es la nuera** de mi padre.

9. **Mis nietos** son los sobrinos de mis papás.

10. Mi padrastro es **el hermano** de mi madre.

EXERCISE M

Match the words in Columns A and B logically, following the example.

EXAMPLE: padre   **hija**

<u>A</u>	<u>B</u>
1. abuelos	*a.* padres
2. sobrina	*b.* suegra
3. yerno	*c.* cuñado
4. niño	*d.* nietos
5. primos	*e.* tío
6. hijos	*f.* madre
7. cuñada	*g.* primas

EXERCISE N

Identify the family relationship in each statement. Write the words in the space provided.

EXAMPLE: La hija de mi padre es mi **hermana**.

1. Los padres de mis tíos son mis _____ .

2. El hermano de mi madre es mi _____ .

3. Los hijos de mis tíos son los _____ de mis padres.

4. El hermano de mi papá es el _____ de mi mamá.

5. Mi padre es el _____ del padre de mi madre.

6. Mis abuelos maternos son los _____ de mi padre.

7. Yo soy el _____ de los hijos de mis tíos.

◆ 4 ◆ Community/Neighborhood

a. Areas

el barrio	*neighborhood*	el pueblo	*town*
el campo	*country*	las afueras	*suburbs*
el centro	*downtown*	el vecindario	*neighborhood*
la ciudad	*city*		

b. Los edificios

el aeropuerto	*airport*	el hospital	*hospital*
el banco	*bank*	el hotel	*hotel*
la biblioteca	*library*	la iglesia	*church*
el café	*coffee shop*	el museo	*museum*
la casa	*house*	el palacio	*palace*
la catedral	*cathedral*	el parque	*park*
el centro comercial	*mall*	la piscina	*swimming pool*
el centro comunal	*community center*	el puente	*bridge*
el cine	*movies, movie theater*	el restaurante	*restaurant*
el correo	*post office*	el teatro	*theater*
el edificio	*building*	la terminal de autobuses	*bus terminal*
la escuela	*school*	el templo	*temple*
la estación	*(train) station*	la universidad	*university*
el estadio	*stadium*		

c. Las tiendas

el almacén	*department store*	el mercado	*market*
la bodega	*grocery store*	la panadería	*bakery*
la carnicería	*butcher*	la pastelería	*pastry shop*
la farmacia	*drugstore, pharmacy*	el supermercado	*supermarket*
la ferretería	*hardware store*	la tienda	*store, shop*
la florería	*flower shop*	la tienda de ropa	*clothing store*
la frutería	*fruit store*	la tintorería	*dry cleaners*
la lavandería	*laundry*	la zapatería	*shoe store*

EXERCISE O

In each group, select the word that is *not* related to the other three.

1. familia, templo, iglesia, catedral

2. carnicería, bodega, panadería, templo

3. universidad, escuela, fiesta, biblioteca

4. lámpara, estación, terminal, aeropuerto

5. parque, estadio, piscina, esquina

6. almacén, zapatería, hospital, tienda de ropa

7. carnicería, puente, panadería, frutería

8. cine, museo, teatro, lavandería

9. café, edificio, museo, palacio

10. casa, centro, palacio, hotel

EXERCISE P

Match each activity in column A with the location where it takes place in column B.

A	*B*
1. comer	*a.* el cine
2. estudiar	*b.* el hotel
3. comprar estampillas	*c.* la piscina
4. ver una película	*d.* el restaurante
5. curar a los enfermos	*e.* la estación
6. nadar	*f.* la biblioteca
7. caminar	*g.* el banco
8. buscar un libro	*h.* el correo
9. rezar	*i.* el estadio
10. ver un partido	*j.* el museo
11. tomar el tren	*k.* la escuela
12. ver una obra de arte	*l.* el café
13. buscar a un turista	*m.* la iglesia
14. tomar el autobús	*n.* el aeropuerto
15. tomar un café	*o.* el hospital
16. cambiar dinero	*p.* el parque
17. viajar en avión	*q.* la terminal

EXERCISE Q

You're running some errands in town. Indicate the stores you'll visit to buy the following items.

1. rosas, claveles y geranios

2. refrescos, leche, queso

3. jamón, biftec, pollo

4. una camisa blanca, una corbata

5. manzanas, peras, uvas

6. aspirinas, algodón, curitas

7. zapatos, pantuflas

8. un pastel de cumpleaños

EXERCISE R

Read the passages below and determine in each case which store the person should go to.

1. Ramón va a pasar el fin de semana en las montañas con unos amigos. Tiene que comprar un suéter grueso porque va a hacer mucho frío allí. ¿Adónde debe ir Ramón?

2. Vamos a tener invitados a cenar el sábado por la noche. Mi mamá prepara una lista de las cosas que necesita para preparar la cena. ¿Adónde debe ir mi mamá?

3. Susana y Alicia van a pasar las vacaciones en Puerto Rico. Su avión sale a las tres de la tarde. ¿Adónde deben ir las chicas?

4. Pablo está enfermo. El médico le da una receta para una medicina. ¿Adónde debe ir Pablo?

5. Mi prima se casa mañana. La ceremonia de la boda es a las doce. ¿Adónde debo ir?

EXERCISE S

You and your family are driving through Mexico in a van. You arrive in a small town around lunchtime. Tell which places the members of your family want to visit in the town.

EXAMPLE. Mi padre **quiere visitar el museo**.

1. Mi madre

2. Mi hermano

3. Mi hermana

4. Mis padres

5. Mi abuela

6. Yo

◆ 5 ◆ Physical Environment

a. La geografía

el cayo   *key (Key West)*

el continente   *continent*

la cordillera   *mountain range*

el estado   *state*

el golfo   *gulf*

la isla   *island*

el país   *country, nation*

la península   *peninsula*

b. La naturaleza

el aire *air*	el mar *sea*
el árbol *tree*	la montaña *mountain*
el bosque *forest*	el mundo *world*
el campo *country*	la naturaleza *nature*
el cielo *sky*	la nieve *snow*
el clavel *carnation*	la nube *cloud*
la estrella *star*	la planta *plant*
la flor *flower*	la playa *beach, seashore*
la hierba *grass*	el río *river*
la hoja *leaf*	la rosa *rose*
el jardin *garden*	el sol *sun*
el lago *lake*	la tierra *earth, land*
la luna *moon*	la violeta *violet*
la lluvia *rain*	

c. Las estaciones y el tiempo

el calor *heat, warmth*	el sol *sun*
la estación *season*	la temperatura *temperature*
el fresco *coolness*	el tiempo *weather*
el frío *cold*	el verano *summer*
el grado *degree*	el viento *wind*
el invierno *winter*	hace (calor, fresco, frío, sol, viento)
la lluvia *rain*	*it's (hot, cool, cold, sunny, windy)*
la nieve *snow*	llover *to rain*
el otoño *autumn*	nevar *to snow*
la primavera *spring*	

d. Los meses

enero *January*	julio *July*
febrero *February*	agosto *August*
marzo *March*	septiembre *September*
abril *April*	octubre *October*
mayo *May*	noviembre *November*
junio *June*	diciembre *December*

e. Los días

el domingo	*Sunday*	el jueves	*Thursday*
el lunes	*Monday*	el viernes	*Friday*
el martes	*Tuesday*	el sábado	*Saturday*
el miércoles	*Wednesday*		

EXERCISE T

In each group, select the word that is *not* related to the other three.

1. mundo, cielo, aire, mercado

2. clavel, lluvia, rosa, violeta

3. tienda, bosque, montaña, campo

4. nieve, viento, estado, lluvia

5. playa, ciudad, estado, país

6. árbol, planta, hoja, cielo

7. primavera, estrella, otoño, invierno

8. estación, abril, noviembre, enero

9. verano, miércoles, sábado, viernes

10. calor, luna, frío, viento

11. tierra, lago, río, mar

12. cielo, estrella, sol, pueblo

13. hierba, flor, mundo, planta

14. día, mes, estación, fresco

15. tiempo, frío, lluvia, tierra

EXERCISE U

If the statement is true, write *Sí*; if it's false, correct it by replacing the word(s) in boldface.

1. Después de abril viene el mes de **mayo**.

2. Hace calor en **el invierno**.

3. Cuando **hace sol** uso un paraguas.

4. El sábado y el domingo son **el fin de semana**.

5. Las rosas y las violetas son **árboles**.

6. Durante la noche vemos **el sol** en el cielo.

7. El verano y el otoño son **meses**.

8. El Misisipí es **un lago**.

9. California es **un país**.

10. Puerto Rico es **una ciudad**.

11. Hay edificios altos en **el campo**.

12. Vemos muchas estrellas en **el bosque**.

13. Nadamos en **las afueras**.

14. Un árbol tiene muchas **nubes**.

15. En el parque hay **un lago**.

EXERCISE V

You're talking about your hometown to your host family in Venezuela. Describe or explain how the following things are where you live.

1. una estación del año

2. tu ciudad o pueblo

3. el mes de febrero

4. las afueras

5. el cielo en una noche de verano

♦ 6 ♦ Meals / Food / Beverages

a. Las comidas

el almuerzo *lunch*	almorzar *to have (eat) lunch*
la cena *supper, dinner*	cenar *to have (eat) supper*
la comida *meal, food*	desayunar *to have (eat) breakfast*
el desayuno *breakfast*	

b. La comida / la bebida

el agua *water*	la naranja *orange*
el alimento *food*	el pan *bread*
el (la) azúcar *sugar*	la papa, la patata *potato*
el café *coffee*	el pastel *pie, pastry*
la carne *meat*	la pera *pear*
la cereza *cherry*	el pescado *fish*
el chocolate *chocolate*	la pimienta *pepper (spice)*
la ensalada *salad*	el pimiento *pepper (vegetable)*
la fruta *fruit*	el pollo *chicken*
la gaseosa *soda, pop*	el postre *dessert*
el helado *ice cream*	el refresco *refreshment, soda*
el huevo *egg*	la sal *salt*
la leche *milk*	la sopa *soup*
la legumbre *vegetable*	el té *tea*
el limón *lemon*	el vino *wine*
la mantequilla *butter*	beber *to drink*
la manzana *apple*	comer *to eat*

EXERCISE W

In each group, select the word that is *not* related to the other three.

1. fruta, manzana, cereza, puente

2. naranja, azul, ensalada, pera

3. vino, hoja, café, agua

4. queso, pan, huevo, burro

5. almuerzo, cena, chocolate, desayuno

6. sopa, azúcar, pimienta, sal

7. comer, almorzar, caminar, beber

8. pollo, refresco, carne, pescado

9. leche, mantequilla, queso, limón

10. legumbre, postre, helado, pastel

11. té, pescado, chocolate, café

12. cereza, pera, helado, naranja

EXERCISE X

Answer your friend's questions about your eating preferences.

1. ¿Cuál es tu comida favorita?

2. ¿Qué desayunas por la mañana?

3. ¿A qué hora comes el almuerzo?

4. ¿Cuál prefieres, el pollo o el pescado?

5. ¿Qué frutas te gustan?

6. ¿Qué tomas con la cena?

7. ¿Cuál es tu postre preferido?

8. ¿Qué comes mientras ves la televisión?

9. ¿Cuándo comes helado?

10. ¿Por qué comes?

EXERCISE Y

You and some friends are planning a barbecue. List the foods and beverages that you have to buy when you go to the supermarket.

♦ 7 ♦ Health and Well-Being

a. El cuerpo

la boca *mouth*	el estómago *stomach*	la nariz *nose*
el brazo *arm*	la garganta *throat*	el ojo *eye*
la cabeza *head*	el labio *lip*	la oreja *ear*
la cara *face*	la lengua *tongue*	el pelo *hair*
el cuerpo *body*	la mano *hand*	el pie *foot*
el dedo *finger, toe*	la muela *molar (tooth)*	la pierna *leg*
el diente *tooth*		

b. Medicina y salud

bien *well*	la medicina *medicine*
el dentista *dentist*	el médico *doctor*
el doctor *doctor*	el paciente *patient*
el dolor *ache, pain*	la receta *prescription*
la enfermedad *illness*	el resfriado *cold (illness)*
la enfermera *nurse*	la salud *health*
enfermo,-a *ill, sick*	doler *to ache*
el hospital *hospital*	tener dolor de *to ache*

EXERCISE Z

In each group, select the word that is *not* related to the other three.

1. labio, muela, pelo, ascensor

2. médico, cortina, enfermera, hospital

3. sopa, pie, dedo, pierna

4. ojos, postre, nariz, orejas

5. dedo, mano, estómago, brazo

6. comida, medicina, receta, dolor

7. doctor, profesor, dentista, enfermera

8. salud, bien, enfermo, frío

EXERCISE AA

If the statement is true, write *Sí*; if it's false, correct it by replacing the word(s) in boldface.

1. Tengo cinco **dientes** en cada mano.

2. Si estoy **enfermo(-a)** mi madre llama al doctor.

3. Llevo zapatos en **los pies**.

4. Comemos con **la nariz**.

5. Usamos **los ojos** para oír.

6. Comemos con **los brazos**.

7. Una enfermera trabaja en **una tienda**.

8. Tomamos **postre** cuando estamos enfermos.

9. El resfriado es una clase de **receta**.

10. Usamos **la lengua** para hablar.

EXERCISE BB

Tell what's wrong with these people. Use *doler* o *tener dolor de* in your responses.

EXAMPLE: Marta no puede oler las flores.
          Le duele la nariz.

1. Roberto no puede comer porque no puede masticar la comida.

2. Mi abuelo tiene dificultad al caminar.

3. José no puede escribir el examen.

4. Graciela no puede hablar.

5. No tengo apetito y no quiero comer nada.

6. Lola no quiere ver la televisión ni leer una revista.

◆ 8 ◆ Education

a. La escuela

la alumna *pupil (f.)*	la nota *mark, grade*
el alumno *pupil (m.)*	la página *page*
la asignatura *subject*	la palabra *word*
el autobús escolar *school bus*	el papel *paper*
la bandera *flag*	el párrafo *paragraph*
el bolígrafo *ballpoint pen*	la pizarra *chalkboard*
el borrador *eraser (chalkboard)*	la pluma *pen*
la cafetería *cafeteria*	el profesor *teacher (m.)*
la clase *class*	la profesora *teacher (f.)*
el colegio *school, college*	la prueba *examination, test*
la computadora *computer*	el pupitre *(pupil's) desk*
el cuaderno *notebook*	la regla *rule, ruler*
el diccionario *dictionary*	la sala de clase *classroom*
el dictado *dictation*	la tarea *assignment*
el error *mistake, error*	la tiza *chalk*
la escuela *(primaria, secundaria)*	la universidad *college, university*
school (elementary, secondary/high school)	los útiles *school supplies*
el (la) estudiante *student*	el vocabulario *vocabulary*
el examen *examination, test*	aprender *to learn*
la falta *mistake, error*	contestar *to answer*
la frase *sentence*	enseñar *to teach*
la goma *eraser*	cscribir *to write*
el horario *schedule, program*	escuchar *to listen (to)*
el lápiz *pencil*	estudiar *to study*
la lección *lesson*	explicar *to explain*
el libro *book*	hacer la tarea *to do homework*
el maestro (la maestra) *teacher*	leer *to read*
el marcador *felt-tip pen*	preguntar *to ask*
la materia *subject*	responder *to answer*
la mochila *backpack*	salir bien (mal) *to pass (fail)*

b. Las materias / asignatures

el álgebra *algebra*	el francés *French*
el arte *art*	la geografía *geography*
las artes industriales *shop*	la geometría *geometry*
la biología *biology*	la historia *history*
las ciencias *sciences*	la informática *computer science*
el coro *choir*	el inglés *English*
el dibujo *drawing*	la música *music*
la educación para la salud *health education*	la pintura *painting*
la educación física *physical education*	la química *chemistry*
el español *Spanish*	el recreo *recess*
la física *physics*	

EXERCISE CC

In each group, select the word that is *not* related to the other three.

1. párrafo, dictado, menú, página
2. aprender, enseñar, nadar, escuchar
3. escuela, papel, lección, leche
4. pizarra, clase, cabeza, pupitre
5. manzana, bolígrafo, lápiz, tiza
6. prueba, tarea, examen, salud
7. receta, dibujo, coro, física
8. asignatura, clase, materia, dolor
9. borrador, tiza, cuaderno, pizarra
10. deporte, química, biología, ciencia

EXERCISE DD

Match the words in column A with their respective synonyms or related words in column B.

A	*B*
1. falta	*a.* maestro
2. escuela	*b.* coro
3. profesor	*c.* pizarra
4. asignatura	*d.* prueba
5. contestar	*e.* error
6. examen	*f.* estudiante
7. alumno	*g.* responder
8. música	*h.* materia
9. biología	*i.* colegio
10. tiza	*j.* ciencia

EXERCISE EE

Using the drawings below, make a list of the school supplies you have to buy for the new school year.

EXERCISE FF

Answer these questions that a new student from Argentina asks you.

1. ¿Cuántas materias estudias este año?

2. ¿Qué lengua aprendes?

3. ¿Qué clase de ciencia tienes?

4. ¿Tomas una clase de informática?

5. ¿Cómo son los exámenes de la clase de matemáticas?

6. ¿Cúal es tu asignatura favorita?

7. ¿Te gusta tu horario este año?

♦ 9 ♦ Earning A Living

a. Las profesiones y los oficios

la abogada, el abogado   *lawyer*

el actor   *actor*

la actriz   *actress*

el agricultor, la agricultora   *farmer*

el / la artista   *artist, entertainer*

la barbera, el barbero   *barber*

el / la bombero   *firefighter*

la carnicera, el carnicero   *butcher*

el / la chófer (chofer)   *chauffeur*

la científica, el científico   *scientist*

el / la comerciante   *businessperson, entrepreneur*

la empleada doméstica   *maid*

el / la dentista   *dentist*

el director, la directora   *director*

el doctor, la doctora   *doctor*

la dueña, el dueño   *owner, boss*

la enfermera, el enfermero   *nurse*

el escritor, la escritora   *writer*

la farmacéutica, el farmacéutico   *pharmacist*

el / la gerente   *manager*

el hombre / la mujer de negocios   *businessperson*

la ingeniera, el ingeniero   *engineer*

la jefa, el jefe   *supervisor, boss*

la maestra, el maestro   *teacher*

la médica, el médico   *doctor*

el oficio   *occupation*

la panadera, el panadero   *baker*

el / la periodista   *journalist*

el / la piloto   *pilot*

el policía / la (mujer) policía   *police officer*

el profesor, la profesora   *teacher, professor*

el programador / la programadora de computadoras   *computer programmer*

la sastra, el sastre   *tailor*

la secretaria, el secretario   *secretary*

el / la soldado   *soldier*

la veterinaria, el veterinario   *veterinarian*

el / la deportista   *sportsman / sportswoman*

el / la cantante   *singer*

el cocinero / la cocinera   *cook*

la zapatera, el zapatero   *shoemaker*

estar desempleado   *to be unemployed*

ganarse la vida   *to earn a living*

trabajar   *to work*

b. Los lugares de trabajo

la barbería   *barber shop*

el consultorio   *doctor's office*

la corte   *court*

la escuela   *school*

la fábrica   *factory*

el hospital   *hospital*

el laboratorio   *laboratory*

la oficina   *office*

la peluquería   *hair salon*

el salón de belleza   *beauty salon*

la tienda   *store*

la universidad   *university, college*

EXERCISE GG

Identify the profession that is associated with the following drawings.

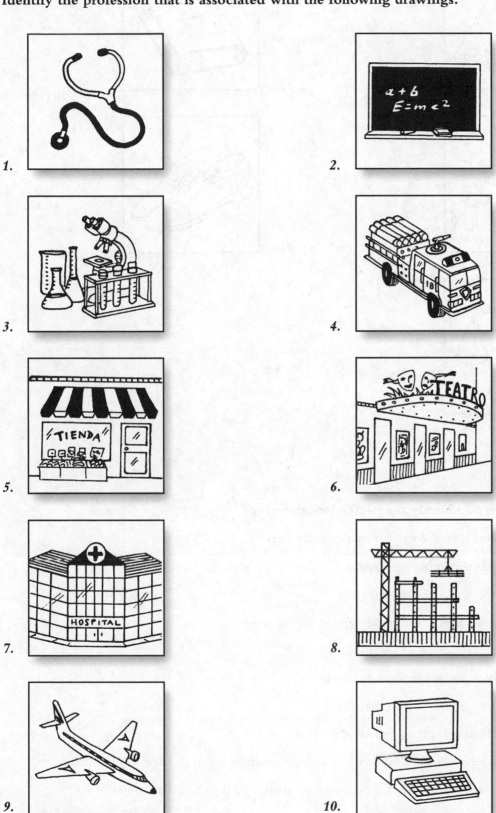

1.

2.

3.

4.

5.

6.

7.

8.

9.

10.

11.

12.

13.

14.

15.

EXERCISE HH

Use the clues below to identify the professions described.

1. Preparo la medicina que el doctor ordena en una receta.

2. Defiendo la patria cuando hay una guerra.

3. Protejo a las personas. Llevo uniforme.

4. Preparo a los jóvenes para el futuro. Me gustan los exámenes.

5. Ayudo a los médicos y cuido a los enfermos.

6. Hago experimentos. Trabajo en un laboratorio.

7. Corto el pelo a los hombres y a las mujeres.

8. Trabajo en las películas. Trato de divertir al público.

9. Me gusta la vida del campo. Cultivo la tierra y tengo animales como las vacas y los pollos.

10. Escribo las noticias todos los días. Las personas compran mi producto diariamente.

11. Trato de mejorar la vida con edificios nuevos y puentes.

12. Ayudo a las personas cuando tienen dolor de muelas.

13. Trabajo en una oficina donde contesto el teléfono y escribo correos electrónicos.

14. Reparo la ropa de las personas. Me gusta coser.

15. Me fascina volar y siempre llevo a muchas personas de una ciudad a otra.

♦10♦ Leisure

el ajedrez *chess*	la grabadora *tape recorder*
el béisbol *baseball*	el instrumento *instrument*
el billar *pool*	la música *music*
el campeón *champion*	el partido *game, match*
la canción *song*	el pasatiempo *pastime, hobby*
el cine *movies*	la película *film, movie*
la cinta *cassette tape*	el programa *program*
el concierto *concert*	el / la radio *radio*
el disco compacto *CD*	el teatro *theater*
las diversiones *amusements*	la televisión *television*
el equipo *team*	el tenis *tennis*
el fútbol *soccer*	el tocadiscos *record player*
andar en bicicleta *to ride a bicycle*	las vacaciones *vacation*
bailar *to dance*	jugar *to play (a game, sport)*
cantar *to sing*	levantar pesas *to lift weights*
coleccionar monedas (estampillas, muñecas, insectos) *to collect coins (stamps, dolls, insects)*	mirar televisión *to watch television*
correr *to run*	nadar *to swim*
dar un paseo *to take a walk*	patinar *to skate*
escuchar *to listen (to)*	practicar el judo *to practice judo*
esquiar *to ski*	sacar fotos *to take pictures*
hacer gimnasia *to do gymnastics*	salir con los amigos *to go out with friends*
hacer yoga *to practice yoga*	ser fanático de *to be a fan of*
ir de compras *to go shopping*	tocar *to play (music)*
	viajar *to travel*

EXERCISE II

In each group, select the word that is *not* related to the other three.

1. leer, disco compacto, tocadiscos, música

2. bailar, cantar, patinar, trabajar

3. película, juego, cine, actriz

4. música, equipo, fútbol, partido

5. esquiar, estudiar, nadar, correr

6. concierto, televisión, escuela, teatro

7. programa, béisbol, tenis, fútbol

8. hacer yoga, levantar pesas, ir de compras, hacer gimnasia

EXERCISE JJ

Identify the pastime that each of these people enjoys most.

1. A Rogelio le gusta conocer otros países y ciudades. Le fascina visitar los museos.

2. Luis siempre me pide los sobres de las cartas que recibo de mi amigo por correspondencia. También le gusta ver las tarjetas postales que recibo de mis amigos cuando visitan otros países.

3. Sarita y Gladys quieren ser bailarinas. Practican mucho y hacen ejercicios especiales.

4. Jorge quiere tener músculos grandes. Es socio de un gimnasio donde hace este ejercicio todos los días.

5. A Enrique le gustan mucho los juegos de mesa. Practica con mucha frecuencia y es el campeón del equipo de la escuela. Prefiere el juego más difícil y exigente.

6. A Sofía le gusta gastar dinero. Compra regalos bonitos para todo el mundo.

7. A Beto le gusta la zoología. Le fascina caminar en el parque y en el bosque. A su hermana no le gustan las cosas que Beto colecciona en sus paseos.

◆11◆ Public and Private Services

autoridad de aqueductos	*water utilities company*
el correo	*mail, post office*
la electricidad	*electricity*
hablar por teléfono	*to speak on the telephone*
hacer una llamada	*to make a call*
llamar	*to call*
la estampilla	*stamp*
el gas	*gas company*
el teléfono	*telephone*
marcar un número	*to dial a number*
pagar el agua (el gas)	*to pay the water (the gas) bill*

EXERCISE KK

Complete each statement with the appropriate words.

1. Para mandar una carta tengo que comprar _____ . Las compro en el _____ .

2. Durante el verano visité un pueblo muy primitivo. Las casas no tienen _____ y tienen que

usar el _____ del río.

3. Mi tío vive en Buenos Aires. Cada domingo nos _____ por teléfono. Es una llamada de

_____ . Él no puede _____ ; tiene que hablar con la operadora primero.

4. No distribuyen _____ en la calle en que vivo hasta las dos de la tarde. Mis padres reciben

mucho _____ : cartas, tarjetas postales, revistas y cuentas.

♦12♦ Shopping

a. Las tiendas

el almacén	*department store, warehouse*	la panadería	*bakery*
la bodega	*grocery store*	la papelería	*stationery store*
la carnicería	*butcher shop*	la pastelería	*pastry shop*
el centro comercial	*mall*	la peluquería	*barbershop, hair salon*
la farmacia	*pharmacy, drugstore*	el salón de belleza	*beauty shop*
la florería	*florist shop*	el supermercado	*supermarket*
la lavandería	*laundry*	la tienda	*store*
la librería	*bookstore*	la tienda de ropa	*clothing store*
el mercado	*market*	la zapatería	*shoe store*
la mueblería	*furniture store*		

b. Palabras relacionadas

barato, -a	*cheap, inexpensive*	la ganga	*sale, bargain*
la caja	*cashier*	grande (mediano, pequeño)	*large (medium, small)*
caro, -a	*expensive*		
el cheque	*check*	el precio	*price*
el/la dependiente	*salesperson*	la queja	*complaint*
el efectivo	*cash*	ahorrar	*to save*
en especial	*on sale*	comprar	*to buy*
la etiqueta	*tag*	devolver	*to return (an item)*

pagar con cheque/tarjeta de crédito
  to pay with check / credit card

pagar en efectivo   *to pay cash*

probarse   *to try (on)*

rebajado, -a   *reduced*

la talla (clothing)   *size*

el tamaño (package)   *size*

la tarjeta de crédito   *credit card*

quedarle bien   *to look well on*

regatear   *to bargain*

vender   *to sell*

¿Cuánto vale (cuesta)?   *How much does it cost?*

¿En qué puedo servirle?   *How may I help you?*

EXERCISE LL

Match the words in column A with their related words in column B.

A	*B*
1. carnicería	**a.** diccionario
2. farmacia	**b.** ropa limpia
3. mueblería	**c.** calcetines
4. librería	**d.** cortar el pelo
5. florería	**e.** sandalias
6. lavandería	**f.** refrescos
7. papelería	**g.** biftec
8. salón de belleza	**h.** muchos departamentos
9. pastelería	**i.** pan
10. tienda de ropa	**j.** sofá
11. bodega	**k.** tiendas
12. centro comercial	**l.** claveles
13. panadería	**m.** postre
14. zapatería	**n.** tarjeta
15. almacén	**o.** receta

EXERCISE MM

Complete each statement with the appropriate word or expression.

1. En una tienda la persona que atiende al cliente es _____ .

2. No tengo ni dinero ni un cheque; voy a pagar con _____ .

3. Busco un suéter, _____ grande.

4. Leo el precio del artículo en _____ .

5. Estos zapatos cuestan mucho; quiero algo más _____ .

6. Este pantalón está _____ , ahora cuesta solamente veinte dólares.

7. Pago por las compras en _____ .

8. No me gusta este artículo. Quiero hablar con el gerente porque lo tengo que _____ .

9. En esta tienda tenemos que pagar el precio indicado; no podemos _____ .

10. El perfume viene en dos _____ : pequeño o grande.

11. No me gusta el suéter. Voy a _____ el suéter a la tienda.

12. Debes _____ el suéter antes de salir de la tienda.

♦ 13 ♦ Travel

a. Medios de transporte

el autobús *bus*	el ferrocarril *railroad*
el automóvil *car, automobile*	la motocicleta *motorcycle*
el avión *airplane*	el tren *train*
el barco *boat*	el vapor *steamship*
la bicicleta *bicycle*	el metro *the subway*
el coche, el auto *car, automobile*	

b. Palabras relacionadas

el aeropuerto *airport*	el pasillo *aisle*
el asiento *seat*	el plano (de la ciudad) *(city) map*
el baúl *trunk*	la puerta *gate, door*
el billete *ticket*	la salida *exit*
el boleto *ticket*	el sur *south*
el camino *road, way*	el viaje *trip, voyage*
la entrada *entrance*	el vuelo *flight*
la estación *station*	la llegada *arrival*
el este *east*	la demora *delay*
la fila *row*	caminar *to walk*
la maleta *suitcase*	hacer la maleta *to pack*
el mapa *map*	regresar *to return*
el norte *north*	salir *to leave, depart*
el oeste *west*	viajar *to travel*
la parada *bus stop*	volver *to return*

EXERCISE NN

In each group, select the word that is *not* related to the other three.

1. avión, sala de clase, bicicleta, coche

2. vapor, ferrocarril, viajar, teatro

3. libro, maleta, baúl, viaje

4. este, pregunta, norte, oeste

5. aeropuerto, calle, parada, estación

6. comer, billete, puerta, boleto

7. tren, vuelo, estación, ferrocarril

8. mapa, calle, plano, número de teléfono

9. asiento, fila, pasillo, baúl

10. vapor, mar, barco, camino

EXERCISE OO

Match the words in column A with their related words in column B.

	<u>A</u>		<u>B</u>
1.	asiento	a.	salir
2.	maleta	b.	aeropuerto
3.	avión	c.	barco
4.	parada	d.	puerta
5.	tren	e.	fila
6.	regresar	f.	autobús
7.	mapa	g.	plano
8.	entrada	h.	coche
9.	automóvil	i.	baúl
10.	vapor	j.	ferrocarril

EXERCISE PP

Complete each of the sentences with the appropriate word or expression.

1. Ponemos la ropa en _____ .

2. El Canadá está al _____ de México.

3. México está al _____ de los Estados Unidos.

4. El avión llega al _____ .

5. En el avión me siento en la _____ 31, _____ C.

6. Para subir al avión tengo que mostrar el _____ .

7. Una bicicleta con un motor es una _____ .

8. En la ciudad uso un _____ para encontrar la calle que busco.

9. Antes de viajar, escojo la ropa para _____ .

10. Tomo el autobús en la _____ .

♦ 14 ♦ Entertainment

el actor	*actor*	el horario	*schedule*
la actriz	*actress*	el locutor	*announcer*
el / la artista	*artist, entertainer, performer*	la noticia	*news item*
el billete	*ticket*	las noticias	*news*
el boleto	*ticket*	el noticiero	*news broadcast*
el cine	*movies*	la obra	*(theater) work, play*
el concierto	*concert*	la película	*film*
el estadio	*stadium*	la taquilla	*box office*
el estreno	*opening (of a performance), showing*	el teatro	*theater*
la función	*performance, showing*	hacer cola	*to wait in line*

EXERCISE QQ

Match the words in column A to their related words in column B.

_A_		_B_	
1. el boleto		**a.** el artista	
2. la película		**b.** el horario	
3. la obra		**c.** el locutor	
4. la taquilla		**d.** el cine	
5. la función		**e.** el teatro	
6. el concierto		**f.** los deportes	
7. el estadio		**g.** hacer cola	
8. el noticiero		**h.** la taquilla	

EXERCISE RR

Complete this story with the appropriate word or expression in the list below. Note that the words or expressions are arranged in alphabetical order, not in order of appearance.

billetes	esperar	hacer cola	película
boletos	estadio	horario	taquilla
cine	estreno	locutor	
concierto	función	música	

Sergio invita a Blanca a acompañarle a un _____ de su grupo favorito. Tiene dos
          1.

_____ para el _____ pero no sabe _____ . Tiene que recoger
      2.   3.   4.

los _____ en la _____ del _____ . Cuando Sergio y Blanca
        5.   6.   7.

llegan allí hay mucha gente y tienen que _____ . Mientras ellos _____ ,
                                              8.   9.

escuchan _____ en un radio portátil. El _____ anuncia que el avión en que
            10.   11.

llegaba el grupo favorito de Sergio no va a llegar a tiempo y que van a cancelar

la _____ . Sergio está enojado y triste pero decide ir con Blanca a ver una
      12.

_____ de ciencia ficción en el _____ .
      13.   14.

⟨⟨ MASTERY EXERCISES ⟩⟩

EXERCISE SS

Ramón's little brother, Pepito, is learning many new words. Write *Sí*, if the sentence is true. If it's false, correct it by replacing the words in boldface with the correct ones.

EXAMPLE: Los médicos trabajan en **una carnicería**.
                Los médicos trabajan en **un hospital**.

OR: Los médicos trabajan en **un consultorio**.

1. **Hago las maletas** antes de viajar.

2. Hay muchos libros en **una florería**.

3. Compramos pan en **la mueblería**.

4. El secretario trabaja en **una oficina**.

5. La química y la historia son **asignaturas**.

6. Tengo los ojos y **las piernas** en la cara.

7. Para **escribir**, uso una pluma o un lápiz.

8. Mi padre cocina en **la sala**.

9. Cuando hace **calor** llevamos abrigo, guantes y botas.

10. La cereza y la pera son **legumbres**.

(EXERCISE TT)

You're going on a vocabulary game show, where you must read each definition and write its corresponding word or words.

EXAMPLE: libro donde se explican las palabras de una lengua   **un diccionario**

1. persona de pelo negro

2. el cuarto donde duermo

3. yo soy su nieta

4. lugar donde se sale a comer

5. tienda donde se venden flores

6. sinónimo de montaña

7. estación en que hace mucho frío en Norteamérica

8. mes entre septiembre y noviembre

9. día antes del sábado

10. fruta amarilla que no es dulce

11. parte del cuerpo donde llevo un sombrero

12. lengua que hablan en Perú

13. persona que estudia

14. lugar donde van los enfermos

15. el deporte más popular de Hispanoamérica

16. medio de transporte necesario para ir de México a Argentina

17. artista de cine

18. tienda donde compro libros

19. objeto para escribir en la pizarra

20. palabras que tengo que aprender

PART

5

Spanish and
Spanish-American
Civilizations

Spanish Influence in the United States

Since the discovery of the New World, there has always been a notable Spanish influence in the United States.

First Spanish Explorers

Cristóbal Colón (Christopher Columbus) is believed to be the Genoese navigator Cristoforo Colombo, who became an explorer for Spain and the first European to reach the New World (1492). He made four voyages, touching on various parts of what is now Spanish America. **Hernán Cortés** conquered Mexico (1519–1521), defeating the Aztecs and their king, Moctezuma. **Francisco Pizarro** conquered Peru (1532–1535), defeating the Incas and their king, Atahualpa. Pizarro founded the city of Lima in 1535. **Juan Ponce de León** was the first Spanish governor of Puerto Rico and the first European to explore what is now Florida (1513) in his search for the Fountain of Youth. He arrived on Easter Sunday (Domingo de Pascua Florida), therefore naming it Florida. **Álvar Núñez Cabeza de Vaca** shipwrecked on the Texas coast in 1528. He was captured by Native Americans, whom he served as a slave and medicine man. He later escaped and wandered for six years, exploring parts of Texas, Kansas, and New Mexico. After traveling thousands of miles, Cabeza de Vaca finally reached Mexico in 1536. His reports from the Pueblo Indians led to the myth of the "Seven Cities of Cibola."

Francisco Vásquez de Coronado was the first Spaniard to explore what are now New Mexico and Arizona (1540, including the Grand Canyon) in his search for the supposedly rich and prosperous "Seven Cities of Cibola." **Hernando de Soto** explored much of Georgia, the Carolinas, Alabama, and Oklahoma. He was the first European explorer to reach the Mississippi River (1541) where he was later buried. **Juan Rodríguez Cabrillo** explored the coast of California in 1542. **Vasco Núñez de Balboa** was the first European explorer to reach the Pacific Ocean (1513).

Early Spanish Settlements

St. Augustine (Florida) is the oldest city in the United States. It was established by the Spaniards in 1565. **Santa Fe** (New Mexico) is the oldest capital city in the United States. It was founded in 1609. Spanish missions were organized by priests in the southwestern part of the United States. **Fray Junípero Serra** was the most famous of the Spanish missionaries. He and his followers established a chain of twenty-one missions from San Diego to San Francisco (California, 1769–1823) along the **Camino Real** (royal road), which is today called Coast Highway 101. Two of the most visited California missions are **San Juan Capistrano** and **Santa Barbara**. The latter is called the "Queen of the California Missions."

Geographic Names of Spanish Origin

A glance at a map of the United States shows the influence of Spanish on the names of states, cities, rivers, and mountains. For example:

States: California, Colorado, Florida, Montana, Nevada

Cities: El Paso, Las Vegas, Los Angeles, Sacramento, Santa Fe, San Francisco

Rivers: Brazos (Texas); Colorado (Colorado, Utah, Arizona); Río Grande (New Mexico, Texas)

Mountains: San Juan (Colorado); Sierra Nevada (California)

Evidence of Spanish Influence in the United States: Architecture

Many modern American homes and buildings, especially in the southwest, show the influence of the old adobe ranch houses and mission buildings constructed by the Spaniards.

Spanish architecture is characterized by a **patio** (inner courtyard), an attractive spot for family relaxation, decorated frequently with flowers, shade trees, and an ornamental fountain. A **reja** (iron grating on windows) is used for security and decoration. A **balcón** (balcony) is used for displaying flags during celebrations, watching processions and parades, and sunning flowering plants. **Tejas** (roof tiles) are made of baked clay and are red in color. An **arcada** (arcade) is a covered passageway along a row of columns in front of commercial buildings. It provides protection from the weather (rain or hot sun) for patrons and strollers.

Economic Life

The earliest economic influence by the Spanish was in **cattle raising**. The Spaniards are credited with bringing the first cows, horses, goats, pigs, and sheep to the New

World. American cowboys copied Spanish cowboys' dress, equipment, vocabulary, and ranching techniques. The Spaniards also developed the first gold and silver mines in the New World. Their methods and success influenced the **mining industry** in America.

Language

Spanish explorers, missionaries, and settlers in North America contributed many Spanish words to our language. Some of these words are identical in English and Spanish. Others have been slightly changed. Common English words of Spanish origin include:

Ranch life: bronco, chaps **(chaparreras)**, cinch **(cincha)**, corral, lariat **(la reata)**, lasso **(lazo)**, mustang **(mesteño)**, ranch **(rancho)**, rodeo, stampede **(estampida)**

Foods: avocado **(aguacate)**, banana, barbecue **(barbacoa)**, chili **(chile)**, potato **(patata)**, tomato **(tomate)**, vanilla **(vainilla)**

Beverages: sherry **(Jerez)**

Clothing: bolero, brocade **(brocado)**, mantilla, poncho, sombrero

Animals and insects: alligator (lagarto), burro, chinchilla, cockroach **(cucaracha)**, coyote, llama, mosquito

Types of people: cannibal **(canibal)**, comrade **(camarada)**, desperado **(desesperado)**, padre, peon **(peón)**, renegade **(renegado)**, vigilante

Nature: arroyo, canyon **(cañón)**, cordillera, lagoon **(laguna)**, mesa, sierra, tornado

Shipping and commerce: armada, canoe **(canoa)**, cargo **(carga)**, contraband **(contrabando)**, embargo, flotilla, galleon **(galeón)**

Buildings and streets: adobe, alameda, hacienda, patio, plaza

Miscellaneous words: bonanza, cigar **(cigarro)**, fiesta, filibuster **(filibustero)**, guerrilla, siesta

Contemporary Life

Spanish influence is evident in many aspects of daily contemporary life in the United States. Mexican foods, for instance, have long been popular in the country. These foods include: **tortilla** (a flat, thin cornmeal pancake); **enchilada** (a rolled tortilla filled with chopped meat or chicken and served with hot chili sauce); **tamal** (seasoned ground meat or chicken rolled in cornmeal dough, wrapped in corn husks, and steamed); **chile con carne** (red pepper, chopped meat, and hot chili sauce); and, **taco** (a crisp tortilla folded over and filled with seasoned chopped meat or chicken, lettuce, and tomatoes). **Salsa and tortilla chips** are welcoming snacks served in many restaurants. Fruits and vegetables that come from Spanish countries can be found in supermarkets and green grocers across the nation. These include **avocados**, **mangos**, and **papayas**, for example. Spanish products are also easily available in supermarkets in cans, and in the frozen food section.

Billboards, printed advertisements, and public announcements in Spanish are readily found and heard throughout the United States.

Hispanic Heritage Month: 15 September – 15 October

In 1968, President Lyndon B. Johnson was authorized by Congress to proclaim a week in September as **National Hispanic Heritage Week**. In 1988, this observance was expanded to a month-long celebration during which the United States celebrates the culture and traditions of U.S. residents who trace their roots to Spain, Mexico, and the Spanish-speaking countries of Central America, South America, and the Caribbean. The starting date, September 15, was chosen for the celebration because it is the anniversary of independence of five Latin American countries: Costa Rica, El Salvador, Guatemala, Honduras, and Nicaragua. Mexico and Chile commemorate their independence days on September 16 and September 18, respectively. October 12, Columbus Day, is known as **El Día de la Hispanidad** and is celebrated throughout the Spanish-speaking world.

Popular Spanish-American Dances and Music

The Spanish-speaking world has given us popular rhythms and dances. For example, **tango** (Argentina), **rumba** (Cuba), **mambo** (Cuba), **cha–cha–cha** (Cuba), and **merengue** (Dominican Republic). Music includes **Latin pop**, **jazz**, **rock,** and **salsa**. **Reggaeton** (a form of urban music with lyrics in Spanish and English), which combines reggae, Latinamerican music, such as merengue or bomba as well as hip hop and electronic music, is also very popular among young people in the United States.

EXERCISE A

If the statement is true, write *Sí*; if it's false, correct it by replacing the word(s) in boldface.

1. Fray Junípero Serra and his followers established **twenty-seven** missions in California.

2. There are many houses of Spanish-style architecture in the **northwestern** United States.

3. The **American** cowboy copied a great deal from the Spanish cowboy.

4. The Spaniards used **adobe** for building.

5. The **Spaniards** established the cattle-raising industry in the New World.

6. The words *rodeo* and *corral* are related to Spanish **city** life.

7. The oldest city in the United States is **San Diego**.

8. In **New Mexico** there are numerous cities that have Spanish names.

9. The **rejas** of Spanish houses have flowers and trees.

10. A **tamal** is a crisp tortilla filled with meat or beans.

EXERCISE B

Match the expressions in column A with their corresponding definitions in column B.

<u>A</u>	<u>B</u>
1. tango	*a.* tortilla with chopped meat and chili sauce
2. De Soto	*b.* roofing material
3. Camino Real	*c.* inner courtyard
4. Santa Fe	*d.* covered passageway
5. Las Vegas	*e.* city in Nevada
6. arcada	*f.* capital city in New Mexico
7. enchilada	*g.* Spanish word related to alligator
8. lagarto	*h.* Argentine dance
9. patio	*i.* road connecting the Spanish missions
10. tejas	*j.* explorer of the Mississippi river
11. Ponce de León	*k.* founder of California missions
12. Fray Junípero Serra	*l.* explorer of Florida

EXERCISE C

Complete the following statements.

1. A mountain range in California with a Spanish name is _____ .

2. A popular dance of the Dominican Republic is the _____ .

3. Two states with Spanish names are _____ and _____ .

4. The river that separates the United States from Mexico is the _____ .

5. A popular Cuban dance is the _____ .

6. An American city with a Spanish name is _____ .

7. One of the animals that the Spaniards brought to the New World is the _____ .

8. The San Juan Mountains are in the state of _____ .

9. A city in Texas with a Spanish name is _____ .

10. The oldest city in the United States is _____ .

EXERCISE D

In each group of words, select the word that isn't related to the other three.

EXAMPLE: rumba, tango, estampida, mambo   **estampida**

1. burro, chinchilla, llama, banana
2. bronco, flotilla, mesteño, rodeo
3. bolero, tornado, arroyo, mesa
4. brocado, tortilla, barbacoa, vainilla
5. sombrero, desesperado, poncho, mantilla
6. patio, hacienda, lazo, alameda
7. taco, tamal, enchilada, bonanza
8. camarada, tomate, patata, chile
9. peón, padre, renegado, embargo
10. armada, contrabando, canoa, sierra

EXERCISE E

Select the words in parenthesis that correctly complete each of the following sentences.

1. (Francisco Pizarro / Juan Ponce de León / Cristóbal Colón) was the first governor of Puerto Rico.
2. (Álvar Núñez Cabeza de Vaca / Hernán Cortés / Hernando de Soto) was the first European explorer to reach the Mississippi River.
3. (Atahualpa / Moctezuma / Cíbola) was the Aztec king conquered by Hernán Cortés.
4. (Fray Junípero Serra /Atahualpa / Juan Rodríguez Cabrillo) was a famous Spanish missionary.
5. (Santa Fe / Santa Barbara / San Francisco) is the oldest capital city in the United States.
6. (San Juan Capistrano / El Paso / St. Augustine) is a famous Spanish mission.
7. The *(tamal / rumba / cincha)* is a popular Spanish-American dance.
8. The tango is a popular dance from (Mexico / Cuba /Argentina).

EXERCISE F

What Spanish influences are there in the area in which you live? Names of state, city, streets? Architecture? Restaurants? Radio/tv station? Write a paragraph in which you describe this influence. You may also wish to use the Internet to identify Spanish influences in the United States. Use the keywords "Spanish influence."

EXERCISE G

Research the celebration of Independence Day, or el Día de la Hispanidad, in one of the Spanish-speaking countries. Prepare a description of the significance of the day and how it is celebrated. Include a brief comparison of how Independence Day or Columbus Day is celebrated in your city.

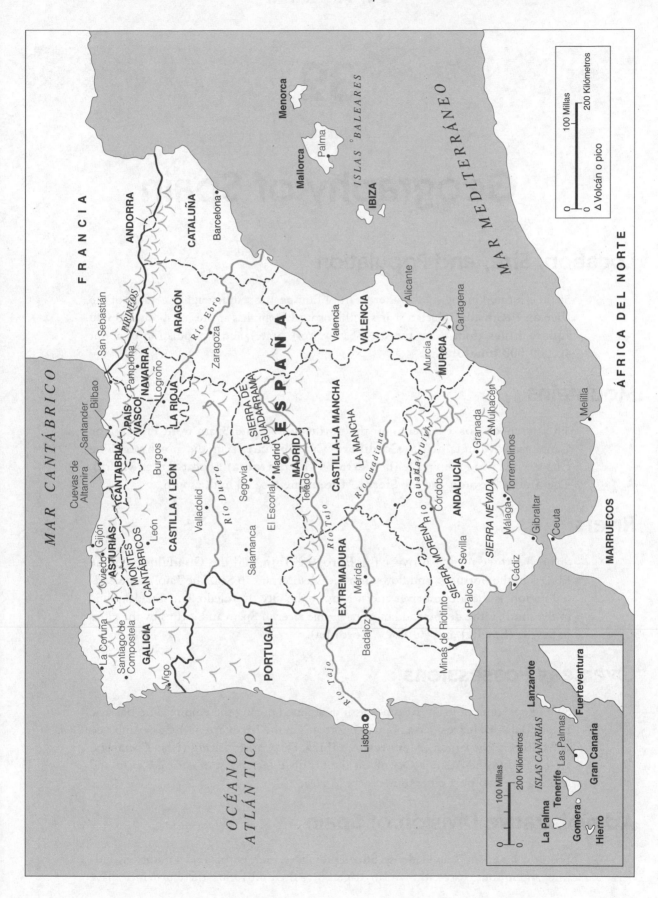

Geography of Spain

Location, Size, and Population

Spain is located in the southwestern part of Europe. It occupies eighty percent of the **Iberian Peninsula**, which it shares with Portugal. Spain has an area of about **200,000 square miles** (four times the size of New York State), and a population of about **40,000,000 inhabitants**.

Mountains

The Pyrenees **(los Pirineos)**, in the northeast, separate Spain from France. The Cantabrian Mountains **(la Cordillera Cantábrica)** is in the northwest. The Guadarrama Mountain range **(la Sierra de Guadarrama)** is located near Madrid. The **Sierra Nevada** and the **Sierra Morena** are located in the south.

Rivers

Spain has three principal rivers: the **Ebro**, the **Tajo**, and the **Guadalquivir**. The Ebro is in the northeast and flows into the Mediterranean Sea. The Tajo, in the central region, is the longest river and it runs by the city of Toledo. The Guadalquivir, in the south, is the deepest and most navigable river in Spain and it runs by the cities of Seville **(Sevilla)** and Cordova **(Córdoba)**.

Overseas Possessions

Spain kept some of its overseas possessions attained during the empire. The Balearic Islands (**Islas Baleares**) are a popular resort area in the Mediterrenean Sea, composed of **Mallorca** (the largest), **Menorca**, and **Ibiza**. The Canary Islands **(Islas Canarias)** are located in the Atlantic Ocean, off the northwestern coast of Africa. **Ceuta** and **Melilla** are two port cities in Morocco, Africa.

Administrative Division of Spain

Historically, Spain is divided into fifteen provinces, each with its own traditions, culture, and in some cases, its own language. Since the mid 1980's, these provinces have been divided into seventeen autonomous communities **(comunidades autóno-mas)**. They are Andalusia **(Andalucía)** in the south; Aragon **(Aragón)** in the northeast; Principality of Asturias **(Principado de Asturias)** in the north; Balearic Islands **(Baleares)** in the Mediterranean Sea; Canary Islands **(Canarias)** in the Atlantic Ocean; **Cantabria** in the north; Castile-La mancha **(Castilla–La Mancha)** in the center; Castile-Leon **(Castilla y León)** in the north center; Catalonia **(Cataluña)** in the northeast; Valencian Community **(Comunidad Valenciana)** in the east; **Extremadura** in the west; **Galicia** in the northwest; **La Rioja** south of Navarra; **Madrid** in the center; Region of Murcia **(Región de Murcia)** in the southeast; Navarre **(Navarra)** in the north; and Basque Country **(País Vasco)** in the north.

Languages

Spanish **(español or castellano)** is the principal language spoken in Spain. However, Galician **(gallego)** is spoken in Galicia; Basque **(vascuence)** is spoken in the Basque Country; and **Catalán** is spoken in Catalonia.

Important Products

Spain is both an industrial and an agricultural country. The principal agricultural products are **olives**, **oranges**, **grapes**, **wheat**, **lemons**, and **cork**, and the country is the third largest **wine** producer in Europe. The wines of **Jerez** (sherry), **Rioja**, and **Málaga** are world-famous. Spain is also one of the world's leading producers of **olive oil**. The nation's mineral resources are **coal**, **iron**, **mercury**, **lead**, and **copper**.

EXERCISE A

Match the words in column A to their related words in column B.

	A		*B*
1.	Asturias	*a.*	Balearic Islands
2.	Spanish	*b.*	Atlantic Ocean
3.	Sierra Morena	*c.*	Spain's longest river
4.	Galician	*d.*	region in the northeast
5.	Tajo	*e.*	wine
6.	Guadalquivir	*f.*	language spoken in the northwest
7.	Jerez	*g.*	most navigable river
8.	Canary Islands	*h.*	mountains
9.	Catalonia	*i.*	region in the north
10.	Mallorca	*j.*	principal language of Spain

EXERCISE B

If the statement is true, write *Sí*, if it's false, correct it by replacing the word(s) in boldface.

1. The Pyrenees separate Spain from **Portugal**.

2. The Mediterranean Sea is situated **west** of Spain.

3. Spain and Portugal form the **Iberian** Peninsula.

4. Some Spanish **wines** are world-famous.

5. Spain has a population of about **60,000,000**.

6. Mallorca is one of the **Canary** Islands.

7. The Cantabrian Mountains are in the **south** of Spain.

8. The most navigable river in Spain is the **Tajo**.

9. **Málaga** is an important wine producing country.

10. The principal language of Spain is **Basque**.

EXERCISE C

Select the word or expression that correctly completes each sentence.

1. The (Guadarrama / Pyrenee / Cantabrian) Mountains separate Spain from France.

2. (Apples / Oranges / Machines) are an important product of Spain.

3. Spain is located in the (southwestern / northeastern / central) part of Europe.

4. Spain has two ports that are situated in (South America / Africa / Mexico).

5. A popular resort area of Spain is (the Balearic Islands / the Canary Islands / Extremadura).

6. The (Tajo / Ebro / Guadalquivir) River passes by Toledo.

7. (Murcia / Aragon / Leon) is in the northwestern part of Spain.

8. An important mineral resource of Spain is (gold / tin / mercury).

9. Spain has an area of (40,000,000 / 200,000 / 1,300) square miles.

10. The (Pyrenee / Guadarrama / Cantabrian) Mountains are near Madrid.

EXERCISE D

Complete the following statements.

1. The _____ is the longest river of Spain.

2. The _____ are islands in the Mediterranean Sea that belong to Spain.

3. _____ is a region of central Spain.

4. Spain is one of the world's leading producers of _____ .

5. _____ is a region that covers most of southern Spain.

6. The Cantabrian Mountains are in the _____ part of Spain.

7. Spain consists of _____ autonomous communities.

8. The Sierra Nevada is a mountain range in the _____ part of Spain.

9. The regional language of Catalonia is _____ .

10. A Spanish river that flows into the Mediterranean Sea is _____ .

EXERCISE E

Research an area of Spain that you would like to visit. Prepare a presentation that you would make to some friends who are also interested in visiting Spain.

CHAPTER

33

History of Spain

Present-day Spain is the product of the diverse peoples that have colonized it since the earliest times. These peoples brought with them their own languages, customs, and inventions, which are still visible in current day Spain.

The earliest inhabitants of Spain were the Iberians **(los íberos)**. Around 1000 B.C., the Celts **(los celtas)** entered the peninsula. The union of the Iberians and the Celts produced the Celtiberians **(los celtíberos)**. The Phoenicians **(los fenicios)** and the Greeks **(los griegos)** established colonies and trading posts in Spain from about the eleventh to the eighth century B.C. The Carthaginians **(los cartagineses)** invaded Spain in the third century B.C. The Romans **(los romanos)** defeated the Carthaginians in about 200 B.C. and ruled Spain for six centuries (until about A.D. 400). During that time, the Romans had a significant impact on the formation of the Spanish culture. They introduced their language, Latin, from which present-day Spanish is derived. They contributed a system of laws and their economic and social structure. They also built bridges, aqueducts, and roads. The Visigoths **(los visigodos)** were a Germanic tribe that defeated the Romans and invaded Spain in A.D. 409. The Moors **(los moros)** attacked Spain, defeating the Visigoths in A.D. 711. The former ruled large areas of Spain for about seven centuries, and were finally driven out of Spain in 1492. The Moors made great contributions to Spanish life and culture in the fields of philosophy, medicine, mathematics, and astronomy. They developed commerce and agriculture, and devised an irrigation system by means of a waterwheel called **noria.** They also introduced many Arabic words into the Spanish language, mostly those beginning with **al–**, such as **algodón**, **alcalde**, and **algebra**.

Heroes of the Reconquest

Don Pelayo was the first leader in the Reconquest of Spain from the Moors. He defeated them in the **Battle of Covadonga** (A.D. 718). **El Cid (Rodrigo Díaz de Vivar)** is Spain's national hero. He continued the struggle against the Moors and captured Valencia from them in 1094.

Important Rulers

Fernando and **Isabel**, the Catholic Rulers **(los Reyes Católicos)**, completed the Reconquest by driving the Moors from Granada, the last remaining Spanish region under Moorish control in 1492. They also financed Columbus' four expeditionary voyages.

Carlos V (1516-1556), grandson of Fernando and Isabel, was one of the most powerful Spanish kings. During his reign, Spain ruled most of Europe and the New World. **Felipe II** was the son of Carlos V. His "Invincible Armada" was defeated in an attempt to invade England in 1588.

Nineteenth and Twentieth Centuries

The **War of Independence** (1808-1814) started with a rebellion of the people against the French ruler, Napoleon.

The Spanish-American War (1898) was an armed military conflict between the United States and Spain. Spain was defeated, and agreed to give up Cuba, Puerto Rico, the Philippines, and Guam.

The Spanish Civil War (1936-1939) was won by General Francisco Franco and his supporters, who overthrew the republic and set up a dictatorship. At Franco's death (1975), Spain became a constitutional monarchy and **Prince Juan Carlos de Borbón**, grandson of **Alfonso XIII**, was proclaimed King. The Spanish throne is hereditary, but the power of the king is symbolic. In 1982, **Felipe González Márquez** became Primer Minister. Spain joined the **European Common Market** in 1985. In 1996, there was a political change in Spain with the election of the **conservative party**, the Popular Party **(el Partido Popular)**. At the head of this party and of the government as Prime Minister was **José María Aznar**.

Twenty-First Century

In the twenty-first century, Spain is a **stable democracy** and is part of the European Common Market. It adopted the **euro** as its currency, replacing the **peseta**. In the last general elections, **José Luis Rodríguez Zapatero**, representing the Spanish **Socialist Workers' Party**, became Spain's Prime Minister. Like other nations, this country faces social challenges that include political terrorism, work stoppages, and uncontrolled immigration, a situation shared by other members of the **European Union**.

EXERCISE A

Match the words in column A with their related words in column B.

	A		*B*
1.	Pelayo	***a.***	early inhabitants of Spain
2.	waterwheel	***b.***	dictator
3.	A.D. 711	***c.***	Catholic Rulers
4.	el Cid	***d.***	Moorish defeat at Granada
5.	Felipe II	***e.***	Rodrigo Díaz de Vivar
6.	1808	***f.***	Invincible Armada
7.	1492	***g.***	brought to Spain by the Moors
8.	Celtiberians	***h.***	War of Independence
9.	Franco	***i.***	Moorish invasion
10.	Fernando and Isabel	***j.***	Covadonga

EXERCISE B

If the statement is true, write *Sí*; if it's false, correct it by replacing the word(s) in boldface.

1. The Spanish "Invincible" Armada, at war with England, was defeated in **1588**.

2. The Moors governed Spain for **two** centuries.

3. The **Celtiberians** established trading posts in Spain.

4. The **Visigoths** invaded Spain in A.D. 711.

5. Carlos V was the father of **Felipe II**.

6. El Cid captured **Valencia** from the Moors.

7. The **Carthaginians** built bridges and aqueducts in Spain.

8. Fernando and Isabel completed the Reconquest from the **Moors**.

9. The **Moors** developed philosophy and the sciences.

10. The **Phoenicians** conquered the Carthaginians.

EXERCISE C

Select the word or expression that correctly completes each sentence.

1. The first leader in the Reconquest of Spain was (Franco / Pelayo / el Cid).

2. The Spanish-American War took place in (1898 / 1936 / 1516).

3. Felipe II was the son of (Fernando and Isabel / el Cid / Carlos V).

4. The Spanish language is derived from (Portuguese / Latin / Basque).

5. The Moors were driven out of Spain in (1588 / 1808 / 1492).

6. The Romans ruled Spain for (two / six / eight) centuries.

7. Many Spanish words that begin with **al–** are of (Greek /Arabic / Portuguese) origin.

8. Prince Juan Carlos de Borbón was proclaimed King in (1898 / 1975 / 1982).

9. Columbus's voyages were financed by (Carlos V / Fernando and Isabel / Felipe II).

10. Spain's national hero is (don Pelayo / el Cid / Franco).

EXERCISE D

a. When did...

   1. the Moors invade Spain?

   2. don Pelayo win at Covadonga?

   3. Fernando and Isabel recapture Granada?

   4. the Spaniards rebel against Napoleon?

   5. England defeat the "Invincible Armada"?

b. Who...

   6. captured Valencia from the Moors?

   7. financed Columbus's voyages?

   8. was the father of Felipe II?

   9. devised an irrigation system called "noria"?

   10. overthrew the Spanish republic in 1939?

EXERCISE E

Create a time line that shows Spain from its earliest inhabitants to today.

CHAPTER

34

Important and Interesting Places in Spain

Madrid is Spain's capital and largest city (population: approximately 5,000,000). In Madrid and its vicinity there are many interesting places to visit. The **Museo del Prado** features one of the world's finest collections of European art. The Royal Palace **(el Palacio Real)**, built in the eighteenth century, is one of the most luxurious palaces in Europe. The Spanish royal family lived there until King Alfonso XIII was forced to leave the country. The palace is now a museum. **La Puerta del Sol** is the central plaza of Madrid. Streets originate from it in all directions, to all parts of the city.

Near Madrid is the **Escorial**, a huge building that combines a palace, art museum, monastery, library, and burial place for Spanish kings. It was built between 1563 and 1584 by order of Felipe II. Also near the capital is the Valley of the Fallen **(el Valle de los Caídos)**, an enormous monument built in memory of the soldiers who died in the Spanish Civil War (1936-1939).

Barcelona is the principal city of Catalonia **(Cataluña)**, and it is the second largest city in Spain (population: approximately 4,000,000). It is Spain's main industrial city and has been an important seaport for more than two thousand years. Many Spanish books are printed in Barcelona. It contains and is known for unique works by master **architect Antonio Gaudí**.

Seville **(Sevilla)** is in Andalusia **(Andalucía)** and is situated on the bank of the Guadalquivir River. Seville is one of Spain's most picturesque cities for its gypsies and flamenco dancers. The Cathedral of Seville **(la Catedral de Sevilla)** is the largest in Spain and one of the biggest in the world. Some historians believe it contains the tomb of Columbus. **The Giralda** is the tower of the Cathedral of Seville and it is an admirable example of Moorish architecture.

Valencia, capital of the Valencian Community, is located in a rich agricultural region on the Mediterranean coast called the "garden of Spain." It is a leading export center for oranges and rice.

Granada is a picturesque city in Andalusia, in the south of Spain. It was the last Moorish possession in Spain and was recaptured by the Christians in 1492. The famous Moorish palace, the **Alhambra**, is the city's main tourist attraction.

Toledo, capital of Castile-La Mancha, is a famous medieval city located on the

Tajo River. It is important in metalworking, especially fine steel and exquisite jewelry. Toledo was the home of the famous painter, **El Greco**, and contains many of his works.

Salamanca, in Castile-Leon, is the site of the **University of Salamanca**, the oldest in Spain, and among the oldest and best universities in Europe. It was established in the thirteenth century.

Cordova **(Córdoba)** is located on the banks of the **Guadalquivir River** in Andalusia. During the tenth and eleventh centuries, it was the Moorish capital of Spain and one of the most important cultural centers of Europe. The city's main tourist attraction is the Mosque **(la Mezquita)**—a Muslim place of worship, built in the eighth century and converted into a Roman Catholic cathedral in 1238.

Burgos, in Castile-Leon, is the home of **el Cid**, Spain's national hero. The **Cathedral of Burgos** is one of the finest in Europe and contains his tomb.

Bilbao, in the Basque Country, is a seaport in the north, where some of Spain's most important mines and steelyards are located. It is also the home of the **Guggenheim Museum**, an art museum designed by architect Frank Gehry and opened in 1997.

Segovia, in Castile-Leon, is an ancient city in central Spain. A Roman aqueduct, known as the Bridge **(el Puente)**, was built there under the Roman Emperor Trajan (A.D. 53–117).

EXERCISE A

If the statement is true, write *Sí*; if it's false, correct it by replacing the word(s) in boldface.

1. Barcelona is an important seaport on the **Atlantic Ocean**.

2. The Royal Palace is in **Segovia**.

3. The largest cathedral in Spain is located in **Seville**.

4. Valencia and Bilbao are important **regions** of Spain.

5. The Escorial was built by order of **Carlos V**.

6. **Madrid** is located on the Guadalquivir River.

7. **Granada** was the last Moorish possession in Spain.

8. Toledo was the home of **El Greco**.

9. Cordova was an important cultural center in the **nineteenth** century.

10. The aqueduct of Segovia is an important **Moorish** monument.

EXERCISE B

Select the word or expression that correctly completes each sentence.

1. A burial place for kings is located in the (Cathedral of Burgos / Valley of the Fallen / Escorial).

2. The Alhambra is located in (Granada / Bilbao / Salamanca).

3. An important mining area of Spain is located near (Segovia / Madrid / Bilbao).

4. The Valley of the Fallen is near (Barcelona / Madrid / Burgos).

5 Cordova is famous for its (castle / mosque / university).

6 The oldest university in Spain is located in (Toledo / Madrid / Salamanca).

7. The second largest city of Spain is (Sevilla / Barcelona / Madrid).

8. Valencia is famous for its (minerals / wines / oranges).

9. The (Prado / Giralda / Alhambra) is a famous art museum in Madrid.

10. The population of Madrid is about (2,000,000 / 5,000,000 / 37,000,000).

EXERCISE C

Match the words in column A with their related words in column B.

	A		*B*
1.	Mosque	*a.*	Madrid
2.	Valencia	*b.*	Alhambra
3.	la Giralda	*c.*	the "garden of Spain"
4.	Granada	*d.*	tower in Seville
5.	Puerta del sol	*e.*	Burgos
6.	el Cid	*f.*	Muslim temple
7.	Toledo	*g.*	steel-manufacturing center
8.	books	*h.*	university
9.	Salamanca	*i.*	medieval city
10.	Bilbao	*j.*	Barcelona

EXERCISE D

Complete the following statements.

1. The cities of Seville and Cordova are located on the _____ River.

2. _____ is Spain's most picturesque city.

3. _____ is a monument to the soldiers who died in the Spanish Civil War.

4. The central plaza of Madrid is called _____ .

5. _____ was one of the most important cultural centers of Europe during the tenth century.

6. Many Spanish kings are buried in _____ .

7. _____ is the capital of Spain.

8. A very important industrial city of Spain is _____ .

9. Toledo is located on the _____ .

10. Granada was recaptured from the Moors in the year _____ .

(**EXERCISE E**)

You and some friends will be traveling throughout Spain. Each of you has agreed to research a different city that you will visit. Using the Internet or guide books, research the city and prepare notes that you will use as the group guide when you are there.

People and Customs of Spain

Names

Spanish family names are different from those in the United States. In addition to a first or given name, every Spanish child has two surnames (last names), the father's family name followed by the mother's family or maiden name. For example, Luis Ortega Ramos marries Elena Sánchez Gómez. They have a son named **Pedro Ortega Sánchez. Pedro's** sister is **Amelia Ortega Sánchez.** When Amelia marries Daniel Zapata Morales, she will add her husband's family name to her own name: **Amelia Ortega de Zapata**.

Most people in Spain and in the rest of the Spanish-speaking countries as well have the name of a saint as their given name. They generally celebrate their saint's day **(el Día del Santo)** instead of, or in addition to, their birthday.

Customs and Traditions

All countries have their own particular customs and traditions, and Spain is not an exception.

The **tertulia** is an informal social gathering for meeting and chatting with friends. It often extends well past midnight. Traditionally, the **siesta** is an afternoon nap or rest following the noon meal. Many stores are closed at this time. Although many Spaniards still stop for siesta, it is less common in big cities, such as Madrid or Barcelona than in small towns. The siesta is gradually disappearing in big cities due to people's hectic lives. The **lotería** is a government-controlled game whose earnings are used to finance many services, such as public assistance for orphans and widows.

The regions of Spain are proud of their tradional **folkloric dances**. The most typical dances are the **bolero**, **fandango**, and **flamenco** from Andalusia, which are generally accompanied by a guitar. The **jota** is a lively dance from Aragon and the **sardana** is a type of circle dance from Catalonia. The **tuna** is a group of strolling musicians, usually university students, who play romantic and animated music. This is a tradition that exists since the sixteenth century. The Gypsies **(los gitanos)** are found mostly in the south, especially around Seville and Granada. It is believed that they came from northern India. Their language is called **romaní**.

Religious Holidays

Spain has been a **Catholic country** for centuries, and religious holidays and traditions continue to be important.

Christmas **(Navidad)** is celebrated on December 25. Christmas trees are not displayed as much as in the United States. Instead, many homes and public establishments have a nativity scene **(nacimiento)**, which consists of small clay figures representing the scene of the birth of Christ. On Christmas eve **(Nochebuena)**, people attend a midnight mass **(Misa del Gallo)**. Children receive gifts on January 6, the Day of the Three Wise Men **(Día de los Reyes Magos)**. The Reyes Magos play the same role in Spanish life as Santa Claus plays in American culture.

Easter **(Pascua Florida)** is celebrated throughout Spain and Spanish America. Holy Week **(Semana Santa)** is observed the week before, with solemn commemorations and processions. The Holy Week celebration in Seville is world-famous. Carnival **(Carnaval)** is a festivity that occurs during the last three days before Lent. All Souls' Day **(Día de los Muertos)** is observed solemnly on November 2. People visit the graves of relatives and friends.

National Holidays

There are three important holidays in Spain. The Day of the Constitution **(Día de la Constitución)** is celebrated on December 6. This commemorates the day in 1978 when the Spaniards voted for the constitution that led to democracy after forty years of dictatorship.

October 12 corresponds to Columbus Day. It is called **Día de la Hispanidad** or **Día de la Raza**. May 1 is Labor Day **(Día del Trabajador)** and is celebrated throughout the European Union.

Festivals

Local and regional festivals abound in Spain. A few of the best known include:

The **Way of Saint James (El Camino de Santiago)** is the pilgrimage to the Cathedral of Santiago de Compostela in Galicia in northwestern Spain. Legend has it that the remains of the apostle Saint James the Great are buried there. While there is not a single route, a few of the routes are considered main ones. Since the 1980s the route has attracted a growing number of modern-day pilgrims from around the globe. In October 1987, the Council of Europe declared the route the first European Cultural Route; in 1993 it was also named one of UNESCO's World Heritage Sites.

The **Tomatina** is the world's largest tomato fight which is held the last Wednesday of August in the town of Buñol, located near Valencia. It coincides with the town's festive celebration of its patron saint.

The **Fiesta de San Fermín**, the bull-running festival, is celebrated in Pamplona on July 6. This fiesta was popularized by Ernest Hemingway in his 1926 novel "The Sun Also Rises."

Typical Foods and Beverages

In Spain, as in the United States, there are three principal meals. **Breakfast** is usually eaten around eight o'clock in the morning and generally consists of **coffee with milk** or **hot chocolate** and **bread with butter and marmalade**. **Lunch** and **dinner** are generally complete meals consisting of **soup**, **salad**, **meat with rice** or **vegetables** and **dessert**. Lunch is usually served about 2:00 P.M. and dinner is served after 8:00 P.M. **Tapas**, morsels or bites that reflect the varied typical culinary dishes of the regions of Spain, generally accompany drinks. Spaniards enjoy **el tapeo,** visiting tapas bars with friends. Popular Spanish dishes include **arroz con pollo**, yellow rice with chicken; **paella**, yellow rice with chicken and seafood; and **cocido**, also known as olla or puchero, a beef stew. Thick hot cocoa, **chocolate**, is usually served at breakfast with **churros**, a kind of cruller. **Horchata** is a cold drink made with crushed toasted almonds or sesame seeds, water, and sugar.

EXERCISE A

Match the words in column A with their related words in column B.

	_A_		_B_
1.	Saint's Day	a.	Aragon
2.	Carnival	b.	afternoon nap
3.	flamenco	c.	beverage
4.	Holy Week	d.	birthday celebration
5.	siesta	e.	Lent
6.	jota	f.	Santa Claus
7.	Three Wise Men	g.	midnight mass
8.	Tertulia	h.	Easter
9.	horchata	i.	Andalusia
10.	Christmas	j.	social gathering

EXERCISE B

Select the word or expression that correctly completes each statement.

1. A popular Spanish dish is (sardana / paella / tertulia).

2. Spaniards usually have (horchata / tea / chocolate) at breakfast.

3. The *lotería* is managed (by the church / privately / by the government).

4. Instead of Christmas trees, Spaniards usually have a (basket / bull / nativity scene) set up in the house.

5. The jota is a Spanish (dance / musical instrument / dish).

6. One of the Spanish national holidays is (May 2 / December 6 / November 2).

7. A gathering for the purpose of talking is a (nacimiento / tertulia / cocido).

8. The city of (Seville / Valencia / Granada) is famous for its Holy Week celebration.

9. Spanish children receive their Christmas gifts on (December 16 / December 25 / January 6).

10. Spaniards visit the cemeteries on (their saint's day / All Soul's Day / Christmas Day).

EXERCISE C

Complete the following sentences.

1. The *fandango* is a regional dance of _____ .

2. Juan López Serrano marries Dolores Moreno Ortega. The wife's full name is now _____ .

3. Juan and Dolores have a son, Carlos, whose full name is _____ .

4. Christmas Eve is called _____ in Spain.

5. A group of university students who sing in the streets is called a _____ .

6. A typical dish of Spain is _____ .

7. A _____ is a Nativity scene.

8. Labor Day is celebrated on _____ .

9. A regional dance of Catalonia is the _____ .

EXERCISE D

Define each of the following.

1. arroz con pollo   **6.** Día de la Raza

2. seis de diciembre   **7.** tertulia

3. Reyes Magos   **8.** misa del gallo

4. cocido   **9.** Nochebuena

5. nacimiento

EXERCISE E

Research how one of the national holidays is celebrated in Spain. Then compare it to how a similar national holiday is celebrated in the United States.

CHAPTER

36

Spanish Literature, Science, and the Arts

Literature

Since the earliest times, Spain has been well represented in world literature.

"El Poema o Cantar de Mio Cid" is the oldest and best example of Spanish epic poetry. Its author is anonymous and it was written around 1140. It tells the deeds of Spain's national hero, **Rodrigo Díaz de Vivar**. Other examples of works produced during the **Middle Ages** include *El libro de buen amor* by **Juan Ruiz**, known as *Arcipreste de Hita* (1283-1351); **Fernando de Rojas** (¿-1541) wrote *La Celestina* (1499); and *Lazarillo de Tormes*, an anonymous work, appeared in 1554.

Spain's **Golden Age (Siglo de Oro)** began in 1560 and ended in 1680. One of Spain's greatest novelists, **Miguel de Cervantes** (1547-1616), wrote the world-famous novel *El ingenioso hidalgo don Quijote de la Mancha*. **Lope de Vega** (1562-1635), a leading Spanish dramatist, wrote hundreds of plays. **Pedro Calderón de la Barca** (1600-1681) was the last notable figure of the Golden Age. He wrote the philosophical play *La vida es sueño (Life Is a Dream)*.

The **eighteenth century** was the age of enlightenment or reason. It was the century in which philosophy flourished more than literature. Spain was influenced greatly by the French philosophers. In 1713, the *Royal Spanish Academy (la Real Academia Española)* was established. Its purpose was and continues to be to maintain the purity of the Spanish language.

Renowned authors of the **nineteenth** and **twentieth centuries** include: **Benito Pérez Galdós**, **Vicente Blasco Ibáñez**, **Jacinto Benavente**, **Juan Ramón Jiménez**, **Federico García Lorca**, and **Vicente Aleixandre**.

Benito Pérez Galdós (1843-1920) was among the most prestigious novelists of the nineteenth century. He wrote *Marianela*. **Vicente Blasco Ibáñez** (1867-1928) was a distinguished novelist who wrote *The Four Horsemen of the Apocalypse (Los cuatro jinetes del apocalipsis)* and *Blood and Sand (Sangre y arena)*. He also wrote many novels about Valencia, of which the most famous is *La barraca*. **Jacinto Benavente** (1866-1954) was a famed dramatist who won the Nobel Prize for Literature in 1922. Another Nobel Prize winner (1956) is the Andalusian poet **Juan Ramón Jiménez** (1881-1958). **Federico García Lorca** (1898-1936) was a famed poet and dramatist whose works deal with folkloric and traditional themes. His plays *Bodas de sangre* and *La casa de Bernarda Alba* continue to be presented in the theater. He died tragically during the Spanish Civil War. **Vicente Aleixandre** (1898-1984) was a renowned essayist and poet. He won the Nobel Prize for Literature in 1977.

As a result of the Spanish American War (1898), Spain lost what remained of its colonial empire. A group of young Spanish intellectuals, who became known as *la Generación del '98 (The Generation of '98)*, began to study the cultural and spiritual state of their country within the modern world and proclaimed a moral and cultural rebirth for Spain. This group includes essayists, novelists, poets, and dramatists. Among the most influential figures of this group are: **Francisco Giner de los Ríos** (1839–1915), **Miguel de Unamuno** (1864–1936), **Ramón del Valle-Inclan** (1866–1954), **Ramón Menéndez Pidal** (1869–1968), and **Pío Baroja** (1872–1956).

A new generation of writers appeared in Spain after the Civil War (1936-1939). Many of them were youths during that time. Their writings address the social and economic problems that faced Spain from the end of the war through today. Included among these famous contemporary authors are: **Camilo José Cela**, **Miguel Delibes**, **Carmen Laforet**, **Ana María Matute**, **Alfonso Sastre**, **Antonio Gala**, **Juan Goytisolo**, and **Arturo Pérez-Reverte**.

Camilo José Cela (1916–2002) was a famous novelist of contemporary Spain who won the Nobel Prize for Literature in 1989. **Miguel Delibes** (1920–   ) is a novelist whose work *The Heretic (El hereje)* received the National Prize for Narrative Literature (1999). **Carmen Laforet** (1921–   ) is a famed author whose novel *Nada* deals with life in Spain immediately after the Civil War. **Ana María Matute** (1926–   ) is a novelist whose works have received numerous national prizes. **Alfonso Sastre** (1926–   ) is a dramatist who writes about society with the purpose of sending a social message to his audience. **Antonio Gala** (1930–   ) is a poet and dramatist who discusses current themes through the eyes of historic characters. **Juan Goytisolo** (1931–   ) is a modern novelist who presents the problems and uneasiness of Spanish society in his works. **Arturo Pérez-Reverte** (1951–   ) is a current author who molds his journalistic experiences in his narratives.

Scientists

Spain has produced several prominent scientists. They are **Santiago Ramón y Cajal** (1852–1934), winner of the Nobel Prize for Medicine in 1906 for his many discoveries about the structure of the nervous system; **Juan de La Cierva** (1895–1936), an aeronautical engineer who invented the autogiro, the forerunner of the helicopter, in 1923; and **Severo Ochoa** (1905–1993), winner of the Nobel Prize for Medicine in 1959 for his studies on enzymes.

Painters

Spain has a rich history in painting. Works by Spanish masters are exhibited in the most important museums world-wide. Included among the Spanish painters with international reputation and fame are: **Doménico Theotocopulos**, **Diego Velázquez**, **Francisco Goya**, **Pablo Picasso**, **Joan Miró**, and **Salvador Dalí**.

Doménico Theotocopulos, known as *El Greco* (1541–1614), was a sixteenth century Greek painter who settled in Toledo, where many of his works can still be found. Most of his paintings deal with religious themes. **Diego Velázquez** (1599–1660) is considered by many to be one of Spain's greatest painters. He was court painter to Felipe IV (seventeenth century). His most famous work is *Las meninas*, which is exhibited in **El Prado**, Spain's foremost museum in Madrid. **Francisco Goya** (1746–1828), is among the most prolific Spanish painters of the eighteenth and nineteenth centuries. His works attack the social and political decay of the period. **Pablo Picasso** (1881–1973) is the most influential painter of the twentieth century and the founder of cubism, a style of painting in which figures are deconstructed into geometrical forms. **Joan Miró** (1893–1983), is one of the best painters of abstract art of the twentieth century. **Salvador Dalí** (1904–1989), is an outstanding twentieth-century painter of surrealist art.

Composers and Musicians

The most celebrated Spanish composers are **Isaac Albéniz** (1860–1909), who wrote music for the piano; **Enrique Granados** (1867–1916), who also composed music for the piano; and **Manuel de Falla** (1876–1946), who is considered one of Spain's greatest composers and foremost representatives of modern Spanish music.

The most notable Spanish musicians are **José Iturbi** (1895–1980), a famous pianist, composer, and conductor; **Andrés Segovia** (1893–1987), considered among the most talented Spanish guitarists who gave concerts all over the world; **Pablo Casals** (1876–1973), a cellist of international fame; and **Alicia de Larrocha** (1923–   ), a contemporary pianist who has gained popular acclaim for her interpretation of Spanish composers as well as other classical composers.

The opera stages of the world have been graced by the talent and skill of the sopranos **Victoria de los Ángeles** (1923–2005) and **Monserrat Caballé** (1933–   ), and the tenors **Alfredo Krauss** (1927–1999), **Plácido Domingo** (1941–   ), and **José Carreras** (1946–   ).

The contemporary Spanish singers of popular music who have gained world fame include **Sara Montiel**, **Lola Flores**, **Julio Iglesias**, **Rafael**, **Camilo Sesto**, **Rocío Jurado**, **Rocío Durcal**, **José Luis Perales**, **Lolita**, **Isabel Pantoja**, **Joan Manuel Serrat**, **Ana Belén**, **Víctor Manuel**, **Joaquín Sabina**, **Enrique Iglesias**, **Ismael Serrano**, and **Alejandro Sanz Rosario**.

EXERCISE A

If the statement is true, write *Sí*; if it's false, correct it by replacing the word(s) in boldface.

1. Andrés Segovia was a world-famous **pianist**.

2. Pablo Casals was one of Spain's greatest **composers**.

3. **Blasco Ibáñez** wrote *The Four Horsemen of the Apocalypse*.

4. Lope de Vega was one of Spain's leading **poets**.

5. **Ramón y Cajal** invented the autogyro.

6. **Cervantes** was one of the greatest Spanish novelists.

7. José Carreras is a famous **painter**.

8. **Velázquez** was the founder of cubism.

9. **Carmen Laforet** wrote plays about Spanish folklore.

10. **Dalí** won a Nobel Prize for Literature.

EXERCISE B

Match the names in column A with their related words in column B.

A	*B*
1. Plácido Domingo	*a.* twentieth-century dramatist
2. Calderón	*b.* religious paintings
3. Ramón y Cajal	*c. Las meninas*
4. Albéniz	*d. El ingenioso hidalgo don Quijote de la Mancha*
5. Jacinto Benavente	*e.* Golden Age dramatist
6. Blasco Ibañez	*f.* studies of the nervous system
7. El Greco	*g.* tenor
8. Miguel de Cervantes	*h.* novels about Valencia
9. Diego Velásquez	*i.* cubism
10. Pablo Picasso	*j.* composer

EXERCISE C

Select the word or expression that correctly completes each statement.

1. The Golden Age occurred during the (eighteenth and nineteenth / nineteenth and twentieth / sixteenth and seventeenth) centuries.

2. One of the most famous Spanish composers is (Pablo Picasso / Manuel de Falla / Pablo Casals).

3. A Spanish novelist who won the Nobel Prize was (Ana María Matute / Camilo José Cela / Federico García Lorca).

4. The last great dramatist of the Golden Age was (Velázquez / Calderón / Cervantes).

5. The autogyro was invented by (Juan de la Cierva / Severo Ochoa / Juan Miró).

6. Juan Ramón Jiménez was a famous (poet / musician / painter).

7. (Lope de Vega / Plácido Domingo / Andrés Segovia) was a great Spanish guitarist.

8. One of the greatest painters of eighteenth-century Spain was (Francisco Goya / Diego Velázquez / Salvador Dalí).

9. One of the greatest novelists of Spain was (Miguel de Cervantes / José Carreras / Vicente Aleixandre).

10. Severo Ochoa received a Nobel Prize in the field of (literature / medicine / economics).

EXERCISE D

Complete the following statements.

1. A sixteenth-century painter who lived in Toledo was _____ .

2. An author who wrote about Spain after the Civil War is _____ .

3. _____ was a famous pianist and orchestra leader.

4. Sangre y arena was written by _____ .

5. _____ was court painter to Felipe IV.

6. _____ is the author of *La vida es sueño*.

7. _____ was among the most prestigious novelists of the nineteenth century.

8. _____ won the Nobel Prize for Literature in 1977.

9. _____ earned his fame as a painter of abstract art.

10. _____ is a famous Spanish soprano.

EXERCISE E

a. **Who wrote...**

1. *El ingenioso hidalgo don Quijote de la Mancha?*

2. *La Casa de Bernarda Alba?*

3. *Nada?*

4. about Valencia?

5. hundreds of plays?

b. **Who was...**

6. Joan Miró?

7. one of Spain's greatest composers?

8. Santiago Ramón y Cajal?

9. the father of cubism?

10. Francisco Goya?

EXERCISE F

Select a Spanish painter and use the Internet to view a painting that he or she created. How would you describe the style of the painting? What impresses you most (least) about the painting?

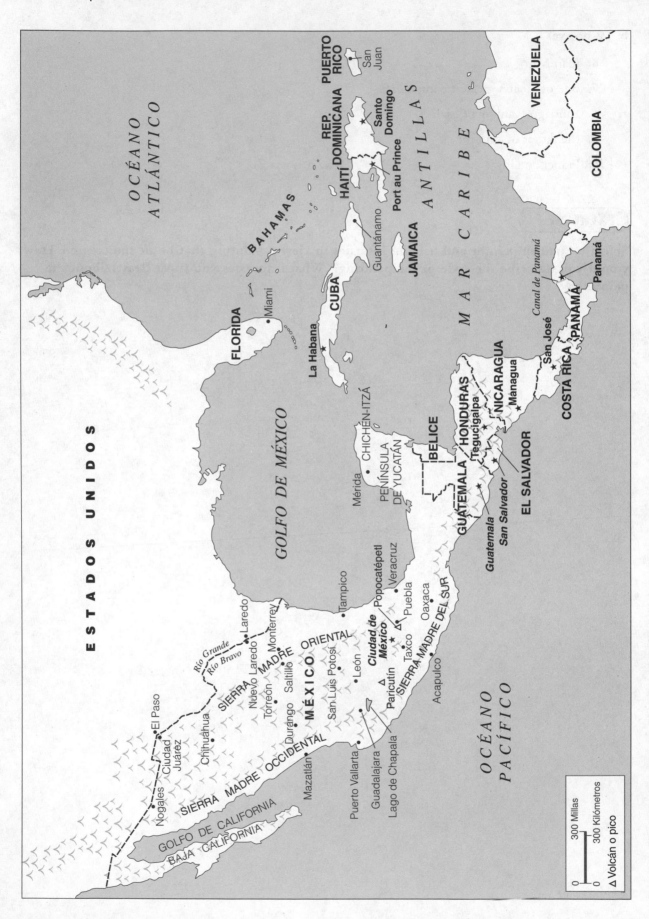

CHAPTER

37

Geography of Spanish America

South of the United States, and occupying an area much larger than that of the United States, live more than three hundred fifty million people whose official native language is Spanish. Spanish America is comprised of nineteen countries, located in three distinct regions: (1) **Mexico** and **Central America**, (2) **las Antillas**, and (3) **South America**.

Mexico and Central America

Mexico (capital: **Federal District of Mexico**) is our nearest Spanish-speaking neighbor. It is located directly south of the western United States and borders the states of Texas, New Mexico, Arizona, and California. It is the land of the **Aztecs** and **Mayas**, two of the most advanced Native-American civilizations. Mexico is part of the North American continent.

Implementation of the **North American Free Trade Agreement** (NAFTA) began on January 1, 1994. Full implementation began on January 1, 2008. Under the NAFTA, all non-tariff barriers to agricultural trade between the United States and Mexico were eliminated.

Guatemala (capital: **Guatemala City**) is located south of Mexico in what is referred to as Central America. It was the center of the old Mayan empire; it boasts the largest population of Central America and the largest percentage of pure indigenous inhabitants (54%). It is the main producer of chicle, which is used in the manufacture of chewing gum.

Honduras (capital: **Tegucigalpa**) is the most mountainous country of Central America. It has important mineral and timber resources. Its principal exports are bananas and coffee.

El Salvador (capital: **San Salvador**) is the smallest country in Central America and the only one that has no coastline on the Atlantic Ocean. Coffee, cotton, and sugar cane are its principal products.

Nicaragua (capital: **Managua**) is the largest country in Central America. Its principal exports are cotton and textiles, coffee, and sugar cane.

Costa Rica (capital: **San José**) is one of the most progressive countries in Central America. It has strict environmental laws and no army. Its developing market economy is largely based on coffee, pineapple, and banana exports.

Panama (capital: **Panama City**) is an ismuth joining Central and South America. It is famous for the Panama Canal, which crosses the country and facilitates travel from east to west and vice versa. Construction of the canal was begun by a Frenchman, Fernando de Lesseps, in 1881. It was completed by the United States in 1914. Its principal port in the Canal Zone is Balboa. Panama's economy has become mainly service-based, with the operation of the Panama Canal, container ports, flagship registry, and tourism all playing important roles.

Las Antillas

Las Antillas are a group of islands in the Caribbean Sea that include **Cuba**, **Hispanola** (the Dominican Republic/Santo Domingo), and **Puerto Rico**. The Dominican Republic shares the island (Hispanola) with French-speaking Haiti. Hispanola was named and discovered by Christopher Columbus. The capital of the Dominican Republic is **Santo Domingo**, the oldest city in the Americas, established in 1496. The University of Saint Thomas Aquinas was founded there in 1538 and is the oldest university in the New World. It is now called the University of Santo Domingo.

Cuba (capital: **Havana**) is the largest island of the Caribbean and was discovered by Columbus on his first voyage. It is referred to as the "Pearl of the Antilles" because of its fertile land and the beauty of its landscape. Its principal products are tobacco and sugar.

Puerto Rico (capital: **San Juan**) is the smallest of the Greater Antilles; it is also called **Borinquen**, its native name. Puerto Rico is a commonwealth of the United States and its inhabitants have been United States citizens since 1917. Its principal products are coffee, sugar cane, tobacco, bananas, and pineapple.

South America

The greater part of **South America** is situated south of the equator and their seasons are the reverse of ours. When it is winter here, it is summer there. The continent is very mountainous which has affected its development. The **Andes Mountains** are in the western part of the continent and include the countries of **Chile**, **Bolivia**, **Peru**, **Ecuador**, **Colombia**, and **Venezuela**. The Andes extend from the Caribbean to Antárctica, more than 4,660 miles. There are many high peaks, the highest, **Aconcagua**, has an altitude of nearly 23,000 feet (more than four miles), and it is the highest peak in the Western Hemisphere.

Argentina (capital: **Buenos Aires**) is the largest of the Spanish-speaking countries in South America. It extends from the Chaco region in the north to the Tierra del Fuego and the Strait of Magellan in the south, from the Atlantic Ocean in the east to the Andes Mountains in the west. Its capital is the largest city in South America and is situated on the Río de la Plata. The population is predominately of Spanish and Italian descent. The greater part of the country is situated in a great plain, called *La Pampa*. It is the home of the *gaucho*, the Argentine cowboy, and is the center for agriculture and cattle-raising.

Uruguay (capital: **Montevideo**) is the smallest Spanish-speaking nation of South America. Its capital is located on the Río de la Plata, opposite Buenos Aires. The population of Uruguay is of European descent, predominately Spanish and Italian. It is a progressive country with little illiteracy.

Paraguay (capital: **Asunción**) is one of two South American countries with no seaport. However, the Río Paraná provides access to the Atlantic Ocean. The country is situated between Bolivia, Brazil, and Argentina. Paraguay has a large Native-American population. Its principal products are soybeans, packed meats, and *yerba mate*, a popular tea.

The Andean countries are found in the western part of the continent. They include **Chile**, **Bolivia**, **Peru**, **Ecuador**, **Colombia**, and **Venezuela**. The Andean Mountains cross almost all of these countries from north to south.

Chile (capital: **Santiago**) is the longest and narrowest country in South America. It is situated between Argentina and the Pacific Ocean. It is a country with a lot of seismic activity. The Atacama Desert in the north is one of the world's driest deserts. The mining region is found in this area. Chile is the second largest producer of copper in the world. The central part of the country has an excellent climate and it is here that the vineyards of Chile are found. The capital, Santiago, and the principal port, Valparaiso, are found in this area. Winter sports such as skiing are practiced in the southern part of the country.

Bolivia (two capitals: **La Paz** and **Sucre**) is the only country in South America without an outlet to the sea. Although Sucre is the official capital, La Paz is the actual seat of the government. It is also the highest capital in the world with an altitude of 12,000 feet above sea level. Bolivia is bordered by Brazil in the north and the east, by Paraguay in the southeast, by Argentina in the south, by Chile in the southwest, and by Peru in the northwest. Lake Titicaca, situated between Bolivia and Peru, is the world's most commercially navigable lake, at an altitude of 12,500 feet. Bolivia's population is fifty percent indigenous: the aimaraesí, the quechuas, and the guaraníes are the most numerous. It is a country rich in minerals and is one of the principal producers of tin.

Peru (capital: **Lima**) is three times larger than the state of California. It is bordered in the north by Ecuador and Colombia, in the east by Brazil and Bolivia, in the south by Chile, and in the west by the Pacific Ocean. The Andes Mountains divide the country into three natural regions: the Pacific coast, which is narrow and desert-like; the mountain, which is comprised of a high plateau and is dominated by the Andes and is where more than half of the population lives; and the jungle near the Amazon, which is an immense plain that covers more than half the country. Agriculture and mining are important to the economy. Peru is the land of the Incas, a Native-American civilization that flourished before the arrival of Europeans in America. They were destroyed by Francisco Pizarro in 1533. Their principal city was Cuzco, located near the sacred city of Machu-Pichu.

Ecuador (capital: **Quito**) is named for its location on the equator. The country is crossed north to south by two parallel ranges of very high volcanic peaks, which are part of the Andes Mountains. The Galapagos Islands, located in the Pacific Ocean, belong to Ecuador. Quito is situated at an altitude of 9,300 feet at the foot of a volcano. Although it is in the torrid zone, its altitude gives it a rather cold climate. Guayaquil is the principal port and center of commerce of the country. Ecuador's most important product today is bananas.

Colombia (capital: **Bogotá**) is the only South American country with two sea-coasts: on the Caribbean Sea (Cartagena and Barranquilla), and on the Pacific Ocean (Buenaventura). Colombia is bounded on the north by the Caribbean Sea, on the south by Ecuador and Peru, on the west by the Pacific Ocean and Panama, and on the east by Venezuela and Brazil. The country can be divided into three regions: the Andean in the west where most of the population lives, the eastern plains, and the jungle of the Amazon. Its most important river is the Magdalena, which crosses the country from south to north. The principal products for export are coffee, bananas, and oil. The capital, Bogotá, is located in the interior of the country and has been the center of the country since its founding in 1538. Medellín is the second largest city and the center of coffee production.

Venezuela (capital: **Caracas**) is the richest oil-producing country in South America. It is also the birthplace of Simón Bolívar, "The Liberator." It is bounded in the north by the Caribbean Sea, in the west by Colombia, in the south by Brazil, and in the east by Guyana. The population is concentrated in the mountainous zones of the west and in the coasts. In addition to oil as a principal product, it also produces coffee and cacao. Caracas is the political and commercial capital of the country. It is a very modern city. Nearby is La Guaira, which is its port on the Caribbean Sea.

Geographic Features

Mountain Ranges: The **Andes** extend the entire length of South America along the west coast. There are many high peaks; the highest, **Aconcagua**, has an altitude of nearly 23,000 feet (more than four miles), and is the highest peak in the Western Hemisphere. There are many other peaks nearly as high. The **Sierra Madre** in Mexico consists of two parallel mountain chains, the **Sierra Madre Oriental** (Eastern) and the **Sierra Madre Occidental** (Western), with a great plateau between them.

Principal Rivers: The longest single river in Spanish America is the **Orinoco**, located in eastern Venezuela. (The **Amazon River**, which is more than twice as long, is in Brazil.) The **Río de la Plata** is located between Uruguay and Argentina. The capitals of both countries, Montevideo and Buenos Aires, are on its banks. The Paraná-Paraguay System is formed by the **Paraná** and **Paraguay Rivers**. It connects with the Río de la Plata to form the chief water outlet from the interior regions to the sea. The **Magdalena River** in Colombia is an important means of transportation.

Climate: Argentina, **Uruguay**, **Paraguay**, and **Chile** are in the **South Temperate Zone**. **Northern Mexico** is in the **North Temperate Zone**. **Southern Mexico** and the **rest of Spanish America** lie in the tropics **(Torrid Zone)**. Most cities that are located in the tropics are very warm, except the ones at high altitudes.

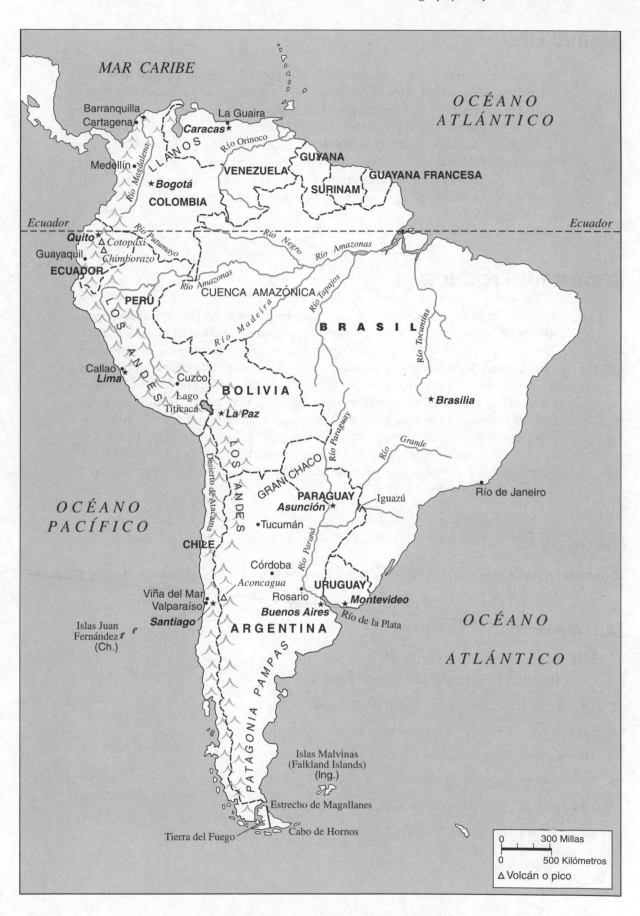

MAR CARIBE

OCÉANO
ATLÁNTICO

Barranquilla
Cartagena
La Guaira
Caracas ★
Medellín
Río Magdalena
LLANOS
Río Orinoco
GUYANA
VENEZUELA
GUAYANA FRANCESA
★ *Bogotá*
SURINAM
COLOMBIA

Ecuador
Ecuador

Quito ★
Río Putumayo
Río Negro
Río Amazonas
△ *Cotopaxi*
Guayaquil
△ *Chimborazo*
ECUADOR
Río Amazonas
PERÚ
CUENCA AMAZÓNICA
Río Tapajós
BRASIL
Río Madeira
Río Tocantins

LOS ANDES

Callao
Lima ★
Cuzco
BOLIVIA
Lago
Titicaca
★ *La Paz*
★ *Brasilia*

Río Paraguay
Río Grande
Río

Desierto de Atacama
LOS ANDES
GRAN CHACO
PARAGUAY
Iguazú
Río de Janeiro
Asunción ★

OCÉANO
PACÍFICO
Tucumán

CHILE
Córdoba
Río Paraná
Aconcagua
URUGUAY
Viña del Mar ★ △
Valparaíso
Rosario
Montevideo
Santiago
Buenos Aires
Río de la Plata
ARGENTINA
OCÉANO

Islas Juan
Fernández
(Ch.)

ATLÁNTICO

PATAGONIA PAMPAS

Islas Malvinas
(Falkland Islands)
(Ing.)

Estrecho de Magallanes
Tierra del Fuego
Cabo de Hornos

0		300 Millas
0		500 Kilómetros

△ Volcán o pico

Animal Life

Two prevalent **birds** in Spanish America are the **condor** and the **quetzal**. The condor is a carrion-eating bird from the Andes. It is probably the largest among flying birds. The quetzal is a brilliant colored bird of Central America. It is the national emblem of Guatemala and gives name to its monetary unit.

Among the **wool-bearing animals** of Spanish America are the **alpaca**, the **guanaco**, the **llama**, and the **vicuña** in the Andes. **Sheep** are found mainly in Argentina and Uruguay. The **burro** is the most common beast of burden in Spanish America. The llama is the principal beast of burden of the Andean countries (Peru, Ecuador, Bolivia).

Important Products

Some of the products that Spanish America gives to the world are **potatoes**, **corn**, **tomatoes**, **chocolate**, **vanilla**, **pineapples**, **peanuts**, **pecans**, and **cashew nuts**. The main producers of other agricultural products are: Chile: **apples** and **peaches**; most Central American countries: **bananas**; Argentina and Uruguay: **beef**; Ecuador and Venezuela: the **cacao bean**, which is used in manufacturing chocolate; Colombia, Costa Rica, and Venezuela: **coffee**; Cuba and the Dominican Republic: **sugar**; Ecuador: **corozo nuts**, which are used in manufacturing buttons; Cuba: **tobacco**; Argentina and Uruguay: **wheat**. The main producers of mining and chemical industries are: Chile and Peru: **copper**; Colombia: **emeralds**; Chile: **nitrates** used for fertilizers; Venezuela and Mexico: **petroleum**; Colombia: **platinum**; Mexico and Peru: **silver**; and Bolivia: **tin**.

EXERCISE A

If the statement is true, write *Sí*; if it's false, correct it by replacing the word(s) in boldface.

1. Two important products of Venezuela are **petroleum** and **coffee**.

2. Lima is the capital of **Argentina**.

3. **Santiago** is the capital of Colombia.

4. Costa Rica and Honduras produce many **bananas**.

5. The Paraná River flows into the **Pacific Ocean**.

6. Spanish is the language of **six** countries in South America.

7. **Montevideo** is the capital of Venezuela.

8. The condor lives in the **Andes**.

9. Mexico and Peru produce **emeralds**.

10. There are **six** countries in Central America.

EXERCISE B

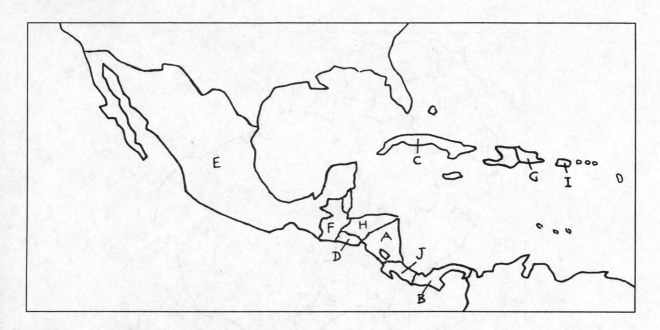

In the map above, identify each of the following countries.

1. Panama

2. Puerto Rico

3. Costa Rica

4. Honduras

5. El Salvador

6. Guatemala

7. Mexico

8. Cuba

9. Nicaragua

10. Dominican Republic

EXERCISE C

In the map above, identify each of the following countries.

1. Bolivia   *6.* Colombia

2. Argentina   *7.* Peru

3. Chile   *8.* Paraguay

4. Ecuador   *9.* Venezuela

5. Uruguay

EXERCISE D

Match the words in column A with their corresponding definitions in column B.

	A		*B*
1.	Sierra Madre	*a.*	river in Colombia
2.	corozo nuts	*b.*	capital of Nicaragua
3.	yerba mate	*c.*	used to manufacture chocolate
4.	Aconcagua	*d.*	fabric borne by the Alpaca
5.	tin	*e.*	mountains in Mexico
6.	Magdalena	*f.*	highest peak in the Western Hemisphere
7.	Managua	*g.*	used to manufacture buttons
8.	cacao	*h.*	bird of the Andes
9.	wool	*i.*	element found in Bolivia
10.	condor	*j.*	popular tea from Paraguay

EXERCISE E

Write the word that is needed to complete each statement.

1. The longest river in Venezuela is the _____ .

2. The Andes are situated in _____ .

3. The quetzal is found mainly in _____ .

4. The main beast of burden in the Andes is the _____ .

5. In Chile, Argentina, and Uruguay it is cold in the months of _____ .

6. The capital of Costa Rica is _____ .

7. The only country in South America without an outlet to the ocean is _____ .

8. The country crossed north to south by two parallel ranges of peaks is _____ .

9. The richest oil-producing country of South America is _____ .

10. The ingredient used to manufacture chocolate is _____ .

EXERCISE F

The geography of a country often affects its social, economic, and political structure. Select a country in Spanish America and explain the effects of its geography on contemporary life there.

CHAPTER

38

Famous Names in Spanish America

National Heroes of Spanish America

All the colonies of the New World were considered possessions of the king of Spain. These colonies were divided into four administrative territories called "virreinatos." They were (1) the Virreinato of New Spain, which included Mexico, Central America, part of what is today the United States, and the Antilles; (2) the Virreinato of Peru, which included Peru and Chile; (3) the Virreinato of New Granada, which included Ecuador, Colombia, Panama, and Venezuela; and (4) the Virreinato of the Río de la Plata, which included Argentina, Bolivia, Paraguay, Uruguay, and part of Brazil. They were governed by viceroys (virreyes), appointed directly by the king of Spain. Spain's crown had a dual purpose: to civilize the Indians by converting them to Catholicism, and to exploit the natural resources of the colonies for the sole benefit of Spain. The colonial period lasted about three centuries.

National heroes emerged as the colonies sought independence from Spain. Among them were: **Simón Bolívar**, **José de San Martín**, **Bernardo O'Higgins**, **Antonio José de Sucre**, **Miguel Hidalgo**, **Benito Juárez**, and **José Martí**.

Simón Bolívar (1783–1830) was one of the main figures in the struggle for South American independence from Spain. He was called the Liberator (El Libertador) as he won independence for the northern part of South America. Bolivia was named in his honor. **José de San Martín** (1778–1850) was an Argentine general who won independence for the southern part of South America, including Argentina and Chile. **Bernardo O'Higgins** (1778–1842) was a Chilean general who helped San Martín in the liberation of Chile. O'Higgins became the first president of Chile.

Antonio José de Sucre (1795–1830) defeated the Spanish army in the battle of Ayacucho in Peru. This was the last battle for South American independence (1824). **Miguel Hidalgo** (1753–1811) was a Mexican priest and patriot who began the struggle for Mexican independence. He is known for the famous "Grito de Dolores," with which he started the revolution on September 16, 1810. **Benito Juárez** (1806–1872) fought against the Archduke Maximilian, Emperor of Mexico. Juárez was later called the "Abraham Lincoln of Mexico." **José Martí** (1853–1895) was a famous Cuban poet and patriot who died fighting for Cuban independence from Spain.

Spanish American Writers

Spanish American writers have also joined the long lists of world class authors and poets.

XIX Century

Andrés Bello (1781–1865) was a Chilean critic and a leading intellectual of Spanish America. He wrote *Gramática de la lengua castellana*. **Domingo Faustino Sarmiento** (1811–1888) was an Argentine educator and statesman. He was known as the "Schoolmaster President." He wrote *Facundo*, which deals with the life of a gaucho (Argentine cowboy) leader. **Ricardo Palma** (1833–1919) wrote *Tradiciones peruanas*, a collection of stories about Peru during colonial times. **Rubén Darío** (1867–1916) was born in Nicaragua. One of the greatest poets of Spanish America, he helped create a new poetic style called "modernism." **Mariano Azuela** (1873–1952) was a Mexican novelist who wrote *Los de abajo*, a novel about the Mexican Revolution of 1910–1920. **Gabriela Mistral** (1889–1957) was a Chilean poetess who won the Nobel Prize for Literature in 1945. **Rómulo Gallegos** (1884–1969) was a Venezuelan novelist and statesman who wrote *Doña Bárbara*, a novel about life on the plains of Venezuela. **Miguel Ángel Asturias** (1899–1974) was a Guatemalan novelist whose books describe the suffering caused by the local dictator Miguel Estrada Cabrera and by the big "Yanqui" companies. He received the Nobel Prize for Literature in 1967.

XX Century

Pablo Neruda (1904–1973) was a Chilean poet and diplomat who received the Nobel Prize for Literature in 1971. **Octavio Paz** (1914–1998) was a Mexican poet and essayist who received the Nobel Prize for Literature in 1990. Among the best known works of the Argentine writer, **Julio Cortázar** (1914–1984), is the novel *Rayuela* whose fragmented structure reflects the incoherence of life and contemporary culture. **Gabriel García Márquez** (1928–   ) is a Colombian novelist who wrote *Cien años de soledad*, the history of an imaginary town in Colombia. He received the Nobel Prize for Literature in 1982. **Guillermo Cabrera Infante** (1929–2005) was a Cuban writer who lived in exile in England since 1996. He is considered one of the great innovators of the novel. His novel *Tres tristes tigres* received many prizes. **Manuel Puig** (1932–1990) is an Argentine writer who is known internationally. He is famous for his novels *Boquitas pintadas* and *El beso de la mujer araña*. This work was banned for many years in Argentina. A successful film and Broadway show were made of this work. **Mario Vargas Llosa** (1936–   ) is a Peruvian writer who has achieved international fame. Among his important works are *La ciudad y los perros* and *La casa verde*. He has received numerous prizes for his literary works and since 1993 he has been a citizen of Spain. He is also a member of the *Real Academia Española*. **Isabel Allende** (1942–   ) is a contemporary Chilean writer who resides in the United States. Trained as a journalist, she is now the most read Latin-American author. Her novels are translated into different languages and they often appear on the best-sellers list. Among her novels are *La casa de los espíritus*, *Eva Luna*, and *Cuentos de Eva Luna*.

Spanish American Painters

It was not until the twentieth century that Spanish American painters achieved any fame or worldwide recognition. One of the three best known Mexican painters is **Diego Rivera** (1886–1957). His early works are in the cubist and post-impressionism style. He then dedicated his work to mural painting in which he dealt with political and social topics. His murals adorn many public buildings throughout Mexico. **José Clemente Orozco** (1883–1949) is another muralist whose works defend the cause of the Mexican Revolution. He painted the murals in the Palacio de Bellas Artes in Mexico City. He also painted murals in Dartmouth College. **David Alfaro Siqueiros** (1896–1974) is the most prominent defender of art as an expression of the political ideology of the second half of the twentieth century. In 1932, Siqueiros organized the Experimental Workshop of New York. His students included painter **Jackson Pollack**. **Rufino Tamayo** (1899–1991) is another Mexican painter and muralist who received several international awards for his work. His murals adorn such buildings as the Palacio de Bellas Artes in Mexico City, the Anthropological Museum of Mexico City, and the UNESCO building in Paris.

Other outstanding Spanish American painters contributed great visual joy to the art world.

The Mexican **Miguel Covarrubias** (1904–1957) is best known for his caricatures of famous people. **Frida Kahlo** (1907–1954), also from Mexico, was the third wife of Diego Rivera. She enjoys great popularity today for her realistic paintings that show great suffering. Scenes of gaucho life were painted by the Argentine **Cesáreo Bernaldo de Quirós** (1879–1969). The indigenous culture of Peru was reflected by **José Sabogal** (1888–1956). **Wilfredo Lam** (1902–1982) was a Cuban painter who was influenced by surrealism. One of his most famous paintings, *La jungla*, hangs in the entrance of the Museum of Modern Art in New York City.

Among the contemporary painters whose works have been exhibited and acquired by galleries and museums in the United States and Europe are: the Argentine cubist painter **Emilio Pettoruti** (1892–1971); the abstract and surrealistic Chilean painter **Roberto Matta** (1911–2002); the Ecuadorian **Oswaldo Guayasamín** (1919–1999); the abstract Colombian painter **Alejandro Obregón** (1920–1992); **Rómulo Macció** (1931–) from Argentina; the Colombian **Fernando Botero** (1932–), and **Gerardo Chávez** (1937–) from Peru.

Composers and Musicians

Carlos Chávez (1899–1978) from Mexico, and **Alberto Ginastera** (1916–1983) from Argentina are two famous composers of classical music. Chávez was a famous orchestra conductor and founder of the Symphonic Orchestra of Mexico and the National Symphony. He is famous for the ballet *Sinfonía India*. Ginastera was a contemporary composer of operas, ballets, and symphonies. His opera *Bomarzo* is well known. **Manuel Ponce** (1882–1948) from Mexico composed numerous works for orchestra that highlight the popular music of his country. **Gonzalo Roig** (1890–1972) was a Cuban—composer and conductor who wrote many zarzuelas. He is well known for his popular song *Quiéreme mucho*. Another Cuban, **Ernesto Lecuona** (1896–1963) composed music for the piano and orchestra and songs such as *Siboney* and *Malagueña*. The Mexican **Agustín Lara** (1897–1970) is famous for songs such as *María Bonita* and *Granada*.

Several singers and instrumentalists from Hispanic America have also gained international acclaim. They include the Chilean opera tenor, **Ramón Vinay**, the Puerto Rican baritone **Justino Díaz**, the great Peruvian singer **Yma Sumac**, the Argentine singer and composer **Atahualpa Yupanqui**, and the famous Chilean pianist **Claudio Arrau**. Enjoying fame in the contemporary opera world are the tenors **Rolando Villazón** and **Ramón Vargas** from Mexico, **Juan Diego Flórez** from Peru, and **José Cura** and **Marcelo Álvarez** from Argentina.

In recent years, Hispanic music has gained great popularity throughout the world. Among the famous singers are **José Luis Rodríguez** (*El Puma*) from Venezuela, the Mexicans **Marco Antonio Muñiz** and **Luis Miguel**, the Cubans **Oswaldo Farrés**, **Antonio Machín**, **La Lupe**, **Celia Cruz** and **Gloria Estefan**. Latin pop music is represented by **Ricky Martin** and **Chayanne** from Puerto Rico, and **Shakira** from Colombia. Latin jazz is represented by the Puerto Ricans **Ray Barreto** and **Eddie Palmieri**. The **Buena Vista Social Club** highlights the Cuban sound. Among the most popular singers of salsa are **Rubén Blades**, **Los Van Van**, and el **Médico de la Salsa**. Latin rock is represented by the Mexican group **Maná** and the guitarist **Carlos Santana**.

EXERCISE A

Identify each of the following names by writing the corresponding letter next to each of them.

a. patriot   *b.* writer   *c.* painter   *d.* composer-musician

1. Mariano Azuela

2. Andrés Bello

3. Rubén Darío

4. Rómulo Gallegos

5. Antonio José de Sucre

6. Benito Juárez

7. Gabriela Mistral

8. Octavio Paz

9. Diego Rivera

10. Bernardo O'Higgins

11. Carlos Chávez

12. Claudio Arrau

13. Cesáreo Bernaldo de Quirós

14. Miguel Ángel Asturias

15. José Clemente Orozco

EXERCISE B

Match the names in column A with their related words in column B.

A		**B**
1. Juárez		*a.* novelist
2. Sarmiento		*b.* great Spanish–American poet
3. San Martín		*c.* *Tradiciones peruanas*
4. Martí		*d.* Schoolmaster President

5. García Márquez   e. murals

6. Darío   f. Mexican patriot

7. Orozco   g. painter

8. Palma   h. Argentina's independence

9. Bolívar   i. Cuban patriot

10. Rivera   j. "the Liberator"

EXERCISE C

Select the name, title, or word that correctly completes each statement.

1. (Siqueiros / Neruda / Martí) was the second writer to win a Nobel Prize for Chile.

2. (Juárez / Hidalgo / San Martín) was called the "Abraham Lincoln of Mexico."

3. One of the greatest Spanish-American poets was (Ricardo Palma / Rubén Darío / Rómulo Gallegos).

4. *(Doña Bárbara / Facundo / Los de abajo)* is a novel about the Mexican Revolution.

5. (Claudio Arrau / Bernardo O'Higgins / Gabriela Mistral) was a famous Chilean pianist.

6. Diego Rivera was a famous (musician / novelist / painter).

7. The last battle in the struggle for South American independence took place at (Lima /Ayacucho / Mexico).

8. (Gabriela Mistral / Jose Martí /Andrés Bello) won the Nobel Prize for Literature.

9. The first president of Chile was (Sucre / O'Higgins /Azuela).

10. Sarmiento wrote *(Facundo / Cien años de soledad / Tradiciones peruanas)*.

EXERCISE D

a. Write the name that would fit each definition.

1. Mexican painter   5. country named for Bolívar

2. Argentine educator   6. Mexican composer

3. Spanish-American novelist   7. a Mexican Nobel Prize winner

4. Spanish-American poet   8. a Colombian Nobel Prize winner

b. Tell who wrote the following titles.

9. *Facundo*   12. *Tradiciones peruanas*

10. *Doña Bárbara*   13. *Los de abajo*

11. *Cien años de soledad*   14. *Gramática de la lengua castellana*

EXERCISE E

Complete the following statements.

1. One of Nicaragua's most famous poets is _____ .

2. San Martín won independence for Chile and _____ .

3. The Mexican movement for independence from Spain was begun by _____ .

4. Bernaldo de Quirós painted scenes of the life of the _____ .

5. The Spanish army was defeated by Sucre at the battle of _____ .

6. José Clemente Orozco was a Mexican _____ .

7. José Martí was killed in the war for the independence of _____ .

8. The Chilean general who helped San Martín win independence for Chile is _____ .

EXERCISE F

Research, explain, and discuss the role of the Latin Grammy Awards in the musical field in the United States today. How has it helped the careers of contemporary Spanish-speaking musicians and composers?

Places of Interest in Spanish America

Spanish America offers many interesting places for tourists. It is rich in natural beauty, history, and traditions.

Mexico

The Federal District of Mexico **(Distrito Federal de México)** is the capital of Mexico. It was built on the site of the original capital of the Aztec empire, **Tenochtitlán**. Today it is a modern city and the largest Spanish-speaking city in the world. Among the interesting places to visit in Mexico City is the Metropolitan Cathedral **(Catedral Metropolitana)**. It is the largest and oldest cathedral on the North American continent. Directly in front of it is the **Zócalo** or main plaza. One of the most beautiful museums in the world is the Museum of Anthropology **(Museo Antropológico)**, located on the famous **Paseo de la Reforma**. Among its greatest treasures is the Sun Stone **(La Piedra del Sol)**, an ancient stone inscribed with the Aztec calendar. Not very far away is **Chapultepec**, a large incredible park with an impressive castle. The Palace of Fine Arts **(Palacio de Bellas Artes)** contains a stunning theater and art museum. **Ciudad Universitaria** is the site of the National University, the oldest university in North America. **Popocatépetl** and **Ixtaccíhuatl** are picturesque volcanoes overlooking the Federal District of Mexico. Popocatépetl is still an active volcano. **Xochimilco** is a town near the Federal District that is famous for its floating gardens. **Taxco** is one of Mexico's most colorful cities. The Spanish colonial atmosphere is still preserved. Taxco is widely known for its silver.

Mexico has many beautiful and fashionable seaside resort towns. Among those are **Cozumel** and **Cancún**, which are located in the region of Mayan temples, such as **Chichén-Itzá**, **Uxmal**, and **Palenque**. On the Pacific coast are the famous resorts of **Acapulco** and **Puerto Vallarta**.

Central and South America

Among the most attractive places of interest in Central America are **Monteverde**, a rain forest in Costa Rica; and **Tikal**, the Mayan ruins in Guatemala.

South America also has many appealing and fascinating places for visitors. **Buenos Aires**, the capital of Argentina, is one of the most beautiful capital cities in the world. Strongly influenced by European culture, Buenos Aires is sometimes referred to as the "Paris of South America." **Lima** is the capital of Peru and its main industrial and cultural center. The **University of San Marcos**, the oldest university in South America, is located here. **Cuzco** (Peru) is the ancient capital of the Incas. Nearby are the enigmatic Inca ruins of **Machu-Picchu**. **Bogotá** is the capital and most important cultural center of Colombia. It has many excellent examples of colonial architecture. **Quito** is the capital and principal textile center of Ecuador. It is located almost at the equator, but it has a pleasant climate due to its high altitude (nearly 10,000 feet). The **Galapagos Islands** are national parks in Ecuador of great interest to visitors. The islands and the surrounding marine reserve were both declared World Heritage sites. They are home to the giant tortoise, marine iguanas, and Darwin finches. **Lake Titicaca** is located in the Andes Mountains between Bolivia and Peru. It is the highest navigable lake in the world. The Iguazú Falls **(Las Cataratas del Iguazú)** are spectacular waterfalls located between Argentina and Brazil. They are higher than the Niagara Falls. On the border between Chile and Argentina in the Andes Mountains stands the Christ of the Andes **(El Cristo de los Andes)**, a giant statue of Christ. It was erected to commemorate the peaceful settlement of a boundary dispute.

EXERCISE A

Match each of the tourist attractions in column A with its description in column B.

A	*B*
1. Monteverde	*a.* floating gardens
2. Tenochtitlán	*b.* seaside resort
3. Cristo de los Andes	*c.* Mayan ruins in Guatemala
4. Popocatépetl	*d.* statue
5. Cuzco	*e.* rain forest
6. Iguazú	*f.* original Aztec capital
7. Xochimilco	*g.* lake
8. Cancún	*h.* volcano in Mexico
9. Titicaca	*i.* Inca capital
10. Tikal	*j.* waterfall

EXERCISE B

If the statement is true, write *Sí*; if it's false, correct it by replacing the word(s) in boldface.

1. The **Piedra del Sol** is a famous theater in Mexico.

2. The city of **Quito** is located near the equator.

3. The University of San Marcos is located in **Bolivia**.

4. Bogotá is the capital of **Colombia**.

5. Taxco is a colorful city in **Argentina**.

6. **Chichén-Itzá** is a famous beach in Mexico.

7. **Iguazú Falls** are located between Bolivia and Peru.

8. The largest Spanish-speaking city in the world is **Buenos Aires**.

9. The oldest university in North America is located in **Peru**.

10. The ruins of Machu-Picchu are located near **Cuzco**.

EXERCISE C

Complete the following statements.

1. The volcanoes *Popocatépetl* and *Ixtaccíhuatl* are located near _____ .

2. The highest navigable lake in the world is _____ .

3. The oldest university in South America is located in _____ .

4. *El Cristo de los Andes* commemorates the settlement of a dispute between Argentina and _____ .

5. The famous rain forest in Costa Rica is _____ .

6. The oldest university in Mexico is _____ .

7. Quito has a pleasant climate because of its _____ .

8. Between Brazil and Argentina there is a waterfall called _____ .

9. Cozumel is a seaside resort in _____ .

10. Cuzco was the ancient capital of the _____ .

EXERCISE D

Identify the country where each of the following is located.

1. Palacio de Bellas Artes
2. Cuzco
3. Cataratas del Iguazú
4. Bogotá
5. Cancún

6. Titicaca
7. Buenos Aires
8. Piedra del Sol
9. Tikal
10. Lima

EXERCISE E

Explain why places such as Monteverde in Costa Rica and the Galapagos Islands in Ecuador are popular destinations for tourists. What is their principal attraction to the visitor? How do the local governments support these sites?

CHAPTER

40

People and Customs of Spanish America

The customs and traditions of Spanish America reflect the Spanish and indigenous influences in all aspects of daily life.

People of Spanish America

Most Spanish-American countries have several racial groups. These include: **Whites**, **Native-Americans**, **Blacks**, **Mestizos**, and **Mulattos**.

Whites are descendants of Spanish settlers and other European immigrants (from Italy, Germany, England, Ireland, and the Slavic countries). Native-Americans, found in great numbers in many Spanish-American countries, especially in Mexico, Central America, Ecuador, Bolivia, Paraguay, and Peru, are descendants of the Aztecs, the Mayas, and the Incas. Blacks are descendants of Africans who were brought to Spanish America. They are most numerous in the Caribbean. Mestizos, people of mixed European and Native-American ancestry, are the largest racial group in Spanish-American countries. Mulattos, people of mixed European and African ancestry, are most numerous in the Caribbean.

National Holidays

Each country has its national holiday or Independence Day that commemorates the date on which the country finally attained its independence from Spain. **September 16** is the Mexican national holiday; in Guatemala, Honduras, El Salvador, Nicaragua, and Costa Rica it is **September 15**; in Chile it is **September 18**; in Paraguay it is **May 14**; in Venezuela it is **July 5**; in Colombia it is **July 20**; in Peru it is **July 28**; in Bolivia it is **August 6**; in Ecuador it is **August 10**; and in Panama it is **November 3**.

In some Spanish-American countries, Independence Day celebrates emancipation from nations other than Spain. The Dominican Republic on **February 27** celebrates its independence from Haiti; Uruguay on **August 25** celebrates its independence from Brazil; three dates are remembered in Cuba: **December 10** marks the independence from Spain, **May 20** marks the independence from the United

States, and **July 26** commemorates the Day of the Revolution. In Puerto Rico, two dates are celebrated: **July 4,** Independence Day in the United States; and **July 25,** the day of the constitution. In Argentina, **May 25** commemorates the revolution against the Spaniards.

There are two holidays that are celebrated throughout the Spanish–Speaking world: **May 1**, which is Labor Day, and **October 12**, which commemorates the discovery of America and is called **el Día de la Raza** or **el Día de la Hispanidad**.

Religious Holidays

One of the goals of Spain was to convert the native population in Spanish America to Catholicism. They succeeded, and the catholic religion has played an important role in the history and daily life of Spanish America. Many of the religious holidays became national holidays, for example, Christmas, is observed in all of the countries of Spanish America, and its celebration varies from country to country. In Mexico, for instance, Christmas festivities begin with **posadas** or visits by neighbors nine days before Christmas Eve. At the parties that follow the posadas, children break a **piñata** (an earthen jug that is colorfully decorated and contains candy, fruit, and toys). In other countries, Christmas is celebrated with a big meal and a religious mass, as it is practiced in Spain. January first is also celebrated throughout Spanish America.

Carnival **(Carnaval)** is a festivity that takes place before Lent. Holy week **(Semana Santa)** is also celebrated in Spanish America and is followed by Easter **(Pascua Florida)**.

All Saints Day **(el Día de Todos los Santos)**, is observed solemnly in almost all of the countries on November 1. It is celebrated in Mexico on November 2 as el **Día de los Muertos** and the event is anything but somber. Sugar figures of skulls are sold in bakeries and families visit the graves of their loved ones at the cemeteries. They decorate gravesites with marigold flowers and candles, and sit on picnic blankets next to the graves where they eat their departed loved ones' favorite foods.

Picturesque Types

Cowboys are found in the great plains where cattle are raised and the principal means of transportation is on horseback. In Colombia and Venezuela, the cowboys are called **llaneros**. In Uruguay and Argentina, they are called **gauchos**.

The **charro**, dressed in his traditional outfit, is the Mexican cowboy. The woman who accompanies him is called the **china poblana**. Her typical dress consists of a wide and long red or green skirt and a white blouse, which represent the colors of the Mexican flag.

The **mariachi** is a group of street musicians and singers who play the music from the state of Jalisco, located in the western part of Mexico.

Clothing

In the cities, people generally dress as we do in the United States. However, traditional dress is often seen. This dress includes the **sarape**, a bright colored Mexican blanket made of wool or cotton. It is worn by men and women, slung over the shoulders.

The **poncho** is a cape worn by the Mexicans, gauchos, and other Spanish Americans as protection from the cold and rain. It is also known as **ruana** in the northern part of South America. The **rebozo** is a shawl worn by Mexican women. **Huaraches** are sandals worn in Mexico. The **sombrero de jipijapa** (Panama hat) is a high-quality straw hat that is hand-made in Ecuador (not Panama).

Sports and Spectacles

Soccer **(el fútbol)** is the most popular sport in Spanish-speaking countries, both as a participatory sport as well as a spectator sport.

Jai-alai is a game that originated in the Basque country of Spain. This sport is popular in Spain, Mexico, Venezuela and Cuba. Jai-alai is similar to handball but it is played in a **frontón**, a three-walled court. The players wear a **cesta** or curved basket strapped to their wrist, in which the ball is caught and thrown against the wall.

Bullfights **(las corridas de toros)** are prohibited in some Spanish-American countries, but they are still popular in Mexico and Colombia.

Monetary Unit

Each of the Spanish-American countries has its own monetary unit. Although the monetary unit of Argentina, Colombia, Cuba, Chile, the Dominican Republic, Mexico, and Uruguay is called the **peso**, the peso does not have the same value in each country. The following monetary units are used in the other Spanish American countries: Bolivia, the **boliviano**; Costa Rica, the **colón**; Guatemala, the **quetzal**; Honduras, the **lempira**; Nicaragua, the **córdoba**; Panama, the **balboa** and the **U.S. dollar**; Paraguay, the **guaraní**; Peru, the **nuevo sol**; Venezuela, the **bolívar**. The U.S. dollar is used in Puerto Rico, El Salvador, and Ecuador.

EXERCISE A

Match the words in column A with their related words in column B.

A	*B*
1. charro	*a.* jai-alai
2. Día de los Muertos	*b.* Lent
3. Las posadas	*c.* candy
4. gaucho	*d.* Argentina

5. fútbol	**e.** Christmas
6. frontón	**f.** china poblana
7. sarape	**g.** soccer
8. Carnaval	**h.** Columbus Day
9. piñata	**i.** November 2
10. Día de la Raza	**j.** blanket

EXERCISE B

If the statement is true, write *Sí*; if it's false, correct it by replacing the word(s) in boldface.

1. The **incas** were the dominant Native American culture in Mexico.

2. **El Día de los Muertos** is celebrated in Mexico.

3. The cowboy of Argentina is the **charro**.

4. The gauchos wear **ponchos** as protection from the rain.

5. Panama hats are made in **Panama**.

6. **El Día de la Raza** is celebrated in Spanish America and Spain.

7. **Jai-alai** originated in the Basque country in Spain.

8. Bullfights are popular in **Mexico**.

9. *Las Posadas* occur immediately **after** Christmas.

10. A **corrida** is a Mexican blanket.

EXERCISE C

Select the word or expression that correctly completes each sentence.

1. Mexican women wear a shawl called a *(rebozo / poncho / cesta)*.

2. In (Argentina / Bolivia / Uruguay) most of the inhabitants are Indians.

3. A three-walled court is used for (bullfighting / jai-alai / soccer).

4. One of the most important religious holidays in Spanish America is *(Navidad / Día de los Muertos / Carnaval)*.

5. The Mexican street singers are called *(charros / gauchos / mariachis)*.

6. The Mexican national holiday is (November 2 / October 12 / September 16).

7. A person of mixed Native American and European ancestry is called a *(china poblana / mestizo / sarape)*.

8. On May 5, Mexicans commemorate the rebellion against (Maximilian / Bolívar / Martí).

9. *El Día de la Raza* corresponds to (All Soul's Day / Easter / Columbus Day).

10. On November 2, Spanish Americans celebrate (Christmas / All Soul's Day / Easter).

EXERCISE D

Define each of the following.

1. mestizos

6. mariachi

2. Día de la Raza

7. gauchos

3. cesta

8. piñata

4. sarape

9. china poblana

5. frontón

10. poncho

EXERCISE E

Research the monetary unit of one of the Central or South American countries that does not use the peso as its currency. Describe the significance of the name of the currency and its current exchange value.

Comprehensive Testing: Speaking, Listening, Reading, Writing

Rating and Scoring the Speaking Section

Rating and Scoring. The rating procedures described below provide for a maximum of five points for the performance of each task. Each utterance is worth a maximum of one point and is rated on the basis of comprehensibility, appropriateness, and the characteristics listed in column 1 below. An utterance is any spoken statement that helps to accomplish the stated task.

Comprehensibility is determined by considering whether the utterance would be understood by a literate native speaker of Spanish who knows no English but is used to speaking with non-native speakers.

Appropriateness is determined on the basis of the utterance's contribution to the completion of the task to be performed.

2 points	1 point	0 points
Utterance is • comprehensible *and* • appropriate *and* is strongly characterized by the following: • initiates and/or sustains and/or advances the conversation • uses common verb tense forms • uses accurate structure • is articulated comprehensibly • uses a variety of vocabulary which may expand or clarify meaning • is extended discourse (may contain more than one short utterance) • uses culturally correct gestures, social conventions and/or idiomatic expressions	Utterance is • comprehensible *and* • appropriate *but* • a single, short, discrete utterance consisting of limited vocabulary/ structures *or* • contains little or no evidence of the characteristics listed in column 1	Utterance is • incomprehensible and/or • inappropriate Disregard if it is a • Yes/No response • Socializing device • Restatement of all or essential parts of what the teacher said • Proper noun(s) in isolation

INFORMAL SPEAKING RUBRIC

Dimension	4	3	2	1
Initiation	**Eagerly** initiates speech. Utilizes appropriate attention-getting devices. Asks questions easily. **Speaks spontaneously.**	**Willing** to initiate speech. Uses appropriate attention-getting devices. Asks questions. **Speaks evenly.**	**Sometimes** initiates speech using attention-getting devices. Sometimes asks questions. **Speaks hesitantly.**	**Reluctant** to initiate speech. Struggles to ask questions. **Speech is halting.**
Response	**Almost always** responds appropriately to questions/statements.	**Frequently** responds appropriately to questions/statements.	**Sometimes** responds appropriately to questions/statements.	**Rarely** responds appropriately to questions/statements.
Conversational Strategies	Clarifies and continues conversation. Uses **all** or **some** of the following strategies: circumlocution, survival strategies, intonation, self-correction, verbal cues.	Uses **all** or **some** strategies but may need occasional **prompting**.	Uses **some** strategies. Needs **frequent prompting** to further the conversation.	Uses **few** strategies. Relies heavily on conversational partner to sustain conversation. **Rarely** responds even with frequent prompting.
Vocabulary	Incorporates a **variety** of old and new vocabulary. Uses idiomatic expressions appropriate to topic. Speaks clearly and imitates accurate pronunciation.	Utilizes a **variety** of old and limited new vocabulary. Attempts to use idiomatic expressions appropriate to topic. Speaks clearly and imitates accurate pronunciation.	Relies on **basic** vocabulary. Speech is comprehensible in spite of mispronunciations.	Uses **limited** vocabulary. Mispronunciations impede comprehensibility.
Structure	Makes **few errors** in the followings areas: Verbs in utterances when necessary with appropriate subject/verb agreement; noun and adjective agreement; correct word order. Errors do not hinder comprehensibility.	Makes **several errors** in structure which do not affect overall comprehensibility.	Makes **several errors** in structure which may interfere with comprehensibility.	Makes utterances which are so brief that there is little evidence of structure. Comprehensibility is impeded.
Cultural Appropriateness	**Almost always** uses/interprets cultural manifestations when appropriate to the task.	**Frequently** uses/interprets cultural manifestations when appropriate to the task.	**Sometimes** uses/interprets cultural manifestations when appropriate to the task.	**Rarely** uses/interprets cultural manifestations when appropriate to the task.

A zero can be given in any of the above dimensions when the student's performance falls below the criteria described for a score of "1."

If a paper scores a zero on purpose/task, the entire response receives a zero.

Conversion Chart				
19–24 = 5	14–18 = 4	10–13 = 3	5–9 = 2	1–4 = 1

1. Speaking: Oral Interpersonal Communication Tasks

Directions: The speaking test consists of communication tasks to be performed by a student with his/her teacher. Each task is a simulated conversation in which the student always plays the role of himself/herself and the teacher assumes the specific role indicated in the task. The tasks may involve one or more of the four communication functions: socializing, providing and obtaining information, expressing personal feelings or opinions, and getting others to adopt a course of action.

You will perform a total of four tasks. Each task consists of a brief statement in English to indicate the purpose and setting of the communication, the role of the teacher, and the person who is to initiate the conversation. Each task should be completed in five interactions between the student and the teacher. These interactions are called utterances.

2. Listening Comprehension

A. MULTIPLE CHOICE (ENGLISH)

For each question, you will hear some background information in English. Then you will hear a passage in Spanish twice, followed by a question in English. Listen carefully. After you have heard the questions, read the question and the four suggested answers in your book. Choose the best suggested answer based on the information you heard.

1. **What did the teacher announce?**
   1. Classes will be canceled tomorrow.
   2. A special program will be held in the auditorium.
   3. Students will be dismissed at one o'clock.
   4. All classes have been lengthened to forty minutes.

2. **What does the announcer advise the people to do?**
   1. Stay at home.
   2. Go to emergency shelters.
   3. Prepare for a hurricane.
   4. Shut off all electrical appliances.

3. **How is your friend going to spend the afternoon?**
   1. Watching television.
   2. Reading a book.
   3. Playing soccer.
   4. Copying his assignment.

4. **Why is Felipe not at home?**
   1. He had an accident.
   2. He went to the store.
   3. He went to the emergency room.
   4. He went to the hospital.

5. **What does the doctor tell you to do?**
   1. Return to school.
   2. Take some medicine.
   3. Take your temperature.
   4. Make an appointment.

B. MULTIPLE CHOICE (SPANISH)

For each question, you will hear some background information in English. Then you will hear a passage in Spanish twice, followed by a question in Spanish. Listen carefully. After you have heard the question, read the question and the four suggested answers in your book. Choose the best suggested answer based on the information you heard.

1. *¿Qué actividad le gusta más a tu amigo?*
1. Ir al centro.
2. Ir al cine.
3. Practicar un deporte.
4. Leer un libro.

2. *¿Por qué te pide perdón tu amiga?*
1. No le gustó tu regalo.
2. Salió con otros amigos.
3. Volvió a casa muy tarde.
4. No devolvió tu llamada.

3. *¿Qué debes hacer ahora?*
1. Limpiar la sala.
2. Descansar en tu cuarto.
3. Arreglar tu cuarto.
4. Pasar la aspiradora.

4. *¿Qué anuncian en el aeropuerto?*
1. Que el avión tiene un problema mecánico.
2. Que los pasajeros deben bajarse del avión ahora.
3. Que los pasajeros deben volver al hotel.
4. Que el avión no puede salir porque hace mal tiempo.

5. *¿Por qué no quiere ver esa película tu amigo?*
1. Tiene mucha violencia.
2. Prefiere los deportes.
3. No tiene ningún dinero.
4. Es una película corta.

C. MULTIPLE CHOICE (VISUAL)

For each question, you will hear some background information in English. Then you will hear a passage in Spanish twice, followed by a question in English. Listen carefully. After you have heard the question, read the question and look at the four pictures in your book. Based on the information you heard, choose the picture that best answers the question.

1. *Who is Manuel?*

1   2   3   4

2. *Where does Gabriel want to go?*

1   2   3   4

3. *What hobby does he prefer?*

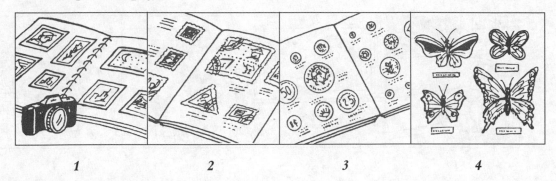

          1   2   3   4

4. *What food does your friend like?*

          1   2   3   4

5. *What is your friend planning to do during her vacation?*

          1   2   3   4

6. *Where does you friend's mother work?*

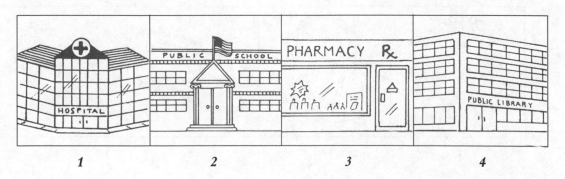

          1   2   3   4

7. *What activity does the doctor restrict?*

1   2   3   4

8. *What did your friend lose?*

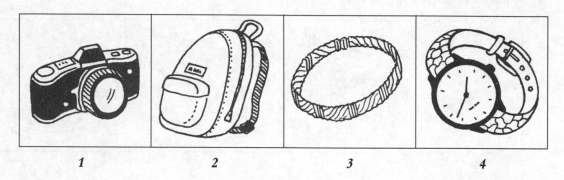

1   2   3   4

9. *What piece of furniture are you going to buy?*

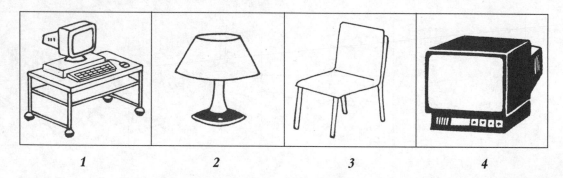

1   2   3   4

10. *What does your friend want to buy?*

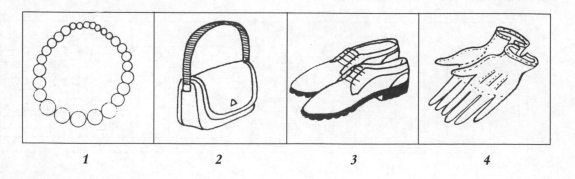

1   2   3   4

3. Reading Comprehension

A. MULTIPLE CHOICE (ENGLISH)

This activity consists of questions or incomplete statements in English, each based on a reading selection in Spanish. Choose the expression that best answers the question or completes the statement. Base your choice on the content of the reading selection.

1. What is Dr. Elizondo's specialty?

1. Allergies.
2. Hearing.
3. Vision.
4. Bones.

¡CUIDE SUS OJOS!

Vaya al oculista una vez al año. Recuerde que el 80% de los casos de ceguera son evitables.

DR. PEDRO ELIZONDO

Le ofrece:
- EXAMEN OCULAR COMPUTARIZADO
- TRATAMIENTOS CON LÁSER

333 Calle Luna
Montevideo, Uruguay
Teléfonos: 04.48.63.01 y 04.40.57.80

¡VACACIONES A CABALLO!

Si Ud. está cansado de quedarse en casa y no salir de vacaciones de invierno: el INSTITUTO ECUESTRE le ofrece clases de equitación, con la posibilidad de continuar con cursos semanales todo el año. Al alumno se le facilita el caballo completamente equipado. Para más información, comuníquese con el:

INSTITUTO ECUESTRE
Avenida Figueroa Alcorta #4
Barcelona, España
Teléfonos: 27.71.55.42 y 27.71.38.28

---

2. What is the advantage of this option?

1. It can be done in the winter.
2. The students receive a free horse.
3. There is a minimal fee for the equipment that is needed.
4. It's an intensive program.

EL GATO CON BOTAS

El espectáculo para niños creado por
Hugo Midón se ha repuesto en cartelera y
constituye una buena opción para llevar
a los chicos en las vacaciones de invierno.

Paseo La Plaza, Calle Corrientes #1600, Buenos Aires
(Funciones a las 5:00 y a las 6:45)

3. What is "El gato con botas"?

1. A shoe store.
2. A pet shop.
3. A television program.
4. A show.

CANAL 13
10:00 **Noticias de América** *Informativo con Juan Carlos Pereira.*
11:00 **Sin Vergüenza** *Entretenimientos, con la participación del público en la calle; con Andrea Martín.*
12:00 **Almorzando con Mirtha Carter** *Interés general, con entrevistas a invitados.*
1:30 **El Desprecio** *Telenovela venezolana-mexicana, con Maricarmen López y Flavio Guzmán.*
2:30 **Visiones** *Magazine de actualidad con Belén Ríos y Sergio Méndez. Colaboran: Catalina Lago (en espectáculos) y Virginia Rivera (en deportes).*

4. On which program does the host interview guests?

1. Noticias de América.
2. Almorzando con Mirtha Carter.
3. Visiones.
4. Sin Vergüenza.

$ $

LA TASA PARA GANAR ESTÁ EN EL PLAZO FIJO DEL

BANCO COMERCIAL DE VENEZUELA

◆

Obtenga desde un **47%** hasta un **55%** de interés colocando su dinero a 30 días. Con una inversión mínima de 250 mil bolívares adquiera su certificado, *¡su más firme aliado!*

$ $

---

5. *This advertisement offers you help in*

  1. buying stocks.

  2. investing your money.

  3. avoiding high interest rates.

  4. investing in industry.

B. MULTIPLE CHOICE (SPANISH)

This activity consists of questions or incomplete statements in Spanish, each based on a reading selection in Spanish. Choose the expression that best answers the question or completes the statement. Base your choice on the content of the reading selection.

VACACIONES DIFERENTES EN EL CAMPAMENTO VACACIONAL RANITA

Para niños entre 8 y 12 años. Situado en Sanare, Falcón, con una extensión de 400 hectáreas, donde sus niños podrán disfrutar el contacto directo con la Naturaleza. Actividades diversas, tales como:

- paseos a caballo
- elaboración de quesos
- cuidado de animales
- paseos diurnos y nocturnos
- juegos de campo
- gimkana
- deportes varios y mucho más

PRIMER GRUPO: del 25 de junio al 10 de julio
SEGUNDO GRUPO: del 15 de julio al 30 de agosto

Para más información, llame a los teléfonos:
08.27.62.14   08.27.62.37   08.27.68.93

1. *¿Qué es lo atractivo de este campamento?*

  1. Ofrece una variedad de actividades.

  2. Los niños pueden vivir en casa mientras asisten al campamento.

  3. Es un programa largo y entretenido.

  4. Los niños no van a estar al aire libre, en compañía de los animales.

2. *¿Qué ofrece este anuncio?*

1. Un trabajo.
2. Una venta.
3. Productos buenos.
4. Sistemas modernos.

¡OFERTA POR TIEMPO LIMITADO!
¿Eres ambicioso?

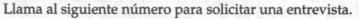

Nosotros te damos el mejor
entrenamiento en ventas y la mejor
comisión. No importa tu experiencia.
Tenemos el mejor producto y el sistema
de ventas más seguro.
Llama al siguiente número para solicitar una entrevista.

09.86.86.51

CONOCE A GENTE INTERESANTE EN
LA LÍNEA LOCA

CHISMES   DEPORTES   FARÁNDULA   ROMANCE

¡Ahora puedes hablar con gente divertida e interesante en nuestra línea de
conversación continua! Llama a cualquier hora a los teléfonos:

31.01.60.09   31.01.67.10   31.01.60.50

(Una llamada a LA LÍNEA LOCA cuesta lo mismo que una llamada
a los Estados Unidos, aproximadamente 126 bolívares por minuto.
La tarifa está sujeta a cambios.)

3. *Esta información les interesa a personas que quieren*

1. visitar los Estados Unidos.
2. hacer amistades por teléfono.
3. conversar en otro idioma.
4. recibir llamadas de otros países.

TALLER MUSICAL VACACIONAL
Para niños de 6 a 12 años

¡FABULOSA INICIACIÓN MUSICAL en un
ambiente ameno y divertido! Tres
semanas, desde el lunes 19 de julio.

**Caurimare, Calle B-2, No. 97
Teléfono: 04.86.62.34**

4. *Este anuncio es para los niños que*

1. cantan bien.

2. tocan instrumentos musicales.

3. quieren aprender música.

4. participan en una orquesta.

GRAN VENTA ESPECIAL

*FALDAS desde **$30**   *BLAZERS desde **$95**

*CAMISAS desde **$45**   *TRAJES DE SEDA desde **$150**

y durante esta semana. . . ¡REGALOS!
1 FALDA Y 1 CAMISA (ó 1 BLAZER), con compras de **$200** o más.

TIENDA MARÍA LISA
PASEO ALCORTA
Local 2046, Segundo Nivel
Salguero 3172, Distrito Federal
Se Aceptan Tarjetas de Crédito

5. *¿Qué debe hacer el cliente para recibir un regalo?*

1. Recomendar a otros clientes.

2. Usar su tarjeta de crédito.

3. Presentar este anuncio en la tienda.

4. Gastar cierta cantidad de dinero.

4. Writing

WRITING RUBRIC

Dimension	4	3	2	1
Purpose/Task	Satisfies the task, connects **all** ideas to task/purpose, and exhibits a logical and coherent sequence of ideas throughout.	Satisfies the task; connections are implied with **few** irrelevancies.	Satisfies the task; connections may be unclear with **some** irrelevancies.	Makes at least one statement which satisfies the task. Remaining statements are irrelevant to the task.
Vocabulary	Utilizes a **wide variety** of vocabulary that expands the topic in the statement/question to include nouns, verbs and/or adjectives, as appropriate to the task.	Utilizes a **variety** of vocabulary relevant to the topic in statement/questions to include nouns, verbs, and/or adjectives, as appropriate to the task.	Utilizes **basic** vocabulary, some of which is inaccurate or irrelevant to the task.	Utilizes **limited** vocabulary, most of which is inaccurate or irrelevant to the task.
Structure/ Conventions	Exhibits a **high** degree of control of structure/conventions: • subject/verb agreement • noun/adjective agreement • correct word order • spelling **Errors do not hinder overall comprehensibility of the note.**	Exhibits **some** control of structure/conventions: • subject/verb agreement • noun/adjective agreement • correct word order • spelling **Errors do not hinder overall comprehensibility of the note.**	Exhibits **some** control of structure/conventions: • subject/verb agreement • noun/adjective agreement • correct word order • spelling **Errors do hinder overall comprehensibility of the note.**	Demonstrates **little** control of structure or conventions. **Errors impede overall comprehensibility of the note.**
Word Count	Uses 30 or more comprehensible words in target language that contribute to the development of the task.	Uses 25–29 comprehensible words in target language that contribute to the development of the task.	Uses 20–24 comprehensible words in target language that contribute to the development of the task.	Uses 15–19 comprehensible words in target language that contribute to the development of the task.

A zero can be given in any of the above dimensions when the student's performance falls below the criteria described for a score of "1."

If a paper scores a zero on purpose/task, the entire response receives a zero.

Conversion Chart					
14–16 = 5	11–13 = 4	8–10 = 3	5–7 = 2	2–4 = 1	0–1 = 0

A. NOTES

Choose two of the three writing tasks provided below.

Your answer to each of the two questions you have chosen should be written entirely in Spanish and should contain a minimum of 30 words. Your answers must be written in your own words; no credit will be given for a response that is a copy or substantially the same as material provided from other parts of this examination.

Place names and brand names written in Spanish count as one word. Contractions are also counted as one word. Salutations and closings as well as commonly used abbreviations are included in the word count. Numbers, unless written as words, and names of people are not counted as words.

Be sure that you have satisfied the purpose of the task. The sentence structure and/or expressions used should be connected logically and demonstrate a wide range of vocabulary with minimal repetition.

1. Your electronic pen pal from Venezuela sent you some photographs. In Spanish, write a note to him or her in which you express your thanks and appreciation for the photographs. You may wish to include:

   ➤ when you received the photographs

   ➤ the quality of the photographs

   ➤ recognition of the people in the photographs

   ➤ questions about where they were taken

   ➤ your gratitude

2. You are an exchange student in Peru. You are planning to spend the day with a Peruvian friend. In Spanish, write a journal entry about your plans. You may wish to include the following:

   ➤ with whom you will go

   ➤ where you will meet

   ➤ at what time

   ➤ what you would like to see

   ➤ where you will have lunch

   ➤ what you will eat

   ➤ when you will return home

3. You attended an event (soccer game, tennis match, museum exhibit, a concert, etc.) in Mexico. In Spanish, write an e-mail message to a friend in which you describe the event. You may wish to include the following:

   ➤ the event you attended

   ➤ where it was held

   ➤ who accompanied you

   ➤ why you went

   ➤ what you liked or disliked about the event

Appendix

♦ 1 ♦ Regular Verbs

INFINITIVE		
cantar	beber	abrir

PRESENT		
canto	bebo	abro
cantas	bebes	abres
canta	bebe	abre
cantamos	bebemos	abrimos
cantáis	bebéis	abrís
cantan	beben	abren

PRETERIT		
canté	bebí	abrí
cantaste	bebiste	abriste
cantó	bebió	abrió
cantamos	bebimos	abrimos
cantasteis	bebisteis	abristeis
cantaron	bebieron	abrieron

IMPERFECT		
cantaba	bebía	abría
cantabas	bebías	abrías
cantaba	bebía	abría
cantábamos	bebíamos	abríamos
cantabais	bebíais	abríais
cantaban	bebían	abrían

FUTURE

cant**aré**	beb**eré**	abr**iré**
cant**arás**	beb**erás**	abr**irás**
cant**ará**	beb**erá**	abr**irá**
cant**aremos**	beb**eremos**	abr**iremos**
cant**aréis**	beb**eréis**	abr**iréis**
cant**arán**	beb**erán**	abr**irán**

COMMANDS

canta
no cant**es** } (tú)

cant**e** (Ud.)

cant**emos** (nosotros)

cant**ad**
no cant**éis** } (vosotros)

cant**en** (Uds.)

beb**e**
no beb**as** } (tú)

beb**a** (Ud.)

beb**amos** (nosotros)

beb**ed**
no beb**áis** } (vosotros)

beb**an** (Uds.)

abr**e**
no abr**as** } (tú)

abr**a** (Ud.)

abr**amos** (nosotros)

abr**id**
no abr**áis** } (vosotros)

abr**an** (Uds.)

◆ 2 ◆ Stem-Changing Verbs

a. –ar Verbs

INFINITIVE	pen**sar** (**e** to **ie**)	mos**trar** (**o** to **ue**)	jug**ar** (**u** to **ue**)
PRESENT	**pienso**	**muestro**	**juego**
	piensas	**muestras**	**juegas**
	piensa	**muestra**	**juega**
	pensamos	mostramos	jugamos
	pensáis	mostráis	jugáis
	piensan	**muestran**	**juegan**

b. –er Verbs

INFINITIVE	per**der** (**e** to **ie**)	vol**ver** (**o** to **ue**)
PRESENT	**pierdo**	**vuelvo**
	pierdes	**vuelves**
	pierde	**vuelve**
	perdemos	volvemos
	perdéis	volvéis
	pierden	**vuelven**

c. –ir Verbs

INFINITIVE	pedir (e to i, i)	sentir (e to ie, i)	dormir (o to ue, u)
PRESENT	**pido**	**siento**	**duermo**
	pides	**sientes**	**duermes**
	pide	**siente**	**duerme**
	pedimos	sentimos	dormimos
	pedís	sentís	dormís
	piden	**sienten**	**duermen**

INFINITIVE	pedir (e to i, i)	sentir (e to ie, i)	dormir (o to ue, u)
PRETERIT	pedí	sentí	dormí
	pediste	sentiste	dormiste
	pidió	**sintió**	**durmió**
	pedimos	sentimos	dormimos
	pedisteis	sentisteis	dormisteis
	pidieron	**sintieron**	**durmieron**

COMMANDS

pide ⎫ (tú) no **pidas** ⎭	**siente** ⎫ (tú) no **sientas** ⎭	**duerme** ⎫ (tú) no **duermas** ⎭
pida (Ud.)	**sienta** (Ud.)	**duerma**(Ud.)
pidamos (nosotros)	**sintamos** (nosotros)	**durmamos** (nostros)
pedid ⎫ (vosotros) no **pidáis** ⎭	sentid ⎫ (vosotros) no **sintáis** ⎭	dormid ⎫ (vosotros) no **durmáis** ⎭
pidan (Uds.)	**sientan** (Uds.)	**duerman** (Uds.)

♦ 3 ♦ Verbs With Spelling Changes

a. –cer and **–cir** Verbs

INFINITIVE	ofrecer (c to zc)	conducir (c to zc)
PRESENT	**ofrezco**	**conduzco**
	ofreces	conduces
	ofrece	conduce
	ofrecemos	conducimos
	ofrecéis	conducís
	ofrecen	conducen

INFINITIVE	ofre**cer** (**c** to **zc**)	condu**cir** (**c** to **zc**)

COMMANDS	ofrece no **ofrezcas** } (tú)	conduce no **conduzcas** } (tú)
	ofrezca (Ud.)	**conduzca** (Ud.)
	ofrezcamos (nosotros)	**conduzcamos** (nosotros)
	ofreced no **ofrezcáis** } (vosotros)	conducid no **conduzcáis** } (vosotros)
	ofrezcan (Uds.)	**conduzcan** (Uds.)

b. Verbs That Change **i** to **y** in the Preterit

INFINITIVE	le**er**	ca**er**	o**ír**	inclu**ir**
PRETERIT	leí	caí	oí	incluí
	leíste	caíste	oíste	incluíste
	leyó	**cayó**	**oyó**	**incluyó**
	leímos	caímos	oímos	incluímos
	leísteis	caísteis	oísteis	incluísteis
	leyeron	**cayeron**	**oyeron**	**incluyeron**

◆ 4 ◆ Verbs With Irregular Forms

NOTE: Irregular forms are printed in bold type.

INFINITIVE	PRESENT	COMMAND	PRETERIT	IMPERFECT	FUTURE
caer *to fall*	**caigo**	cae no **caigas** } (tú)	caí	caía	caeré
	caes		caíste	caías	caerás
	cae	**caiga** (Ud.)	**cayó**	caía	caerá
	caemos	**caigamos** (nosotros)	caímos	caíamos	caeremos
	caéis	caed no **caigáis** } (vosotros)	caísteis	caían	caerán
	caen		**cayeron**		
		caigan (Uds.)			
dar *to give*	**doy**	da no des } (tú)	**di**	daba	daré
	das		**diste**	dabas	darás
	da	**dé** (Ud.)	**dio**	daba	dará
	damos	demos (nosotros)	**dimos**	dábamos	daremos
	dais	dad no deis } (vosotros)	**disteis**	dabais	daréis
	dan		**dieron**	daban	darán
		den (Uds.)			

INFINITIVE	PRESENT	COMMAND	PRETERIT	IMPERFECT	FUTURE
decir *to say*	**digo**	**di** } (tú)	**dije**	decía	**diré**
	dices	no **digas**	**dijiste**	decías	**dirás**
	dice	**diga** (Ud.)	**dijo**	decía	**dirá**
	decimos	**digamos** (nosotros)	**dijimos**	decíamos	**diremos**
	decís	decid } (vosotros)	**dijisteis**	decíais	**diréis**
	dicen	no **digáis**	**dijeron**	decian	**dirán**
		digan (Uds.)			
estar *to be*	**estoy**	**está** } (tú)	**estuve**	estaba	estaré
	estás	no **estés**	**estuviste**	estabas	estarás
	está	**esté** (Ud.)	**estuvo**	estaba	estará
	estamos	estemos (nosotros)	**estuvimos**	estábamos	estaremos
	estáis	estad } (vosotros)	**estuvisteis**	estabais	estaréis
	están	no estéis	**estuvieron**	estaban	estarán
		estén (Uds.)			
hacer *to do,* *to make*	**hago**	**haz** } (tú)	**hice**	hacía	**haré**
	haces	no **hagas**	**hiciste**	hacías	**harás**
	hace	**haga** (Ud.)	**hizo**	hacía	**hará**
	hacemos	**hagamos** (nosotros)	**hicimos**	hacíamos	**haremos**
	hacéis	haced } (vosotros)	**hicisteis**	hacíais	**haréis**
	hacen	no **hagáis**	**hicieron**	hacían	**harán**
		hagan (Uds.)			
ir *to go*	**voy**	ve } (tú)	**fui**	**iba**	iré
	vas	no **vayas**	**fuiste**	**ibas**	irás
	va	**vaya** (Ud.)	**fue**	**iba**	irá
	vamos	**vayamos** (nosotros)	**fuimos**	**íbamos**	iremos
	vais	id } (vosotros)	**fuisteis**	**ibais**	iréis
	van	no **vayáis**	**fueron**	**iban**	irán
		vayan (Uds.)			
oír *to hear*	**oigo**	**oye** } (tú)	**oí**	oía	oiré
	oyes	no **oigas**	**oíste**	oías	oirás
	oye	**oiga** (Ud.)	**oyó**	oía	oirá
	oímos	**oigamos** (nosotros)	**oímos**	oíamos	oiremos
	oís	oid } (vosotros)	**oísteis**	oíais	oiréis
	oyen	no **oigáis**	**oyeron**	oían	oirán
		oigan (Uds.)			

INFINITIVE	PRESENT	COMMAND	PRETERIT	IMPERFECT	FUTURE
poner *to put*	**pongo**	**pon** ⎱ (tú)	**puse**	ponía	**pondré**
	pones	no **pongas** ⎰	**pusiste**	ponías	**pondrás**
	pone	**ponga** (Ud.)	**puso**	ponía	**pondrá**
	ponemos		**pusimos**	poníamos	**pon–dremos**
	ponéis	**pongamos** (nosotros)	**pusisteis**	poníais	**pondréis**
	ponen	poned ⎱ (vosotros)	**pusieron**	ponían	**pondrán**
		no **pongáis** ⎰			
		pongan (Uds.)			
saber *to know*	**sé**	sabe (tú)	**supe**	sabía	**sabré**
	sabes	**sepa** (Ud.)	**supiste**	sabías	**sabrás**
	sabe	**sepamos** (nosotros)	**supo**	sabía	**sabrá**
	sabemos	sabed (vosotros)	**supimos**	sabíamos	**sabremos**
	sabéis	**sepan** (Uds.)	**supisteis**	sabíais	**sabréis**
	saben		**supieron**	sabían	**sabrán**
salir *to go out*	**salgo**	**sal** ⎱ (tú)	salí	salía	**saldré**
	sales	no **salgas** ⎰	saliste	salías	**saldrás**
	sale	**salga** (Ud.)	salió	salía	**saldrá**
	salimos	**salgamos** (nosotros)	salimos	salíamos	**saldremos**
	salís	salid ⎱ (vosotros)	salisteis	salíais	**saldréis**
	salen	no salgáis ⎰	salieron	salían	**saldrán**
		salgan (Uds.)			
ser *to be*	**soy**	**sé** ⎱ (tú)	**fui**	**era**	seré
	eres	no seas ⎰	**fuiste**	**eras**	serás
	es	sea (Ud.)	**fue**	**era**	será
	somos	seamos (nosotros)	**fuimos**	**éramos**	seremos
	sois	sed ⎱ (vosotros)	**fuisteis**	**erais**	seréis
	son	no seáis ⎰	**fueron**	**eran**	serán
		sean (Uds.)			
tener *to know (how to)*	**tengo**	**ten** ⎱ (tú)	**tuve**	tenía	**tendré**
	tienes	no **tengas** ⎰	**tuviste**	tenías	**tendrás**
	tiene	tenga (Ud.)	**tuvo**	tenía	**tendrá**
	tenemos	**tengamos** (nosotros)	**tuvimos**	teníamos	**tendremos**
	tenéis	tened ⎱ (vosotros)	**tuvisteis**	teníais	**tendréis**
	tienen	no **tengáis** ⎰	**tuvieron**	tenían	**tendrán**
		tengan (Uds.)			

INFINITIVE	PRESENT	COMMAND	PRETERIT	IMPERFECT	FUTURE
traer *to bring*	**traigo**	trae ⎱ (tú)	**traje**	traía	traeré
	traes	no **traigas** ⎰	**trajiste**	traías	traerás
	trae	**traiga** (Ud.)	**trajo**	traía	traerá
	traemos	**traigamos** (nosotros)	**trajimos**	traíamos	traeremos
	traéis	traed ⎱ (vosotros)	**trajisteis**	traíais	traeréis
	traen	no **traigáis** ⎰	**trajeron**	traían	traerán
		traigan (Uds.)			
venir *to come*	**vengo**	**ven** ⎱ (tú)	**vine**	venía	**vendré**
	vienes	no **vengas** ⎰	**viniste**	venías	**vendrás**
	viene	**venga** (Ud.)	**vino**	venía	**vendrá**
	venimos	**vengamos** (nosotros)	**vinimos**	veníamos	**vendremos**
	venis	venid ⎱ (vosotros)	**vinisteis**	veníais	**vendréis**
	vienen	no **vengáis** ⎰	**vinieron**	venían	**vendrán**
		vengan (Uds.)			
ver *to see*	**veo**	ve ⎱ (tú)	**vi**	**veía**	veré
	ves	no veas ⎰	**viste**	**veías**	verás
	ve	vea (Ud.)	**vio**	**veía**	verá
	vemos	veamos (nosotros)	**vimos**	**veíamos**	veremos
	veis	ved ⎱ (vosotros)	**visteis**	**veíais**	veréis
	ven	no veáis ⎰	**vieron**	**veían**	verán
		vean (Uds.)			

♦ 5 ♦ Punctuation

Spanish punctuation, though similar to English, has the following major differences:

(a) Questions are preceded by an additional question mark, in inverted form (¿).

    ¿Quién es?   *Who is it?*

(b) Exclamatory sentences are preceded by an additional exclamation point, in inverted form.

    ¡Qué día!   *What a day!*

(c) The comma is not used before a conjunction (**y**, **e**, **o**, **u**, or **ni**) in a series.

    Hay clases el lunes, el martes   *There are classes on Monday, Tuesday,*
    y el miércoles.   *and Wednesday.*

(d) Cardinal numbers are set off by periods, and decimal numbers by commas.

    3,5 (tres coma cinco)   *3.5 (three point five)*

    1.200 (mil doscientos)   *1,200 (twelve hundred or one thousand two hundred)*

(e) Final quotation marks precede commas and periods; however, if the quotation marks enclose a complete statement, they follow the period.

Cervantes escribió	*Cervantes wrote*
«Don Quijote».	*"Don Quijote."*
«Escribe pronto.» Con esas	*"Write to me soon." With those words*
palabras terminé mi carta.	*I ended my letter.*

◆ 6 ◆ Syllabication

Spanish words are divided at the end of a line according to units of sound or syllables.

(a) Syllables generally begin with a consonant and end with a vowel. The division is made before the consonant.

te-**n**er   di-**ne**-**r**o   a-**me**-**r**i-**c**a-no   re-**f**e-**r**ir

(b) **Ch**, **ll**, and **rr** are never divided.

pe-**rr**o   ha-**ll**a-do   di-**ch**o

(c) If two or more consonants are combined, the division is made before the last consonant, except in the combinations **bl**, **br**, **cl**, **cr**, **dr**, **fl**, **fr**, **gl**, **gr**, **pl**, **pr**, and **tr**.

tran**s**-**p**or-**t**e   de**s**-**c**u-bie**r**-to   co**n**-**t**i-nuar   a**l**-**b**er-**c**a

BUT

ha-**bl**ar   a-**br**ir   des-**cr**i-bir   a-**pr**en-**d**er

(d) Compound words, including words with prefixes and suffixes, may be divided by components or by syllables.

sud-a-me-ri-ca-no   *OR*   su-da-me-ri-ca-no
mal-es-tar   *OR*   ma-les-tar

◆ 7 ◆ Stress

In Spanish, word stress follows three general rules.

(a) Words ending in a vowel, **n**, or **s** are stressed on the next-to-the-last syllable.

es**cue**la   des**as**tre   **jo**ven   se**ño**res

(b) Words ending in a consonant that is not **n** or **s** are stressed on the last syllable.

compren**der**   ala**bar**   reci**bir**   se**ñor**

(c) All exceptions to the above rules have an accent mark on the stressed syllable.

sábado   **jó**venes   A**dán**   **Cé**sar   fran**cés**

Spanish-English Vocabulary

The Spanish-English Vocabulary is intended to be complete for the context of this book.

Nouns are listed in the singular. Regular feminine forms of nouns are indicated by **(-a)** or the ending that replaces the masculine ending: **abogado(-a)** or **alcalde(-esa)**. Irregular noun plurals are given in full: **voz** *f.* voice; (*pl.* voces). Regular feminine forms of adjectives are indicated by **-a**.

ABBREVIATIONS			
adj.	adjective	*m.*	masculine
f.	feminine	*m./f.*	masculine or feminine
inf.	infinitive	*pl.*	plural
irr.	irregular	*sing.*	singular

abajo below, downstairs
abierto open
abogado(-a) lawyer
abrigo *m.* overcoat
abrir to open
abuela *f.* grandmother
abuelo *m.* grandfather
aburrido bored; boring
acá here
acabar to end; **acabar de** to have just
acompañar to accompany
acostarse (ue) to go to bed
actor *m.* actor
actriz *f.* actress

acuerdo *m.* agreement; **estar de acuerdo** to agree
además besides; in addition
adiós good-bye
admirar to admire
¿adónde? where to?
aeropuerto *m.* airport
afeitar: afeitarse to shave
aficionado(-a) fan, devotee
afueras *f.* suburbs
agrio, -a sour
agua *f.* water
ahí there
ahora now
ahorrar to save

aire *m.* air; **al aire libre** outdoors, in the open
alcalde(-esa) mayor
alcoba *f.* bedroom
alemán, (*f.* alemana) German
alfombra *f.* rug, carpet
algo something
algodón *m.* cotton
algún some
alguno someone
alimento *m.* food
almacén *m.* department store
almohada *f.* pillow

almorzar (ue)   to have (eat) lunch

alquilar   to rent

alto, -a   tall; high

alumno(-a)   student, pupil

amable   nice

ancho, -a   wide

andar *(irr.)*   to walk, go

anillo *m.*   ring

año *m.*   year

anoche   last night

ansioso, -a   anxious

anteayer   the day before yesterday

anteojos *m. pl.*   eyeglasses

antes de   before

antiguo   old; ancient

antipático   unpleasant, disagreeable

anuncio *m.*   announcement

apagar: apagarse   to extinguish, put out

aparecer (zc)   to appear

apellido *m.*   family name, last name

aplicado, -a   diligent, studious

aprender   to learn

aquel, -ella   that; (*pl.* **aquellos, -ellas** those)

aquí   here

árbitro *m.*   referee, umpire

árbol *m.*   tree

arena *f.*   sand

arete *m.*   tree

armario *m.*   closet

arreglar   to arrange; to fix

arriba   above, upstairs

arroz *m.*   rice

ascensor *m.*   elevator

asiento *m.*   seat; **tomar asiento** to sit down

asignatura *f.*   class, subject

asistir (a)   to attend

aspiradora *f.*   vacuum cleaner; **pasar la aspiradora** to vacuum

atracción *f.*   (amusement) ride

aula *f.*   (el aula) classroom

ausente   absent

autobús *m.*   bus

automóvil (auto) *m.*   automobile, car

avión m.   airplane; **en avión** by plane

ayer   yesterday

ayudar   to help

azúcar *m./f.*   sugar

bailar   to dance

baile *m.*   dance

bajar   to go down; to descend; to lower

bajo, -a   low; short

balcón *m.*   balcony

banco *m.*   bank; bench

bañar: bañarse   to take a bath, bathe

bandera *f.*   flag

barato, -a   cheap, inexpensive

barbero(-a)   barber

barco *m.*   boat

barrio *m.*   neighborhood

basura *f.*   garbage

batido, -a   shaken; **leche batida** milkshake

baúl *m.*   trunk

beber   to drink

bebida *f.*   drink; beverage

beca *f.*   scholarship

biblioteca *f.*   library

bien   well

biftec *m.*   beefsteak

billete *m.*   ticket

billetera *f.*   wallet

boca *f.*   mouth

boda *f.*   wedding

bodega *f.*   grocery store

boleto *m.*   ticket

boliche *m.*   bowling

bolígrafo *m.*   ballpoint pen

bolsa *f.*   bag, purse

bombero *m.*   fireman

bondad *f.*   kindness; **tener la bondad de** please…

bonito, -a   pretty

borrador *m.*   (chalkboard) eraser

borrar   to erase

bosque *m.*   forest, woods

brazo *m.*   arm

broma *f.*   joke

bueno, -a   good

bufanda *f.*   scarf

buscar (qu)   to look for

butaca *f.*   armchair

caballo *m.*   horse

cabeza *f.*   head

cacto *m.*   cactus

cada   each, every

cadena *f.*   chain

caer *(irr.)*   to fall; **caerse** to fall down

caja *f.*   box; cashier

calcetín *m.*   sock

caliente   hot

calle *f.*   street

calor *m.*   heat; **hace calor** it is hot

cama *f.*   bed; **guardar cama** to stay in bed

cámara *f.*   camera

camarero(-a)   waiter

cambiar   to change

caminar   to walk

camino *m.*   road, path

camión *m.*   truck

camiseta *f.*   t-shirt

campana *f.*   bell

campeón (*f.* **campeona**)   champion

campesino(-a) *m.*   farmer

campo *m.*   country, countryside

canción *f.*   song

cansado, -a   tired

cantante *m./f.*   singer

cantar   to sing

cara *f.*   face

cárcel *f.*   prison

cariñoso, -a   loving, affectionate

carne *f.*   meat

carnicería *f.*   butcher shop

carnicero(-a)   butcher

caro, -a   expensive; dear

carrera *f.*   career; race

carro *m.*   car

carrusel *m.*   carrousel

carta *f.*   letter

cartel *m.*   poster

cartera *f.*   wallet, purse

caso *m.*   case; **hacer caso de** to pay attention to, to heed

castañuelas *f. pl.*   castanets

catedral *f.*   cathedral

celebrar   to celebrate

celoso, -a   jealous

cena *f.*   dinner; supper

cenar   to eat supper

centro *m.*   center; downtown; **centro comercial** mall

cepillar   to brush; **cepillarse** to brush oneself

cerca de   near; close to

cerdo *m.*   pork

cereza *f.*   cherry

cerrado, -a   closed

cerrar (ie)   to close

cesar (de)   to stop

chaqueta *f.*   jacket

chofer (also **chófer**) *m. / f.* driver

chuleta *f.*   chop; **chuleta de cerdo** pork chop

cielo *m.*   sky

cien (ciento)   one hundred

científico,(-a)   scientist

cine *m.*   movie theater, movies

cinta *f.*   tape

cinturón *m.*   belt

cita *f.*   appointment, date

ciudad *f.*   city

ciudadano(-a) *f.*   citizen

claro, -a   light (color)

clase *f.*   class; kind, type

clavel *m.*   carnation

clima *m.*   climate

coche *m.*   car

cocido, -a   cooked; **bien cocido** well cooked (done)

cocina *f.*   kitchen

cocinar   to cook

cocinero(-a)   cook

cola *f.*   line; tail

colegio *m.*   school

colocar   to place, to put

comedor *m.*   dining room

comenzar (ie)   to begin; to start

comer   to eat

comerciante *m. / f.*   merchant, businessperson

cómico, -a   comical, funny

comida *f.*   food; meal

como   as, like; **¿cómo?** how?, what?

cómoda *f.*   bureau, dresser

cómodo, -a   comfortable

compañero(-a)   friend, pal

compartir   to share

competencia *f.*   competition

compra *f.*   purchase; **ir de compras** to go shopping

comprar   to buy

concurso *m.*   contest

conducir (zc)   to drive; to lead

confesar (ie)   to confess

conocer (zc)   to know (someone), to be familiar with (something)

consejero(-a)   adviser

consentido, -a   pampered, spoiled

construir (y)   to build

contador(-ora)   accountant

contar (ue)   to count; to tell

contento, -a   happy, content

contestar   to answer

contra   against

coro *m.*   chorus

correo *m.*   mail; post office; **correo electrónico** e-mail

correr   to run

correspondencia *f.* correspondence; **amigo por correspondencia** pen pal

cortar   to cut

corte *f.*   court, tribunal

cortés   polite

cortina *f.*   curtain

corto, -a   short

cosa *f.*   thing

coser   to sew

costar (ue)   to cost

creer (y)   to believe; to think

criado(-a)   servant

crudo, -a   raw

cuaderno *m.*   notebook

cuadro *m.*   painting, picture

¿cuál? (pl. ¿cuáles?)   which?, what?

cuando   when; **de vez en cuando** from time to time, sometimes; **¿cuándo?** when?

¿cuánto, -a?   how much?; *pl.* **¿cuántos, -as?** how many?

cuarto *m.*   room; quarter, fourth; **una cuarta parte de** a quarter of, a fourth of

cubeta *f.*   pail

cubrir   to cover

cuchara *f.*   spoon

cucharita *f.*   teaspoon

dalia *f.*   dahlia

dama *f.*   lady; **jugar a las damas** to play checkers

dar *(irr.)*   to give; **darse la mano** to shake hands

debajo de   beneath, under

deber   to owe; should, ought to

débil   weak

decidir   to decide

decir *(irr.)*   to say; to tell

decorar   to decorate

dedo *m.*   finger, toe

defender (ie)   to defend

dejar   to leave; to allow; **dejar de** to fail to; to stop; to neglect to

delante de   in front of

delgado   thin, skinny

demasiado   too much; excessively; too

dentro de   within

dependiente(-a)   salesperson

deporte *m.*   sport

deportista *m. / f.*   athlete

derecha *f.* right; **a la derecha** to the right

derretido, -a   melted

desaparecer (zc)   to disappear

desayunarse to have (eat) breakfast

descansar to rest

describir to describe

descubrir to discover

desear to wish; to want

desilusionado, -a disappointed

despacio slowly

despertador *m.* alarm clock

despertar (ie) to wake (someone) up; **despertarse** to wake up

después de after

desván *m.* attic

detrás de behind

devolver (ue) to return; to give back

día *m.* day

dibujar to draw

diccionario *m.* dictionary

dictado *m.* dictation

diente *m.* tooth

dificultad *f.* difficulty

dinero *m.* money

dirección *f.* address

disco *m.* record; **disco compacto** *m.* CD, compact disc

disculpa *f.* excuse, apology; **pedir disculpa** to ask for forgiveness, apologize

diseño *m.* design

distancia *f.* distance; **larga distancia** long distance

distribuir (y) to distribute

diversión *f.* amusement **divertido, -a** fun; funny, amusing

divertir (ie) to amuse; **divertirse (ie)** to enjoy oneself, have fun

dividir to divide

doler (ue) to be painful, to cause sorrow

dolor *m.* ache, pain

domingo *m.* Sunday

donde where; **¿dónde?** where?

dormir (ue) to sleep; **dormirse** to fall asleep

dormitorio *m.* bedroom

dueño(-a) owner, boss

dulce *m.* sweet, candy

durante during

durar to last, endure

duro, -a hard

echar to throw; to throw out, dismiss; **echar de menos** to miss (someone or something)

edad *f.* age

edificio *m.* building

egoísta *m./f.* selfish person; *adj.* selfish

emocionante exciting

empezar (ie) to begin, start

encantar to like a lot, love; **me encanta** I like it a lot, I love it

encontrar (ue) to find; to meet

enero January

enfermedad *f.* sickness, illness

enfermería *f.* infirmary

enfermero(-a) nurse

enfermo, -a sick, ill

enfrente opposite, facing

ensalada *f.* salad

enseñanza *f.* teaching

enseñar to teach

entender (ie) to understand

entonces then

entrada *f.* entrance; ticket

entrar (en) to enter

entre between, among

entrenador(-ora) *m.* coach, trainer

entrevista *f.* interview

equipaje *m.* baggage

equipo *m.* team

escalera *f.* staircase, stairs

esconder to hide

escribir to write

escritor(-ora) writer

escritorio *m.* desk

escuchar to listen (to)

escuela *f.* school

ese, -a that; *pl.* **esos, -as** those

espalda *f.* back (body)

esperar to wait for; to hope

esposa *f.* wife

esposo *m.* husband

esquiar to ski

esquina *f.* corner

estación *f.* season; (train) station

estadio *m.* stadium

estado *m.* state

estampilla *f.* stamp

estante *m.* shelf

estar to be

este *m.* east

este, -a his; (*pl.* **estos, -as** these)

esto this

estómago *m.* stomach

estrecho, -a narrow

estrella *f.* star

estreno *m.* opening (of a performance), show

etiqueta *f.* label, tag

excursión *f.* trip

explicar to explain

extranjero *m.* foreign; **al extranjero, en el extranjero** abroad

fábrica *f.* factory

falda *f.* skirt

falta *f.* mistake, error

faltar to lack, need

fanático(-a) fan

farmacéutico(-a) pharmacist

farmacia *f.* drugstore, pharmacy

fascinar to fascinate

favor *m.* favor; **por favor** please

fecha *f.* date (month, day, and year)

feliz happy

feroz ferocious

ferrocarril *m.* railroad

fiesta *f.* party; holiday

fijarse (en) to pay attention, to note

fila *f.* row
flan *m.* custard
flor *f.* flower
florería *f.* flowershop
fotografía *f.* photograph;
   sacar fotografías to take
   pictures
frecuencia *f.* frequency; **con**
frecuencia frequently
fresa *f.* strawberry
frijol *m.* bean
frío *m.* cold; **frío, -a** (*adj.*)
   cold
frutería *f.* fruit store
fumar to smoke
función *f.* performance, show
funcionar to function; to work

galleta *f.* cracker
gallo *m.* rooster
gana *f.* desire, will; **tener**
   ganas de (cantar). to feel
   like (singing)
ganar to win, earn; **ganarse**
   la vida to earn a living
garaje *m.* garage
garganta *f.* throat
gaseosa *f.* soda pop
gastar to spend; **gastar**
   dinero to spend money
gasto *m.* expense
gato(-a) cat
gemelos *m. pl.* twins
geranio *m.* geranium
gerente *m. / f.* manager
globo *m.* balloon
goma *f.* (pencil or ink)
   eraser
gozar (de) to enjoy
grabadora *f.* recorder
gracias *f. / pl.* thanks; thank you
grado *m.* degree, grade
graduarse (ú) to graduate
gran great
grande large, big
granja *f.* farm
gritar to shout
grueso, -a thick
guante *m.* glove

guapo handsome
guayaba *f.* guava
guerra *f.* war
guía *m.* guide
gustar to please
gusto *m.* pleasure; **mucho**
   gusto my pleasure

habitante *m. / f.* inhabitant
hablar to speak
hacer to do; to make
hacha *f.* **(el hacha)** ax
hacia toward
hallar to find
hambre *f.* hunger; **tener**
   hambre to be hungry
hasta until; as far as; up to
helado *m.* ice cream
hermana *f.* sister
hermano *m.* brother
hielo *m.* ice
hierba *f.* grass
hija *f.* daughter
hijo *m.* son
historia *f.* history; story
historietas *f. / pl.* comics book,
   comic strip
hoja *f.* leaf
hombre *m.* man
hora *f.* hour; **¿a qué hora?** at
   what time?
horario *m.* schedule
horno *m.* oven
hoy today
huevo *m.* egg

ida y vuelta *f.* round trip
iglesia *f.* church
importar to matter
incluir (y) to include
independiente independent
ingeniero(-a) engineer
inglés English
insistir (en) to insist on
invierno *m.* winter
invitado(-a) guest
ir to go; **irse** to go away
isla *f.* island

jabón *m.* soap
jalea *f.* jelly
jamón *m.* ham
japonés (*f.* **japonesa**)
   Japanese
jardín *m.* garden
jaula *f.* cage
jefatura *f.* headquarters
jefe(-a) chief, boss
joven *m. / f.* young person
juego *m.* game
jueves *m.* Thursday
jugada *f.* play
jugador(-a) player
jugar (ue) to play
jugo *m.* juice
juguete *m.* toy
junto together
justo, -a fair, just
juventud *f.* youth

labio *m.* lip
ladrar to bark
ladrido *m.* bark
ladrillo *m.* brick
lago *m.* lake
lana *f.* wool
lápiz *m.* pencil; (*pl.* **lápices**)
largo, -a long
lavandería *f.* laundry
lavar to wash; **lavarse** to wash
   (oneself)
lección *f.* lesson
leche *f.* milk
lechuga *f.* lettuce
leer (y) to read
legumbre *f.* vegetable
lejos (de) far (from)
lengua *f.* tongue; language
lento, -a slow
levantar to lift; **levantarse** to
   get up
libra *f.* pound
librería *f.* bookstore
libro *m.* book
limón *m.* lemon
limpiar to clean
limpio, -a clean

listo, -a ready; **estar listo** to be ready; **ser listo** to be clever, smart

llamada *f.* call; **hacer una llamada** to make a call

llamar to call; **llamarse** to be named, be called

llave *f.* key

llegada *f.* arrival

llegar to arrive

lleno, -a full

llevar to carry; to take; to wear

llorar to cry

lluvia *f.* rain

locutor(-ora) announcer

luego then, next; afterwards; **hasta luego** until then, good-bye

lugar *m.* place

luna *f.* moon

lunes *m.* Monday

madrastra *f.* stepmother

madre *f.* mother

madrina *f.* godmother

maestro(-a) teacher

mal badly

maleta *f.* suitcase

malo, -a bad

maltratar to mistreat

mañana tomorrow

manera *f.* way, manner; **de ninguna manera** no way

mano *f.* hand

mantequilla *f.* butter

manzana *f.* apple

máquina *f.* machine

mar *m.* sea

marcador *m.* felt-top marker

marcar (un número) to dial (a number)

marco *m.* frame

martes *m.* Tuesday

más more; plus

máscara *f.* mask

materia *f.* subject

mayor older; oldest

medianoche *f.* midnight

medio, -a half

mediodía *m.* noon, midday

medir (i) to measure

mejor better

melancólico, -a sad

melocotón *m.* peach

memoria *f.* memory; **de memoria** by heart

menor younger; minor

menos less; except

menudo tiny, minute; **a menudo** often, frequently

mercado *m.* market

mes *m.* month

mesa *f.* table

mesero(-era) waiter

miedo *m.* fear; **tener miedo** to be afraid, fear

miércoles *m.* Wednesday

mil one thousand

millón *m.* million

mirar to look

mismo same

mitad *f.* half

mochila *f.* knapsack

molestar to bother, to annoy

moneda *f.* coin

mono *m.* monkey

montaña *f.* mountain

montar to ride; **montar en bicicleta** to ride a bicycle

moreno, -a brunette; dark-skinned

morir (ue) to die

mostrar (ue) to show

mozo (-a) waiter

mucho, -a a lot

mueble *m.* piece of furniture; **muebles** *m./pl.* furniture

muela *f.* molar (tooth)

mujer *f.* woman

mundo *m.* world; **todo el mundo** everybody

muñeca *f.* doll

nada nothing; **de nada** you're welcome

nadar to swim

naranja *f.* orange

nariz *f.* nose; (*pl.* **narices**)

natación *f.* swimming

naturaleza *f.* nature

Navidad *f.* Christmas

negro, -a black

nevar (ie) to snow

ni neither; **ni... ni...** neither...nor..., either

nieta *f.* granddaughter

nieto *m.* grandson

nieve *f.* snow

niña *f.* girl, child

ninguno none, not any

niño *m.* boy, child

noche *f.* night; **esta noche** tonight

nombre *m.* name

norte *m.* north

nota *f.* grade; note

noticia *f.* news item; (*pl.* **noticias** news)

noticiero *m.* news broadcast

novia *f.* girlfriend; bride

novio *m.* boyfriend, groom

nube *f.* cloud

nuera *f.* daughter-in-law

nuevo, -a new; **de nuevo** again

nunca never

obedecer (zc) to obey

obra *f.* work, play

ocupado, -a busy

oeste *m.* west

oficio *m.* occupation

ofrecer (zc) to offer

oído *m.* ear

olmo *m.* elm tree

olvidar to forget

oración *f.* sentence

orden *f.* order

oreja *f.* ear

oro *m.* gold

orquídea *f.* orchid

oscuridad *f.* darkness

oso *m.* bear; **oso de peluche** teddy bear

otoño *m.* autumn, fall

otro other, another

oveja *f.* sheep

paciente *m./f.* patient
padrastro *m.* stepfather
padre *m.* father
padrino *m.* godfather
pagar to pay (for)
página *f.* page
país *m.* country
pájaro *m.* bird
palabra *f.* word
palacio *m.* palace
pálido, -a pale
palomitas (de maíz) *f.*
    popcorn
pan *m.* bread
panadería *f.* bakery
panadero(-a) baker
pantalón *m.* pants, trouser
pantufla *f.* slipper
pañuelo *m.* handkerchief
papa *f.* potato; **papas fritas**
    French fries
papá *m.* father, dad
papel *m.* paper
para for, in order to
parada *f.* stop
paraguas *m. sing. & pl.* umbrella
parecer (zc) to seem
pared *f.* wall
pariente *m.* relative
parque *m.* park
párrafo *m.* paragraph
parte *f.* part; **en ninguna**
    parte nowhere
particular private
partido *m.* game, match
partir to leave; to depart
párvulo(-a) child; **escuela de**
    párvulos nursery school
pasado, -a past; **el año**
    pasado last year; **la semana**
    pasada last week
pasar to pass; to spend (time)
pasatiempo *m.* hobby,
    pastime
paseo *m.* stroll; outing
pasillo *m.* hall; aisle
pastel *m.* cake
pastelería *f.* pastry shop
patata *f.* potato

patín *m.* skate
patinar to skate
patio *m.* courtyard
pato *m.* duck
patria *f.* native land,
    fatherland, motherland
pavo *m.* turkey; **pavo real**
    peacock
pedazo *m.* piece
pedir (i) to ask for; to request;
    to order (food)
peinar to comb; **peinarse** to
    comb one's hair
peine *m.* comb
pelear to fight
película *f.* film
pelirrojo, -a redheaded
pelo *m.* hair
pelota *f.* ball
peluquería *f.* hairdresser's,
    barbershop
pensar (ie) to think; to intend
pequeño, -a small
pera *f.* pear
perder (ie) to lose; to waste;
    to miss (train, bus, and so on)
perezoso, -a lazy
periódico *m.* newspaper
periodista *m./f.* reporter
permiso *m.* permission; **con**
    permiso excuse me
permitir to permit; to allow
perro *m.* dog
pesa *f.* weight; **levantar pesas**
    to lift weights
pescado *m.* fish (food)
pescar to fish
pez *m.* fish
pie *m.* foot; **a pie** on foot; **de**
    pie standing
piedra *f.* stone
pierna *f.* leg
pimienta *f.* pepper (spice)
pimiento *m.* pepper
    (vegetable)
piña *f.* pineapple
pintura *f.* paint; painting
piscina *f.* swimming pool
piso *m.* floor, story (building)

pizarra *f.* chalkboard
plano *m.* map (city)
plátano *m.* plantain
plato *m.* plate; dish
playa *f.* beach
pluma *f.* pen
pobre poor
poco little
poder *(irr.)* to be able; can,
    may
policía *m./f.* police officer
pollo *m.* chicken
poner *(irr.)* to put; **poner la**
    mesa to set the table;
    ponerse to put on (clothing)
por for, by, through; times;
    dividido por divided by
porque because; **¿por qué?**
    why?
poseer (y) to possess; own
postre *m.* dessert
practicar (qu) to practice
precio *m.* price
preferir (ie, i) to prefer
pregunta *f.* question
preguntar to ask
premio *m.* prize; award
prendedor *m.* pin
preocupado, -a worried
preparar to prepare
preparativo *m.* preparation
prestado, -a lent; **pedir**
    prestado to borrow
prestar to lend; **prestar**
    atención to pay attention
primavera *f.* spring
primero, -a first
primo (-a) cousin
prisa *f.* hurry, haste; **de prisa**
    quickly; **tener prisa** to be in
    a hurry
producir (zc) to produce
programador(-ora)
    programmer
prometer to promise
pronóstico *m.* forecast
pronto soon; **de pronto**
    suddenly
propina *f.* tip

propio,-a own
próximo, -a next
proyecto *m.* project
prueba *f.* test, exam
pueblo *m.* town
puente *m.* bridge
puerta *f.* door, gate
pulsera *f.* bracelet
punto *m.* point; **en punto** sharp (time)
pupitre *m.* (pupil's) desk

que who, whom, which, that; than; **¿qué?** what?, which?; **¡qué... !** what a…!, how…!
quedar to be left; **quedarse** to stay, remain
queja *f.* complaint
querer *(irr.)* to want; wish; to love
querido, -a dear
queso *m.* cheese
quien who, whom; **¿quién?** who?, whom?; **¿de quién?** whose
química *f.* chemistry
quitar to take away; **quitarse** to take off (clothing)

rama *f.* branch
rato *m.* while; (short) time; **pasar un buen rato** to have a good time
razón *f.* reason; **tener razón** to be right
receta *f.* recipe; prescription
recibir to receive
reconocer (zc) to recognize
recordar (ue) to remember
recreo *m.* recess
recuerdo *m.* remembrance; souvenir
referir (ie) to tell; to narrate
refresco *m.* refreshment; soft drink, soda
regalo *m.* gift, present
regatear to bargain
regla *f.* ruler; rule

regresar to return
reloj *m.* watch; clock
remar to row
remedio *m.* remedy; **no hay más remedio** it can't be helped
reñir (i) to quarrel; to scold
reparar to repair, mend
reparto *m.* cast
repente *m.* sudden movement; **de repente** suddenly
repetir (i) to repeat
resfriado *m.* cold (illness)
resolver (ue) to solve; to resolve
responder to answer
responsable responsible
respuesta *f.* answer
reunión *f.* meeting
revista *f.* magazine
rezar to pray
rico, -a rich
río *m.* river
rompecabezas *m. sing. & pl.* puzzle
romper to break
ropa *f.* clothing
rosado, -a pink
rubio, -a blonde
ruido *m.* noise

sábado *m.* Saturday
saber *(irr.)* to know
sabroso, -a delicious
sacar to take out; **sacar fotografías** to take photos
sal *f.* salt
sala *f.* living room
salchicha *f.* sausage, frankfurter
salida *f.* exit, departure
salir to go out; to leave; **salir bien (mal)** to pass (fail)
salón *m.* room, salon; **salón de belleza** beauty shop; **salón de clases** classroom
salsa *f.* sauce
saltar to jump
salud *f.* health

saludar to greet
saludo *m.* greeting; regards
sandía *f.* watermelon
santo(-a) saint
sastre(-a) tailor
sed *f.* thirst; **tener sed** to be thirsty
seda *f.* silk
segundo, -a second
semana *f.* week
señor *m.* mister, sir
señora *f.* madam, missus
señorita *f.* miss, young lady
sentado, -a seated
sentarse (ie) to sit down
sentir (ie) to regret; to be sorry; **sentirse** to feel sorry
ser *(irr.)* to be
serpiente *f.* snake
servilleta *f.* napkin
servir (i) to serve
siempre always
siguiente following; **al día siguiente** on the following day
silbar to whistle
sillón *m.* chair
simpático, -a nice
sin without
sobre on top of, over
sobrina *f.* niece
sobrino *m.* nephew
sol *m.* sun
solamente only
soldado *m./f.* soldier
solo alone
sonar (ue) to sound; to ring
sopa *f.* soup
sorprendido, -a surprised
sorpresa *f.* surprise
sótano *m.* basement, cellar
subir to go up, climb; to raise
sucio, -a dirty
suelo *m.* ground; floor
sufrir to suffer
sur *m.* south

tacaño, -a stingy
talla *f.* (clothing) size

tamaño *m.* size
también also, too
tampoco neither, not either
tanto so much, as much; **no es para tanto** it is not a big deal
taquilla *f.* box office
tardar to delay
tarde *f.* afternoon; evening; late
tarea *f.* assignment; chore
tarjeta *f.* card; **tarjeta postal** post card
teatro *m.* theater
tela *f.* cloth; fabric
telenovela *f.* soap opera
televisión *f.* television (industry); television (set)
televisor *m.* television set
temprano early
tenedor *m.* fork
tener *(irr.)* to have
tercero, -a third
tercio *m.* third (fraction)
terminal *f.* terminal; **terminal de autobuses** bus terminal
terminar to finish; to end
tía *f.* aunt
tiempo *m.* time; weather; **a tiempo** on time
tienda *f.* store
tierra *f.* earth, land
tigre(-esa) tiger
tintorería *f.* dry cleaner
tío *m.* uncle
tirar to throw
tiza *f.* chalk

tocadiscos *m.* record player
tocar (qu) to touch; to play (a musical instrument); **tocar (a uno)** to be one's turn
todavía still, yet
todo, -a all
tomar to take; to drink
tonto, -a dumb, foolish
trabajar to work
trabalenguas *m. pl.* tongue twister
traducir (zc) to translate
traer *(irr.)* to carry; to bring
traje *m.* suit; **traje de baño** bathing suit
tratar (de) to try to
travieso, -a naughty, mischievous
triste sad
tulipán *m.* tulip

uña *f.* nail (body)
unos, -as *pl.* some
usar to use; to wear
uva *f.* grape

vaca *f.* cow
vacío, -a empty
valer *(irr.)* to be worth
valor *m.* value
vapor *m.* steamship
vaso *m.* glass
vecino(-a) neighbor
vender to sell
venir *(irr.)* to come
venta *f.* sale; **en venta** on sale

ventana *f.* window
ver *(irr.)* to see; to watch
verano *m.* summer
verdad *f.* truth
verde green
vestido *m.* dress
vestir (i) to dress; **vestirse** to get dressed
veterinario(-a) veterinarian
vez *f.* time; **otra vez** again; **a veces** sometimes; **en vez de** instead of
viajar to travel
viaje *m.* trip; **hacer un viaje** to travel
vida *f.* life
viejo, -a old
viento *m.* wind; **hacer viento** to be windy
viernes *m.* Friday
visitar to visit
vista *f.* sight
vivir to live
vivo, -a vivid, bright (colors)
volar (ue) to fly
volver (ue) to return; to come (go) back
voz *f.* voice; *pl.* **voces**

ya already
yerno *m.* son-in-law

zapatería *f.* shoe store
zapatero *m.* shoemaker
zapato *m.* shoe
zoológico *m.* zoo

English-Spanish Vocabulary

The English–Spanish Vocabulary includes only those words that occur in the English-to-Spanish exercise.

able: to be able poder *(irr.)*; **to be able to** poder + *inf.*
about de, acerca de
absent ausente; **to be absent** estar ausente
acquaint: to become acquainted with conocer a
activity actividad *f.*
address dirección *f.*
after después de
afternoon tarde *f.*; **in the afternoon** por la tarde; P.M. de la tarde
again de nuevo; otra vez
age edad *f.* **your age** su edad
agree: to agree with estar de acuerdo con
airplane avión *m.*; **by plane** en avión
airport aeropuerto *m.*
alone solo; **to be alone** estar a solas, estar solo
always siempre
amusing divertido
angry enojado
animal: stuffed animal animal de peluche *m.*
another otro
answer contestar, responder
any ninguno, ninguna
anyone alguien
appear aparecer (zc)

arrive llegar (gu)
art arte *f.* (el arte)
ask preguntar; **to ask a question** hacer una pregunta; **to ask for** pedir (i)
assignment tarea *f.*
attend: to attend school asistir / ir a la escuela
August agosto *m.*
avenue avenida *f.*
awake despierto; **to awaken (wake up)** despertarse (ie)

bank banco *m.*
bath baño *m.*; **to take a bath (bathe)** bañarse
beach playa *f.*
beautiful hermoso, bello
because porque
become llegar (gu) a ser; ponerse *(irr.)* + *adj.*; hacerse *(irr.)*
bed cama *f.*; **to go to bed** acostarse (ue)
before antes de
begin empezar (ie, c), comenzar (ie, c)
behind detrás de
better mejor
bicycle bicicleta *f.*
big grande
birthday cumpleaños *m.*

black negro
blue azul
boring aburrido
born: to be born nacer (zc)
box caja *f.*
boy niño, muchacho *m.*
boyfriend novio *m.*
breakfast desayuno *m.*; **to have (eat) breakfast** desayunarse
bring traer *(irr.)*
brother hermano *m.*
bus autobús *m.*
business negocio *m.*
but pero
by por; **by (bus, train)** en (autobús, tren)

call llamada *f.*; **to call** llamar
camp campamento *m.*
car auto *m.*, carro *m.*, coche *m.*
card tarjeta *f.*; **credit card** tarjeta de crédito
careful cuidadoso; **to be careful** tener cuidado
celebrate celebrar
chair silla *f.*
change cambio; **to change** cambiar
check cheque *m.*; **traveler's check** cheque de viajero *m.*
chicken pollo *m.*
childhood niñez *f.*

city   ciudad *f.*
class   clase *f.*
close   cerrar (ie)
clothes   ropa *f.*
coach   entrenador *m.*
cold   frío; **to be cold**
  (weather) hacer frío; **to be**
  cold (person) tener frío
comb   peine *m.*; **to comb**
  one's hair peinarse
come   venir *(irr.)*
compact disc   disco
  compacto, CD
company   compañía *f.*
computer   computadora *f.*
confess   confesar (ie)
cook   cocinar
cost   costar (ue)
counselor   consejero *m.*,
  consejera *f.*
count   contar (ue)
country   país *m.*; **countryside**
  campo *m.*
cry   llorar

dance   baile *m.*; **to dance**
  bailar
dark   oscuro
day   día *m.*
deal: a great deal   mucho
decide   decidir
defend   defender (ie)
desk (pupil's)   pupitre *m.*;
  escritorio *m.*
dictionary   diccionario *m.*
difficult   difícil
dinner   cena *f.*
directly   directamente
disagreeable   desagradable
disappear   desaparecer (zc)
discover   descubrir
do: to do   hacer
dog   perro *m.*
doll   muñeca *f.*
door   puerta *f.*
downtown   centro *m.*
dress   vestido *m.*; **to get**
  dressed vestirse (i)
during   durante

each   cada
early   temprano
earn   ganar
eat   comer; **to eat breakfast**
  desayunar; **to eat dinner**
  cenar; **to eat lunch** almorzar
electronic   electrónico
e-mail   correo electrónico
employee   empleado *m.*,
  empleada *f.*
end: to end   terminar
English   inglés *m.*
enjoy   divertirse (ie, i)
evening   noche *f.*
every   cada, todos los, todas las
everyone   todos; todo el
  mundo
everything   todo, todas las cosas
exercise   ejercicio *m.*
explain   explicar (qu)

face   cara *f.*
fall   caer *(irr.)*; **to fall down**
  caerse
family   familia *f.*
father   padre *m.*
favorite   favorito
feel   sentir(se) (ie, i); **to feel**
  like tener ganas de
few   unos
fifth   quinto
film   película *f.*
find   encontrar (ue), hallar
fine   fino; bien; *(weather)* hacer
  buen tiempo
first   primero
flower   flor *f.*
fly   volar (ue)
follow   seguir (i)
food   comida *f.*
football   fútbol *m.*
for   para
forget   olvidar
free   libre
friend   amigo *m.*, amiga *f.*

game   partido *m.*; juego *m.*
get up   levantarse
gift   regalo *m.*

girlfriend   novia *f.*
give   dar *(irr.)*
go   ir *(irr.)*; **to go away**
  irse *(irr.)*
gold   oro *m.*
good   bueno
grade   nota *f.*, calificación *f.*
grandfather   abuelo *m.*
grandmother   abuela *f.*
great   gran
green   verde
greet   saludar
ground   suelo *m.*
guitar   guitarra *f.*
gym   gimnasio *m.*
gymnastics   gimnasia *f.*

half   mitad *f.*; **one-half** (un)
  medio
happily   alegremente
happy   contento, alegre
have   tener *(irr.)*; **to have to**
  tener que + *inf.*
hear   oír *(irr.)*
here   aquí, acá
hide   esconder(se)
home   casa *f.*; **at home** en casa
hot   caliente
hour   hora *f.*
how   ¿cómo?
hunger   hambre *f.* (el hambre);
  to be hungry tener hambre
hurry   prisa *f.*; **to be in a**
  hurry tener prisa

ill   enfermo
include   incluir (y)
insist: to insist on   insistir en
intend   pensar (ie) + *inf.*
interesting   interesante
island   isla *f.*

just   justo; **to have just** acabar
  de + *inf.*

key   llave *f.*
kitchen   cocina *f.*
know   saber *(irr.)*; conocer (zc);
  to know how saber + *inf.*

last último; **last (month, year)** (el mes, el año) pasado

late tarde

learn aprender

leave irse *(irr.)*; dejar

library biblioteca *f.*

like gustarle (a uno)

line cola *f.*, fila *f.*

listen escuchar

little (quantity) poco; *(size)* pequeño

live: to live vivir

long largo

look: to look at mirar; **to look for** buscar (qu)

lose perder (ie)

lot: a lot mucho

loud en voz alta; **louder** en voz más alta

love querer *(irr.)*

luck suerte *f.*; **to be lucky** tener suerte

lunch almuerzo *m.*; **to have (eat) lunch** almorzar (ue, c)

magazine revista *f.*

make hacer *(irr.)*

man hombre *m.*

many muchos, muchas; **how many?** ¿cuántos?, ¿cuántas?

matter asunto *m.*; **what's the matter?** ¿qué tiene?

meal comida *f.*

mean querer decir

meet conocer (zc), encontrar (ue)

member miembro *m.*, socio *m.*

midnight medianoche *f.*; **at midnight** a medianoche

minute minuto *m.*

miss echar de menos

Monday lunes *m.*

money dinero *m.*

month mes *m.*

more más

morning mañana *f.*; **in the morning** por la mañana

most más

mother madre *f.*

mountain montaña *f.*

movies cine *m.*

much mucho; **too much** demasiado; **how much?** ¿cuánto?

music música *f.*

name nombre *m.*; **to be named** llamarse

near cerca (de)

need necesidad *f.*; **to need** necesitar, hacerle falta (a uno), faltarle (a uno)

nervous nervioso

never nunca

new nuevo

newspaper periódico *m.*

nice simpático

night noche *f.*; **at night** por la noche

no ninguno, ninguna, ningún; **no longer** ya no

no one nadie

noise ruido *m.*

noon mediodía; **at noon** al mediodía

north norte *m.*

now ahora

number número *m.*; **telephone number** número de teléfono

obey obedecer (zc)

October octubre

offer ofrecer (zc)

often a menudo

old viejo; **to be...old** tener... años *(irr.)*

open abierto

or o, u; ni

other otro

parents padres *m. pl*

park parque *m.*

party fiesta *f.*

passport pasaporte *m.*

patience paciencia *f.*

pay pagar (gu); **to pay attention** prestar atención;

to pay attention to hacerle caso a *(irr.)*

pen pluma *f.*; **ballpoint pen** bolígrafo *m.*

people gente *f.*; personas *f.*; **young people** jóvenes *m. pl.*

photograph fotografía *f.*; **to take pictures** sacar fotografías

phrase frase *f.*

pilot piloto *m.*

place lugar *m.*

plan: to plan pensar + *inf.*

play: to play (music) tocar (qu); **(game)** jugar (ue, gu)

pleasant agradable, simpático

please por favor; tener la bondad de, hacer el favor de

point punto *m.*

police policía *f.*

pool piscina *f.*

popcorn palomitas *f. pl.*

poster cartel *m.*

practice practicar (qu)

prefer preferir (ie, i)

pretty bonito

produce producir (zc)

program programa *m.*

purse bolsa *f.*

put poner *(irr.)*; **to put on** ponerse

quarter cuarto; **one quarter** un cuarto, una cuarta parte

rapid rápido; **rapidly** rápidamente

rare raro

rarely raramente

read leer (y)

recognize reconocer (zc)

record disco *m.*

red rojo

remember recordar (ue)

repeat repetir (i)

respond responder, contestar

rest descansar

return volver (ue), regresar; (give back) devolver (ue)

rice   arroz *m.*

ride: to ride a bicycle
  montar en bicicleta

room   cuarto *m.*, habitación;

roommate   compañero de
  cuarto

row   fila *f.*; **to row** remar

rule   regla *f.*

salary   sueldo *m.*; salario *m.*

Saturday   sábado *m.*

save   ahorrar

school   escuela *f.*, colegio *m.*;
  high school escuela
  secundaria

scold   reñir (i)

sea   mar *m.*

seat   asiento *m.*; **seated**
  sentado

second   segundo

see   ver *(irr.)*

seem   parecer (zc)

sell   vender

serve   servir (i)

several   varios

sharp (time)   en punto

shoe   zapato *m.*

short   corto

show   mostrar (ue), enseñar

silly   tonto

sing   cantar

sister   hermana *f.*

sit   sentarse (ie)

skit   escena *f.*

sky   cielo *m.*

sleep   dormir (ue, u); **to fall
  asleep** dormirse (ue, u); **to
  be sleepy** tener sueño

small   pequeño

snow   nieve *f.*; **to snow**
  nevar (ie)

soccer   fútbol *m.*

soda   refresco *m.*, gaseosa *f.*

some   alguno, algún, unos,
  unas; **sometimes** a veces

song   canción *f.*

soon   pronto

soup   sopa *f.*

Spanish   español *m.*

spend (time)   pasar; **(money)**
  gastar

spoiled   consentido

star   estrella *f.*

start   empezar (ie, c),
  comenzar (ie, c)

station   estación *f.*

stay   quedarse; **to stay in bed**
  guardar cama

still   todavía

stop   dejar de + *inf.*

store   tienda *f.*

street   calle *f.*

strict   estricto

student   alumno *m.*, alumna *f.*,
  estudiante *m./ f.*

study   estudiar

suitcase   maleta *f.*

summer   verano *m.*

sun   sol *m.*; **to be sunny** hacer
  sol

Sunday   domingo *m.*

sweater   suéter *m.*

table   mesa *f.*

take   tomar; **to take pictures**
  sacar fotografías

tall   alto

teacher   maestro *m.*, maestra *f.*,
  profesor *m.*, profesora *f*,

team   equipo *m.*

tell   decir *(irr.)*; **to tell about**
  referir (ie, i) de; **to tell the
  truth** decir la verdad

tennis   tenis *m.*

test   prueba *f.*, examen *m.*

that   ese, esa; aquel, aquella

there   ahí, allí, allá; **there is
  (there are)** hay

thing   cosa *f.*

think   pensar (ie)

thirst   sed *f.*; **to be thirsty**
  tener sed

this   este, esta

those   esos, esas; quellos,
  aquellas

through   por

Thursday   jueves *m.*

ticket   boleto *m.*, billete *m.*,
  entrada *f.*

time (hour)   hora *f.*; **(in a
  series)** vez *f.* (*pl.* veces);
  tiempo; **on time** a tiempo;
  to have a good time
  divertirse (ie), pasar un
  buen rato

tired   cansado; **to be tired**
  estar cansado

today   hoy

together   junto

tomorrow   mañana

tonight   esta noche

tooth   muela *f.*, diente *m.*;
  toothache dolor de muela

train   tren *m.*

translate   traducir (zc)

travel   viajar

tree   árbol *m.*

trip   viaje *m.*; **to make (take)
  a trip** hacer un viaje *(irr.)*

try   tratar de

Tuesday   martes *m.*

turn   turno *m.*; **to be one's
  turn** tocarle (a uno)

typewriter   máquinilla *f.*

understand   comprender,
  entender (ie)

university   universidad *f.*

use   usar

vacation   vacaciones *f./pl.*

very   muy

visit   visitar

voice   voz *f.*; (*pl.* voces)

wait   esperar

walk   caminar, andar *(irr.)*; **to
  take a walk** dar un paseo

wallet   cartera *f.*

want   desear, querer *(irr.)*

wash   lavar; **to wash oneself**
  lavarse

watch   reloj *m.*; **to watch**
  mirar

wear   llevar, **usar;** ponerse *(irr.)*

weather   tiempo *m.*

Wednesday   miércoles *m.*

week   semana

well   bien

what?   ¿qué?

when   cuando; **when?**
  ¿cuándo?

where   donde; **where?**
  ¿dónde?; (from) **where?**
  ¿de dónde? **(to) where?**;
  ¿adónde?

while   mientras

white   blanco

whom   ¿a quién?

whose   ¿de quién?

why   ¿por qué?

wide   ancho

win   ganar

wind   viento *m.*; **to be windy**
  hacer viento

with   con; **with me**
  conmigo

without   sin

woods   bosque *m.*

word   palabra *f.*

work   trabajo *m.*; **to work**
  trabajar

worry   preocupación *f.*;
  to be worried estar
  preocupado

write   escribir

wrong: to be wrong   no
  tener razón

year   año *m.*

yesterday   ayer

young   joven; **younger** menor

Index